RELATIONAL

— INTELLIGENCE —

THE FIVE ESSENTIAL SKILLS YOU NEED TO
BUILD LIFE-CHANGING RELATIONSHIPS

Adam C. Bandelli, Ph.D.

ISBN 978-1-63885-672-6 (Paperback)
ISBN 978-1-63885-674-0 (Hardcover)
ISBN 978-1-63885-673-3 (Digital)

Covenant Books
11661 Hwy 707
Murrells Inlet, SC 29576
www.covenantbooks.com

Mom, you have taught me all I know about relationships. You are genuine and authentic with all the people in your life. Your love, care, and compassion have helped transform the way I look at people and relationships. Thank you for showing me how to have a positive impact on others.

WHAT PEOPLE ARE SAYING

Adam Bandelli, a leading expert on human behavior and relationships, provides a simple guide to building the five essential skills necessary for connecting with people in meaningful ways. This set of skills will enable you to develop genuine and long-lasting relationships with others that can pay off in all walks of life from romantic relationships to the workplace.

—Dr. Paul Spector
Professor Emeritus at Muma College of Business
University of South Florida

I highly recommend any of Adam's books, and especially his latest, *Relational Intelligence: The Five Essential Skills You Need to Build Life-Changing Relationships*. I first met Adam when I was the Chief Administrative Officer of a billion-dollar retailer that was acquired by a private equity firm. Adam was brought in to help us become an even stronger team, and not only was he successful in that engagement, but I have kept him close to me professionally ever since. It's a testament to his ability to build relationships and teach others the value of individuals and teams to drive success. I'm proud to continue working with him today as the head of People and Culture for a $6 billion global retailer. He has been a true trusted advisor for many years.

—Stacy Siegal
Executive Vice President, General Counsel, People and Culture
American Eagle Outfitters

High EQ doesn't always translate to success in the workplace. It is more about how we build relationships and get things done together with others. Adam is a master at teasing out the subtle differences between the two and coaching executives at maintaining and navigating important relationships to achieve their goals while living their purpose.

—Michael Katz
Chief Strategy, Planning, and Investor Relations Officer
Voya Financial

Adam's consulting work and research on relational intelligence delivers on the importance of investing in the personal and professional development of others. In our coaching work together, he has helped me to identify, unlock, and unleash the critical skills needed for cultivating sustainable and impactful relationships with my colleagues. As a result of our relationship, he has helped me to work on my leadership brand and become a greater inspiration to my people and teams.

—Mike Dube
Group Vice President, East Strategic
Splunk Inc.

Life is not about perfection. It's about learning, growth, and progression. We do most of this through our relationships. Adam is a courageous thought leader and has a strong desire to help support his clients. It takes authenticity to be vulnerable and real. Life throws us curve balls and we all make mistakes. In the end, it's what we do with those mistakes and how we grow from them. This book is a masterful blend of relationship concepts and theory supported by research, personal growth, and stories of clients that exemplify the five key relational intelligence skills.

—Dr. Lyne Desormeaux
Master Coach and CEO
Desormeaux Leadership Consulting

My friend and colleague Adam Bandelli introduces the concept of relational intelligence as the master key for business success, personal growth, and lifelong fulfilling relationships. In his new book, *Relational Intelligence: The Five Essential Skills You Need to Build Life-Changing Relationships*, Adam outlines a practical guide to developing genuine and authentic relationships with coworkers, friends, family, and life partners. The book follows the author's life experiences and professional development as an organizational psychologist while drawing on research and practice from many different areas and disciplines. *Relational Intelligence* will show you how to have a deep and meaningful influence on others by establishing stronger and more trusting interpersonal relationships.

—Dr. Randall P. White
Chair of Leadership, eMBA HEC Paris
Coauthor of the book *Breaking the Glass Ceiling*

Adam possesses a raw honesty and transparency that pulls you into his writings and world. In his book, *Relational Intelligence: The Five Essential Skills You Need to Build Life-Changing Relationships*, he shares powerful skills and techniques that you can apply in all aspects of your life from your personal relationships to your professional ones. Adam shows that it is possible to lead with empathy and authenticity to have a lasting positive impact on others. In our coaching work together, he has helped me bring these skills to life. Our discussions have ignited a passion in how I approach connecting with people and influencing others.

—Emmanuelle Cuny
Senior Vice President, Video Production
Capitol Records

Dr. Bandelli takes his clients and readers for an exploration of awareness, creating a deeper understanding of who we are and our "why." This awareness, coupled with his coaching and insights, cultivate opportunities to unleash one's best self, ultimately elevating our understanding of and relationship with ourselves and others. Dr. Bandelli empowers a deeper understanding of one's ability to not only improve in the essential area of relational intelligence but to maximize its application for positive and successful outcomes in our personal, familial, marital, and professional lives.

—Debbie Wishart
Vice President—Public Sector North America
Twilio

Adam Bandelli captures the essence of living a full, effective, and enjoyable life by having more meaningful connections with people. He lays out the five essential skills needed to develop, cultivate, and sustain strong relationships with your colleagues, associates, family, and friends...and improve your ability to make a positive and purposeful impact on others!

—Brannigan Thompson
Senior Vice President, Corporate and Organizational Development
Voya Financial

Working with others requires psychological safety, cocreating trust, leading with vision, and focusing on the picture of what cultivating influence looks like in all our relationships. Adam's research supports how these aspects of leadership matter now more than ever before. He powerfully and clearly articulates how critical it is for leaders to learn, adapt, tune in, and demonstrate relational competency at work. Moreover, he lives and practices what he writes about and really walks the talk!

—Dr. Michael de Vihil
Global Leadership Development Practitioner
Certified executive coach and licensed clinical psychologist

CONTENTS

Introduction..xi

Part 1: The Skills of Relational Intelligence
    Establishing Rapport...1
    Understanding Others...27
    Embracing Individual Differences 53
    Developing Trust...90
    Cultivating Influence..120

Part 2: The Applications of Relational Intelligence
    Family Relationships 151
    Friendships..170
    Professional Relationships 188
    Romantic Relationships and Marriage 211
    The Call to Action 236

INTRODUCTION

The greatest pains and pleasures that you will experience
in life will be in the context of relationships.
—Steven Furtick

I've always been fascinated by the power of relationships. Since my early childhood years, I have marveled at the way people build connections with one another. This started by observing the way my mother interacted with people. She was a special education teacher and worked with fifth- and sixth-grade students. Her compassion for children and the way she built relationships were genuine and authentic. She taught me the meaning of empathy and having a deep understanding of others. She built trust with her students by showing care. She touched so many people's lives through her teaching, so much so that many of her former students still keep in touch with her to this day.

I also learned how to connect with people through sports. I played basketball throughout my adolescent and high school years. I quickly learned that the most impactful coaches built lasting bonds with their players. They worked with players to help them understand their strengths and weaknesses and learn, develop, and grow. I grew up in a single-parent household and didn't get to see my father much growing up. One of my coaches took the time to learn about this and always went out of his way to work one-on-one with me after practice. He taught me about more than just basketball. He taught me about life and the importance of building strong partnerships with my teammates. He taught me the power of teamwork, and that when we worked together collectively, we were always better than a group of talented individuals. This valuable lesson has stuck with me throughout my career.

In college, I continued to learn about the value of relationships. It was the late nineties, and Daniel Goleman's book *Emotional Intelligence* was starting to circulate among professional and academic communities. As an industrial-organizational psychology student, I was intrigued by the concept of EQ and how it affected the way we understood our feelings and the emotions of others. I was working with my mentor at the time, and we were actively conducting research on EQ. One of our early studies focused on the lack of EQ in bullies. This was several years before bullying became a subject that garnered national attention. We hypothesized that bullies lacked self-awareness, did not understand the emotions of others, and had difficulty self-regulating their behaviors. But we later discovered that bullies did, in fact, have high self-awareness. This enabled them to manipulate situations and understand how to get a rise out of others. They also had a good understanding of others' underlying emotions. This helped them find the right button to push on their targets. What I learned quickly was that EQ was a powerful component of relationship building—for both good and bad purposes.

In graduate school, my focus on emotional intelligence grew. I did my master's thesis on EQ and Machiavellianism. The premise of the work was whether Machiavellians were inherently bad people or if they just used EQ to influence people as a means to an end. I discovered that it was more the latter than the former. Machiavellians are not bad people. They just know how to influence people and use relational power to achieve their desired outcomes. This got me thinking about the dynamics in relationships. How do people ingratiate themselves with others? What are some of the first things people do to get buy-in and agreement? How do people connect over similarities? How do they evaluate differences? How do they develop trusting relationships? How do some develop influence over others?

This led me to focus my doctoral dissertation on what, at the time, I called socio-affective competence. The idea behind my dissertation was that when leaders developed relationships, they focused on several important skills that enabled them to connect and build strong partnerships with others. My dissertation outlined the conceptual model, and I developed a psychological assessment test to measure these skills in people. I hypothesized that great leaders knew how to use certain skills to develop long-lasting relationships with others. These types of people knew how to establish rapport. They took time to understand people, then placed value on individual differences. They practiced behaviors that garnered trust. They were effective at cultivating influence over time. My dissertation results indicated that certain leaders did practice these skills, and this enabled them to create greater loyalty and organizational commitment from others. It also fostered environments where people were aligned on a shared vision, which led to greater job performance. The dissertation proved I was on to something—something different from EQ, something that outlined how people built successful relationships with others.

Early in my career, I put the skills I had developed in my research into practice. Upon completing my doctoral program, I began interviewing with management consulting firms. I found a firm that aligned with my personal values and beliefs. The consultants at this firm were mission driven and committed to relationships with their clients. Relationships were their capital for developing new business and lasting partnerships with clients. The interview process was rigorous. For several months, I met with different leaders across the firm in one-on-one discussions, where I had the opportunity to establish rapport and make early connections with my future colleagues. The conversations covered many things. We talked about my background, the nature of their work, and my goals and ambitions as an organizational psychologist. I made sure to learn about each person with whom I met by doing research prior to our interviews, finding out about their interests both inside and outside of work, and asking questions when I met with them—not only questions that focused on the business but also questions about their personal journeys as psychologists and management consultants.

When I received an offer letter from the firm, I was elated. I would be joining a firm where I would have the opportunity to learn from many knowledgeable and intelligent people. Later, I would discover I was one of the youngest hires in the firm's history. I was selected for my potential as a consultant, but more importantly, they chose me for how I was able to connect on a deep, personal level with others. I was selected because of my ability to build relationships with colleagues from different backgrounds and experiences. This strength wasn't an act on my part. I knew if I was going to be successful, I had to develop trusting partnerships. I was also genuinely curious about others and thought I had so much to learn from my colleagues, people who had been doing consulting work for twenty to thirty years.

The first six months of my tenure with the firm were a whirlwind of activity as I learned how to be a management consultant. From selection assessments to team development to executive coaching, there was much to learn. Beyond acquiring knowledge on how to do our work, I started to notice something about many of the senior partners. They all had a way with people and were exceptionally skilled at building relationships with clients. I watched firsthand how they established connections early on with prospects, then turned them into clients. I got to see how they grew accounts by developing trusting partnership with key stakeholders in client organizations. They used more than charm and charisma. These partners took time to learn and understand the needs of their clients. They placed high value on the relationships they built, where loyalty and commitment were key. I knew I had to further develop my relational skills if I was to follow their lead.

Around the six-month mark, I was asked to take on my first executive coaching engagement. The client was an electronic retailer with a leader who was struggling to have a positive impact on others. He led with an iron fist and had difficulty cultivating trusting partnership with his people and teams. Before I sat down with the leader, I had a meeting with his direct manager to discuss the engagement. Little did I know, this conversation would have a tremendous impact on my first few years with my firm. I met with the client's executive vice president of the Northeast US. We were scheduled for a quick thirty-minute face-to-face meeting at her corporate offices.

At the time, I knew nothing about being a coach. All I knew was that I had to apply the same skills I had used to build relationships with my colleagues to my communication with this leader. I started the conversation by asking about her direct reports but opened the dialogue to learn more about her leadership. I invested time to establish rapport and learn about her role and the challenges she faced. The meeting ended up being two and a half hours, and by the end of the discussion, she wanted me to be her coach and work with her team. I hadn't plan for that. It wasn't my goal going into the meeting. I had known, however, that I wanted to build a strong relationship and partnership with her.

Over the next two years, I served as her executive coach and trusted advisor. We worked on many programs together. I ended up building relationships with each member of her direct report team, seventeen leaders—thirteen district managers and a regional staff of four people. With each relationship, I had to adapt and adjust my style to fit the needs of the respective leader. However, I used the same process to build a relationship with each leader. I took time to establish rapport and build a connection. I invested time to learn about and understand each of them. I placed a strong emphasis on acknowledging and valuing the unique leadership skills they brought to the table. I built trust and supported each of them, even when this involved keeping information private and confidential. I exerted my influence on each of them to help support their growth. When I started the account with the single coaching engagement, it was a $20,000 program. I grew the account to over $750,000 within eighteen months. I say this not to impress you but to impress upon you that this growth was the result of building individual relationships with every one of her leaders.

I started applying these relational skills to develop partnerships with all my clients. It wasn't rocket science. I genuinely wanted to improve my clients' leadership skills and help them have a consistently positive impact on their people, teams, and organizations. Relational intelligence is not about driving results. Results are one of the important outcomes of investing in how you develop relationships with others, but relational intelligence goes deeper. It's about using your relational skills to build successful, long-lasting relationships with others. It is the way to have a positive impact on people.

You may be asking yourself, why focus on relationships, and why is that so important to do right now? We are living in a post-COVID-19 world. For close to two years, most of us were socially isolated. We had to shelter in place and keep our distance from others. Many of us had minimal face-to-face contact with people. We lived on conference calls and meetings conducted by video. Some of us lost the art of making connections and developing intimate relationships. Others, particularly early-career professionals, missed out on important opportunities to learn how to network and form new relationships.

In my work as a management consultant, I saw business leaders struggle with keeping their teams engaged and motivated. Successful leaders tried to keep bonds with their people strong despite the challenges. However, people's interaction and communication with others substantially declined. Employees lost focus. They were too busy, worried about their families, or anxious about when COVID-19 would end. This introduced major challenges to the onboarding and integration of new leaders. Such processes don't work in a virtual environment. Nothing replaces genuine, in-person, face-to-face time with others. For example, one of my clients last year onboarded a new CMO. This new leader needed to meet with all her different teams and spend time at different locations and facilities. She couldn't do that because of the pandemic, which damaged her ability to connect with people and gain traction. The circumstance had a negative impact on her ability to influence others.

Similarly, many children had school canceled for most of 2020. This prevented them from interacting face-to-face with others. Relationship building is critical to the positive growth and development of children. Even before the pandemic, challenges have existed that prevented children from interacting with others and learning to build successful relationships. Advances in technology and social media have given younger generations unlimited access to others, but research has shown that children are more isolated than ever before. A recent study conducted by researchers from the University of San Diego found that young people who spent seven or more hours a day on iPads, iPhones, or other technology devices were more than twice as likely to be diagnosed with depression or anxiety.[1] The data came from more than forty thousand kids ages two to seventeen and was collected as part of the survey of the US Census Bureau in the 2016 National Survey of Children's Health.

In other research, behavioral scientists from California State University found that media and technology predicted poor health and well-being in children between the ages of four and eighteen.[2] The study examined the impact of technology on four areas of health and well-being: psychological issues, behavioral problems, attention, and physical health. Their results indicated that for children and pre-teens, total media consumption predicted all four of the variables. For teenagers, nearly every type of technological activity predicted poor health and well-being. The research also found that it had a negative impact on the way teenagers built relationships with others. It's easy to see that our children are not being taught how to establish genuine, meaningful relationships. We are seeing the evolution of a generation that will struggle with how they connect with people. Given how technology has made an impact on the way we communicate and COVID-19 has prevented us from face-to-face interactions with others, I believe relationships are more important now than ever before. We all have to relearn how to connect with others. Our success as people and as a society depends on it. The future growth, development, and vitality of our children will suffer without it.

In business, a connected world and the responsibilities therein require leaders to master many relational and interpersonal skills. Leaders must have a comprehensive awareness of the pressing issues facing their teams and organizations. They must understand the dynamics of social processes and how to get the most out of their people. They must have mature interpersonal skills and high EQ to relate adequately to stakeholders both inside and outside their organizations. They need to do business by building relationships based on trust and mutual accountability. They need to build cultures that are relationship oriented and foster engagement from their employees. Without these things, leaders may have short-term successes, but their long-term influence and impact will fail. That is why relational intelligence is critical to the success of any leader.

In our personal lives, the connections we have with others lead to a life of fulfillment. Our relationships dictate how we view people. They influence our perspectives on critical and important issues in society. They determine how successfully we can grow and develop. When people have strong relationships with others, their levels of self-esteem improve. They have greater feelings of acceptance and an appreciation for others. They are less likely to feel isolated and alone. Relationships help us battle anxiety and depression. Our mental health improves by being around people who love and support us. Relationships help us cope with life's adversities. They help people get through challenging and difficult times. They enable us to overcome obstacles and learn from both good and bad experiences.

Relational intelligence is the ability to successfully connect with people and build strong, long-lasting relationships. It enables you to effectively engage and interact with people from different backgrounds and diverse cultures and experiences. It allows you to understand and appreciate the different interests, values, and beliefs of others. It's relevant at work, at home, and in all aspects of life. It helps leaders better fulfill their roles of cultivating inclusive, stimulating, and respectful work environments. It helps families deepen the bonds of trust and commitment. It helps parents raise children who value and appreciate the connections they have with others. It helps in romantic relationships by allowing individuals to learn and grow with their partners. It helps in friendships by enabling us to identify people who share our beliefs and passions in life. It gives us empathy for and an understanding of people different from us. Relational intelligence helps make us better people with more satisfying and fulfilling lives.

This book will focus on **five essential skills** for building positive, long-lasting, life-changing relationships with others. These skills are **establishing rapport, understanding others, embracing individual differences, developing trust, and cultivating influence**. All five of these skills you can learn, develop, and put into action in all your relationships. Whether you're interacting with colleagues at work, raising a family, or looking for a romantic partner, the skills apply to all walks of life. If you want to build stronger relationships with others, these skills must be put into practice. When applied, you will start to see the quality of your relationships improve. You will have more meaningful connections with people. Your ability to have a positive impact on others will grow.

The first part of this book will cover each of the five skills of relational intelligence. We will start with **establishing rapport**. This skill focuses on the initial stages of building a sustaining relationship. Rapport is often viewed as a starting point for developing trust and having influence on others by using empathy and respect to create an environment of mutual understanding. If you are going to build a relationship with another person, you have to take time in the early stages to establish a positive connection. When two people establish rapport, a state of affinity starts to take shape. This helps make communication more effective.

When establishing rapport, many factors come into play. Similarities between two people can impact the interaction. How much you like or are interested in the other person plays a role. The views you hold about yourself can impact how you come across to others. The perspectives you have about different types of people can affect initial interactions. Words used early on make important statements. Nonverbal cues you use can display attention toward the person and what they are discussing. Humor lightens the mood and puts people at ease.

Once rapport has been established, the focus shifts to **understanding others**. To build a strong relationship, you need to make an effort to learn about the other person. Curiosity plays a role. Your ability to ask questions and gather information helps you identify similarities and differences. Understanding how to read social cues and tone has an impact on how others perceive you. The process of understanding others takes time. It must be a genuine and sincere process. It doesn't happen overnight. You need to spend time with the other person. When people invest the time to understand others, they set the foundation for a relationship to grow.

Understanding people is just the start, though. To truly develop lasting relationships, you must embrace individual differences. **Embracing individual differences** is about tolerating, being approving of, and having a favorable reception of people different from us. When you acknowledge and appreciate the differences of other people, you're able to communicate more effectively with them. This helps build a connection that will strengthen the relationship. There are a variety of factors that play a role in embracing individual differences. Some of these include age, ethnicity, gender, race, sexual orientation, physical abilities, religious and spiritual beliefs, educational backgrounds, personal values, and hobbies and interests. In organizational settings, the concept of embracing individual differences has become prevalent with diversity and inclusion programs. When companies put these types of programs in place, employees' job performance improves. People are also more likely to engage in creative problem-solving and innovation. In our personal lives, embracing individual differences helps us develop friendships with people from different backgrounds and experiences. It strengthens family ties and enables us to have an appreciation for the perspectives of others.

As we continue to embrace individual differences, we begin **developing trust** with others. Trusting people takes time. It involves taking a risk to expose yourself to the actions and behaviors of another. It's allowing yourself to be vulnerable in a situation based on positive expectations about another's intentions. Without a strong foundation of trust, relationships cannot thrive long-term. When trust develops, people are able to let their guards down and share more about themselves.

Trust has important benefits for people in all aspects of life. In the business world, trust leads to individual and team productivity, higher levels of cooperation, and more effective job performance. It enables leaders to have a positive impact on their people. In our personal lives, trust helps us identify true friends. It helps couples plan for the future. It helps families flourish and grow. Damaged trust has a detrimental effect on any relationship. Married couples get divorced when they lose trust in each other. Careers can be destroyed when the trust of colleagues and customers is lost. Friendships can be ruined when people lie and are deceitful. Out of all the relational intelligence skills, trust is the most critical. It deepens the bonds between two people. It also opens the door for us to cultivate influence on others.

Cultivating influence is the final skill of relational intelligence. In relationships, influence is the capacity to have an effect on the character, development, and behaviors of others. For businesspeople, leadership is all about influence. Influence is the use of noncoercive tactics that direct and coordinate others' activities. It is used to accomplish goals and guide people to desired outcomes. If you are going to impact another person's life in a positive fashion, you have to influence them. The most successful people use their influence for good. They are able to connect with people by establishing rapport, understanding others' needs, embracing individual differences, and developing trusting relationships.

In organizational settings, cultivating influence takes time. Leaders have to earn the respect of their employees; but once they do, their influence leads to greater organizational commitment, job satisfaction, collaboration, and employee well-being. It also helps people identify with their leader and the organization. It has been shown to have a positive effect on job performance and productivity. When leaders build strong, solid relationships with employees, they can help them accomplish goals and drive positive organizational outcomes.

With families, parents use influence to help shape children's values. The influence parents have on their children can help lead children toward the pursuit of goals and dreams. In friendships, cultivating influence enables people to share hobbies and interests. Influence can help guide how our friends think and feel about different things. In romantic relationships, the influence partners have on each other can help set the course for their lifelong commitments. Similar to the business world, influence can only happen when our personal relationships are built on a solid foundation.

The second part of this book will focus on the applications of relational intelligence. We will talk about how the five skills can be used to strengthen family ties. I'll touch on the relationships between parents and their children. We will focus on the influence siblings have on one another. We will explore how relationship building can impact extended families. I'll also focus on the impact negative relationships can have on a family—for example, how problems can occur when trust is damaged or influence is used for manipulative purposes.

We will also discuss how relational intelligence can strengthen friendships and the people in our social circles. I'll discuss how friendships are developed in high school and college years. We will touch on how similar hobbies and interests bring people together. I'll cover how lifelong friendships develop and what relationally intelligent people do to influence and have a positive impact on others. I'll also focus on destructive friendships and the challenges associated with dealing with difficult people.

Then we'll cover the business world and how leaders can use relational intelligence to maximize the effectiveness of their employees. I'll talk about the job interview and selection process. We will discuss how teams are formed and the power relational intelligence has on helping groups achieve collective goals and objectives. We'll talk about the relationships that senior executives build with their people, teams, and organizations. We'll focus on how organizations that build strong partnerships with external stakeholders can have a positive impact on society.

Lastly, we will look at romantic relationships and marriage. We'll explore the honeymoon phase and how relationships start to develop and flourish. We will look into the reality phase and the challenges and difficulties that surface as two people truly get to know each other. We'll focus on the adjustment phase, where people accept one another for who they are and embrace their individual differences. We'll conclude this chapter on developing lasting intimacy. I'll focus on the power of influence in helping our partners achieve their full potential.

The stories and people I will discuss throughout this book come from my personal and professional life experiences. Names and organizational information will be changed to respect the anonymity of the people, teams, and companies I have worked with. It is my hope that this book will be a guide for how you can build long-lasting relationships in all areas of your life. As humans, we are all wired to have meaningful connections with others. The quality of our relationships can lead to a life of purpose and fulfillment. By learning these skills and putting them into practice, you'll have a deeper appreciation for others. You'll know how to be more empathetic to family, friends, and coworkers. You'll discover how to connect with people from all walks of life. You will also learn more about yourself along the journey. You'll understand what's important to you and the types of people with whom you want to surround yourself. Relational intelligence is so important to success in life. Our relationships impact how we think and feel about all aspects of our lives. Learning to harness the power of relationships will help shape your purpose, calling, and destiny.

---

1   J. M. Twenge and W. K. Campbell, "Associations between Screen Time and Lower Psychological Well-Being among Children and Adolescents: Evidence from a Population-Based Study," *Preventive Medicine Reports* 12 (2018): 271–283.

2   L. D. Rosen, A. F. Lim, J. Felt, L. M. Carrier, N. A. Cheever, J. M. Lara-Ruiz, J. S. Mendoza, and J. Rokkum, "Media and Technology Use Predicts Ill-Being among Children, Preteens, and Teenagers Independent of the Negative Health Impacts of Exercise and Eating Habits," *Computers in Human Behavior* 35 (2014): 364–375.

THE SKILLS OF
RELATIONAL
INTELLIGENCE

ESTABLISHING RAPPORT

Rapport is the ability to enter someone else's world,
to make a person feel that you understand them,
that you have a strong common bond.
—Tony Robbins

Rapport building is critical to the success of any relationship. When people first meet, establishing rapport allows them to create an initial connection. It sets the stage for two people to develop affinity with and appreciation for each other. Building rapport enables you to understand where someone else is coming from. It helps you begin to understand a person's likes and interests. It can set the foundation for how leaders impact their people. It can create the early sparks for romantic relationships to take shape. It helps us meet friends and develop personal connections.

The concept of establishing rapport—a process of building a sustaining relationship of mutual trust, harmony, and understanding—has been studied in the field of psychology for over seventy years. Researchers have found that rapport is often viewed as a starting point for developing trust in and influence on others by using empathy and respect to create an environment of mutual understanding. Rapport between two people can be instantaneous or developed in a short period of time. This typically occurs based on two important factors: enjoyable interactions and personal connection.

We have all experienced hitting it off immediately with someone we have just met. The very first time you may have spoken with a person with whom you share rapport, a little voice in the back of your mind may have said, "I like this person. I trust them. We have things in common." You may not have been able to identify any spe-

1

cific reason why you felt this way at the time, but you just did. After a few minutes of conversation, when rapport is built, you can quickly get a feel for who a person is and whether you want to continue to get to know them. This is why rapport is simple yet complex. You can establish it quickly with some people, whereas with others, it can be challenging to make an initial connection. I see this often when leaders are working with new teams. If they invest the time needed for getting to know people early on, they can set the stage to have a lasting, positive impact on others. If they miss out on opportunities to build rapport, people can become guarded and skeptical about the leader's motives.

Establishing rapport is also critical in the early stages of dating. When two people meet, there is a sizing-up period that can last throughout the entire first date. This is where first impressions play a crucial role. How are you dressed? What verbal signs are you sending if you are interested and having a good time? What nonverbal gestures are you communicating? Are you asking questions and actively listening, or are you dominating the conversation? Each of these factors plays a role in developing initial connection or rapport. When it's done well, it will usually lead to a second date. When it is managed poorly, the date will end quickly.

Great rapport builders have empathy for people. They know how to relate to others' needs and can see things through their eyes. They have the ability to walk in someone else's shoes. They are also enthusiastic. Enthusiasm is contagious. People gravitate toward those who have a passion for life. Such passion doesn't have to be over-the-top energy and excitement. It can be as simple as a genuine smile. Dale Carnegie, in his timeless classic *How to Win Friends and Influence People*, had this to say about the power of a smile: "Your smile is a messenger of your good will. Your smile brightens the lives of all who see it. It can be like the sun breaking through the clouds."

People who know how to build rapport are also curious. They tend to ask a lot of questions. They use this to gather information but also listen attentively to further develop a connection. They know how to use humor to lighten the mood, which can make people open up and share more about themselves. Part of human nature is the way we are more comfortable and open with people whom we perceive to be like ourselves. People who are skilled at establishing rapport know how make others feel appreciated and understood. They invest time to make others feel comfortable and accepted.

BEDSIDE MANNER: THE DOCTOR-PATIENT RELATIONSHIP

Life in my early twenties was both exciting and challenging. I was new to my doctoral program and was learning many things about the field of organizational psychology. My first year went by in a flash. I had to balance a difficult course load with teaching an undergraduate class of three hundred students in the field of personality psychology. I enjoyed every minute of it! Seeing undergraduates develop interest and desire to learn sparked my creative passion. At the same time, I was learning how to navigate the different personalities and quirks of mentors and professors.

The demands of graduate school can cause a lot of stress and anxiety on its students. Our professors warned us about taking on too much responsibility and the risk of burnout. They advised us to stick to a three-course curriculum per semester. Between this and teaching our own classes to undergraduates, our plates were full. During the first two years of the program, they warned graduate students about seeking jobs and internships outside the university. If we did so, we could spread ourselves too thin.

I have a Type A personality. I am very competitive and goal-oriented. I'm a fast talker, and I move quickly. Interrelated with this is the presence of a significant life imbalance. I'm a workaholic, and during that period of my life, I struggled with finding time for things outside of my studies. I was always operating with a constant sense of urgency. I was impatient then, and I still struggle with impatience now. In my second year of doctoral program, I felt I needed to take on more. The course load was challenging but not overbearing. I knew that if I was to become a consultant, I needed work experiences. So against the counsel of my academic advisor, I pursued internships outside the university. That fall semester, I was able to secure a twenty-hour-a-week part-time internship. I took this on while taking four graduate courses and teaching two undergraduate classes. For three months, I worked close to eighteen hours a day. On top of this, I got into marathon running and started running five to six miles every day. I probably slept two to three hours a night if I was lucky. This took a massive toll on my mental, physical, and emotional well-being. I was determined, though. I was just going to push through the exhaustion and complete the semester.

Winter break could have been a chance for relief. I had a few weeks to rest and rejuvenate. However, I didn't do that. I kept working and actively pursued a second, more prestigious internship. This second internship was halfway across the country. Because I had completed most of my graduate classes, I was able to pack my things and take the six-month internship. Within several weeks of arriving at a new company in a different state, I began to feel signs of anxiety and depression. I saw my energy levels decline rapidly. I found little interest in engaging in the activities that brought me happiness and joy. I started to have difficulty falling asleep and getting the much-needed rest I required. My job performance on the internship started to suffer dramatically. I didn't know what was happening. I was scared and frightened. I didn't know how to get out of the negative spiral of despair and anguish.

It was around this time that my father came for a weekend visit. As soon as he saw me, he knew something was wrong. I was miserable and in the throes of a major depression. He tried to cheer me up like any parent would have, but nothing worked. He was scheduled to stay a few days but ended up extending his visit for a whole week. The day before he was supposed to leave, I told him I didn't want to be alone. I didn't know what I would do to myself if no one was around. Then he was scared. We quickly packed up my things and headed home together. I needed help, and my father wanted to do all he could.

Upon returning home, he scheduled me an appointment with a psychiatrist. I vividly remember my visit to the doctor's office. There was a waiting room full of patients. It was loud and disturbing. We arrived fifteen minutes before my appointment and had to wait close to an hour before we met the psychiatrist. When we finally got in with him, he was cold, aggressive, and abrasive. He quickly asked what was going on and had me explain what I was feeling. He asked me about the last year and what life stressors I dealt with. Within a few minutes of sharing, he cut me off. "You have bipolar disorder," he said. "I'm going to prescribe you these three medications. Start taking them immediately, and I will see you in one week." I was in shock. How could I, a doctoral student in psychology, have a psychological disorder? To compound the problem, the psychiatrist didn't answer any of our questions. He quickly wrote out my scripts and alerted the nursing staff to schedule my next appointment.

That experience made my diagnosis all the worse. On the ride home from his office, I rejected the diagnosis outright. "There's no way I have bipolar. Crazy people have that disease. I'm not crazy." It took me close to ten years to finally accept my diagnosis. Much of that time could have been saved had the psychiatrist established rapport in that first session. Had he answered our questions, explained more about the diagnosis, and outlined treatment options, he would have prevented a lot of pain and heartache—heartache not only for myself but for my loved ones as well.

For years, researchers in the field of medicine have explored how the relationships between doctors and their patients impact the diagnosis of serious illnesses and the efficacy of their treatments. The patient's first visit with a new provider is critical because it has the potential to shape attitudes and behaviors that foster and strengthen the patient-provider relationship.[1] In health care, the first few minutes of an initial patient-provider encounter are important for establishing rapport. Doctor-patient relationships characterized by trust and rapport not only contribute to better care experiences but can also alleviate anxiety and enhance patients' involvement in decisions about their care.[2] Patients' initial care experiences can also impact behaviors such as the likelihood of taking medications as prescribed and returning for follow-up visits.[3] Adherence to medications and retention in care are particularly important for the proper management of chronic diseases.

The skills of rapport building and reflective listening, along with the ability to calmly deal with a wide variety of emotions, are critical to the success of any doctor-patient relationship. Patient-centered care is an important contributor to a positive patient care experience. A large body of literature on patient-centered communication cites rapport building as critical to fostering positive doctor-patient relationships.[4] From a patient's perspective, the first interactions with a doctor can dictate how they will handle their diagnosis and manage their treatment. Patients entering a new relationship with a provider can experience heightened psychological distress ranging from feelings of vulnerability as a new patient to fear, situational anxiety, and panic, especially when the condition is life altering. I witnessed this firsthand with my bipolar diagnosis. Had the psychiatrist taken the time to establish rapport and to demonstrate compassion, the outcome could have been different.

In the medical profession, the task of giving bad news to patients is often avoided or, at best, done reluctantly. However, because the bad news may dramatically change a family's outlook for the future, especially when it involves a medical diagnosis, it is essential to do it well. To deliver bad news well, a therapeutic relationship must first be built. Then and only then will the bad news shared with the patient or family be received in the best possible context. This takes a concerted effort and thoughtfulness on the part of the doctor or medical practitioner, but the end result will be a much more compassionate and effective interaction. Before embarking on the task of delivering bad news to families, physicians must establish rapport to lay the groundwork to facilitate future conversations. It must be kept in mind that the family is about to experience a significant loss of control in their lives. They are being thrust into an environment that is often foreign or, at best, unfamiliar. Anything that can be done to give them back a bit of control will be beneficial to their coping with the situation. Research has shown that creating a setting where the family has some control is the first step to constructing a productive partnership.[5]

My firm has consulted with many physicians and medical professionals. The ones who excel at establishing rapport do several important things. First, they are skilled at creating the right environments for their patients. They find secure, private settings where patients can have direct, face-to-face interaction with their medical professional. Privacy provides freedom for patients to get to know the doctor and express their thoughts and emotions. Second, they build a solid foundation of trust. Good doctors start this process the moment they begin to interact with a patient and their families. Nowhere are rapport and trust more important than while delivering bad news. Patients vividly recall details about the manner in which they are informed of a serious diagnosis. In multiple studies of patients who have received bad news, they preferred that the doctor delivering this information is one who engenders trust, exhibits caring, and remains open throughout the process.[6] Lastly, the most important elements of building rapport in a therapeutic relationship are empathy and compassion. Doctors who impart understanding and compassion can help patients navigate their health challenges and any negative news that will alter their quality of life.

Making the Right Hire: The Job Interview

Early in my career, I worked as a human resources business partner (HRBP) for a small technology company. Like most HR departments, we were responsible for the recruitment and selection of new employees. I worked for the HR lead, who did all the company's job interviewing and hiring. Although I had learned job interviewing theory in graduate school, Cindy taught me how to effectively interview job candidates in the real world. She taught me how to conduct a structured behavioral interview. I learned about behaviorally anchored rating scales and how to assess candidates against the organization's different role requirements and leadership competencies.

She also taught me many tricks of the trade not taught in graduate school. But most importantly, she educated me on the power of rapport building and the information that could be extrapolated from the first five to ten minutes of an interview. I learned how to assess verbal and nonverbal behaviors when we first met candidates from simple things like how a candidate was dressed. For example, if the candidate was a man, was he wearing a suit and tie? If not, what information could I determine based on how he was dressed? She had me look for things like if they were friendly and engaging. Did they articulate themselves well? Were they energetic and passionate about the role? We looked for nonverbal behaviors. Were they leaning in and expressive? Did they ask us questions? Were they smiling? Amazingly, we could often determine job fit based on the first few minutes of the interview. She could quickly determine if the candidates would be a good fit for the company's culture.

In many cases, candidates who did best in interviews knew how to establish rapport quickly. They made us more interested in learning about their past experiences. They knew how to use humor to draw us into conversation. They were curious and inquisitive. They wanted to learn about us and the organization. This went beyond impression management tactics. Obviously, they knew they were being interviewed and had to present themselves in the best possible way. However, it was their ability to build rapport that helped them land the job. It also contributed to how they integrated into the organization. The candidates who took time to learn about others and build relationships were typically the ones who were successful in the long term.

What I learned a few years later in my doctoral program was how powerful the rapport-building stage was in helping candidates get hired by organizations. For years, research in the field of organizational psychology has shown that initial impressions developed during the rapport-building stage influence subsequent interviewer ratings on interviewees. Much of this work shows that meaningful, accurate assessments of competence, warmth, and biographical data can be extracted from brief, initial impressions. In fact, in many instances, hiring managers often make selection decisions within the first five minutes of a conversation.[7]

Rapport building in the interview has been linked to the phenomenon assessed in seminal zero-acquaintance research in social psychology literature. Researchers in this field have found that people routinely form impressions of others from thin slices of expressive behavior. Multiple studies confirm that a substantive amount of valid information is perceived by strangers, even when the interactions last only a few seconds.[8] Many different rapport-building tactics, including altering person-job fit perceptions, exhibiting good social and emotional intelligence, responding to situational strengths, and displaying self-monitoring, can impact how candidates are perceived by interviewers.[9]

The possibility of conveying information that overlaps with job-related interview content during rapport building can be explained by social signaling. Social signaling argues that verbal and nonverbal social signals (e.g., enthusiasm, social fluency, and wittiness) sent by strangers can predict wide-ranging interpersonal characteristics, like marital satisfaction, professional competence, and even personality.[10] For years, research has indicated that in virtually all social interactions, people will attempt to influence others via some form of self-presentation tactic.[11] Whether a friendly bartender making small talk with a customer or a candidate during an interview with a potential employer, people consistently strive to elicit favorable reactions or perceptions from others.

For the applicant, rapport building can influence interviewers' decision-making time. When rapport building takes place, it encourages candidates to be more open in providing information that is more predictive of future performance on the job. This, in turn, impacts the decisions interviewers make when hiring people. In a study conducted by psychologists from several different prestigious universities, researchers have found that initial impressions were related to job applicants' personality and verbal skills during the rapport-building stage.[12] For example, extroverts are characterized as friendly, talkative, and socially adept, all features important to rapport building. These characteristics tend to positively influence their speech production. Similarly, verbal skill is reflective of both spontaneous and consciously controlled expressions of thoughts and emotions. It includes both the candidate's style of delivery (e.g., speech rate and pitch) and verbal fluency. A powerful style of speech results in positive attributions of competence and employability.

For the interviewer, rapport building can provide an initial understanding of how candidates are wired. It gives interviewers a glimpse into how the candidate will mesh with other employees and if their interpersonal style will be a good fit for the company. It also has an impact on how they will rate and score candidates in the interview. Job candidates skilled at building rapport are more likely to positively influence hiring decisions. Similar to other walks of life, the ability to establish rapport plays a critical role in how employers initially form relationships with their employees.

FORENSIC INTERVIEWING: EYEWITNESS TESTIMONY

As a business psychologist, I get the opportunity to work with a variety of leaders. One of my firm's service offerings is executive assessment and feedback. The assessment process is a robust approach to learning about a leader's journey and the events in their life that have shaped who they are today. In executive assessment interviews, we go into a leader's past and explore how childhood events have made an impact on their values and beliefs. Many of these conversations focus on major life events that have given leaders the perspective through which they view the world. Such perspective shapes how they interact with others, the relationships they build, and the people who serve as role models for their growth and development.

Many years ago, I worked with Tony, a senior executive in the retail industry who was being groomed for an executive vice president role in sales and marketing. Tony was a disciplined and hardworking leader who had worked his way up through the organization. People gravitated to him because of his steady leadership and ability to connect with others from all walks of life. When we met for his interview, Tony was open and candid about how several early childhood experiences left a lasting impact on his life. One of these experiences was the death of his older brother. Tony grew up in the projects of Chicago. Drugs and gang violence were the norm in his community. Although Tony was a good student and tried to stay clear of the drug scene, his brother got pulled in when they were in high school. Tony excelled in sports, particularly football, and this helped shield him from the activities of his brother.

One night, when Tony was returning from football practice, he saw his brother across the street from their house with a large group of people. He heard yelling before things turned violent. Then Tony watched another gang member pull out a gun and shoot his brother several times in the chest. Tony raced out of the house as people screamed and ran in all directions. His heart raced as he came up to his brother, who was lying on the ground, covered in a pool of blood. He was in shock and began to call for help. When the paramedics and police arrived, it was already too late. His brother had passed away before anyone could get there.

The next several weeks were a whirlwind. Tony had to deal with the devastating loss of his brother, someone to whom he had looked up and idolized. He also became one of the primary eyewitnesses to the events that had occurred. When he met with the police officers a few days later, he remembered how calm and supportive they were. They showed his family empathy and emotional support. They took the time to provide comfort during a difficult period. They wanted to make sure Tony felt safe and supported before they asked him to recall the events that had taken place. This wasn't what he had thought cops in his community were like. Kids his age were taught to fear the police. They were warned to steer clear of them. Reflecting on this, he was amazed at how the police took time to build rapport with him before asking him to recall details from the night of his brother's death. This left a mark on him and ultimately inspired him to join the police force right out of high school. He spent twenty years as a cop in Chicago and credited his decision to become a police officer because of how those officers made him feel during a difficult period in his life.

The ability of investigative interviewers and police officers to obtain accurate eyewitness information is of paramount importance when solving crimes. Effective interviewing methods that retrieve the greatest amount of accurate information from a witness's memory allow investigators to maximize the number of investigative leads. One of the most often recommended techniques is the use of rapport building. Establishing rapport is perceived by law enforcement as essential to a successful investigative interview. Rapport building establishes harmony in the interview, leads to an open and candid discussion, and creates willingness in the interviewee to provide insights to the criminal investigators. Major police interviewing guidelines recommend that interviewers build rapport with cooperative witnesses.[13] Because establishing rapport has been shown to reduce anxiety, it allows eyewitnesses to allocate additional cognitive resources to recalling criminal events.

Many forensic-interviewing researchers and practitioners have conceptualized rapport building as developing a relationship that provides eyewitnesses with a warm feeling and a positive attitude by establishing a friendly and comfortable environment. The most extensive research of specific rapport-building techniques with cooperative adult witnesses exists within the cognitive interview protocol, which recommends building rapport via two major outlets: personalizing the interview and developing and communicating empathy.[14] Both of these outlets involve the use of verbal and nonverbal techniques. When personalizing the interview, the interviewer is encouraged to use the interviewee's name, repeat the interviewee's statements, follow up with additional questions, and self-disclose personal and biographical information. When developing and communicating empathy, interviewers are encouraged to take a nonjudgmental approach, maintain eye contact, and display interest in the interviewee, such as by slightly leaning forward and verbally indicating an understanding of the interviewee's situation by saying, "I understand how you feel."

The research supporting rapport building by police officers and criminal investigators is compelling. Recent studies have shown that many investigators do it during both adult and child witness interviews. Regarding adult witnesses, a survey of law enforcement's perceptions of their interviewing practices in the United Kingdom revealed that rapport building was one of the most commonly used interviewing techniques with over 87 percent of investigators stating that they almost always built rapport with cooperative witnesses.[15] In a similar study in the United States, researchers surveyed local law enforcement agencies to determine how their officers and detectives defined and built rapport with criminal witnesses. The study specifically assessed the type and frequency of verbal and nonverbal techniques used by law enforcement. The rapport-building techniques were split into twenty different categories. Some of the nonverbal categories included displaying understanding, portraying a friendly demeanor or attitude, offering open and engaging body language, making good eye contact, and using a pleasant tone of voice. Some of the verbal categories included discussing common interests, engaging in self-disclosure, providing an explanation of the case, being honest with the interviewee, and being courteous and thanking the eyewitness.[16] In a separate line of research, investigators identified fourteen different rapport-building techniques used with eyewitnesses during criminal investigations. Some of these techniques included building a bond with the witness, finding common ground, making oneself appear similar to the source, using similar language as the witness, and showing empathy and concern for the interviewee and their situation.[17]

As rapport building is recommended for adult witnesses, it is of even greater importance with child eyewitnesses. Several experimental studies have examined the impact of rapport building on children's subsequent witness accuracy and have found that it helps promote more accurate recall and disclosure of information.[18] Additionally, researchers have found that during the initial part of a child eyewitness interview, interviewers are encouraged to build rapport in two sections. In the first section, the general, free-narrative phase, it is suggested that interviewers build rapport through a series of open-ended questions to elicit personally meaningful information from the child ("Tell me about something fun that happened to you"; "Tell me about the things you like to do"). In the second section, rapport building should continue until the interviewer perceives that the child witness feels comfortable talking about negative events they have experienced. These supportive techniques have been shown to reduce anxiety and help children cope with feelings of shame and guilt during investigative interviews. Tony's experience helped him to navigate the grieving period following his brother's death. When criminal investigators and police officers show compassion and empathy, rapport building creates a powerful experience that can leave a positive, long-lasting impact on eyewitnesses.

CLOSING THE SALE: THE EMPLOYEE-
CUSTOMER RELATIONSHIP

My first job after high school was with Sears. I started working in their paint department the summer after my senior year. Friends told me it was a good side job to have during college. The money was good, and you got a chance to interact with a vast array of people. When I first started, I had no idea how to interact with customers. I knew I had to be knowledgeable about my role, including studying different painting products and information. Were customers painting the interior or exterior of their homes? Were they looking for acrylics, watercolor, or oil-based paint? What type of project were they hoping to do? I had to determine if they were beginners or if painting was their profession. There were many details and nuances I had to learn.

Once I had a good understanding of my role's technical aspects, I had to figure out how to engage customers in a discussion to ascertain their underlying needs. I had to learn to ask questions to help them determine the product that would work best. What I started to realize was that there were different aspects to interacting with customers. First, I had to look the part. The nonverbal areas of rapport building in this role included how I was dressed, whether or not I smiled and made eye contact during the conversation, and if I leaned in to show interest and a desire to help. The verbal aspects involved welcoming them to the store, complimenting them on something to draw them in, probing at their underlying needs, and making sure their questions and concerns were answered. I learned that the relational, communication-related aspects of a sale were more important than my product knowledge. Once I began to understand this, I started to thrive.

Within six months, I was promoted to the hardware department. The stakes were higher there. There was a larger portfolio of products I had to learn. There were handheld tools, power tools and saws, garage door openers, shop vacs, building materials, locks, hinges, and electrical supplies. Knowing the difference between these areas was critical to an employee's success. I had to learn about different product models, brands, and solutions that fitted a variety of customer needs. Customer interactions and relationships became even more critical. I continued to strengthen my ability to initially connect with people. I made customers feel welcome and important. I used humor to lighten the mood and make them comfortable and relaxed. I asked questions to learn about their projects. Over time, I started getting regulars and repeat customers. People came to the store to see me. I had to remember names and aspects of their lives I could reference or inquire about when we interacted. All these rapport-building techniques enabled me to continue to shine as an employee.

Nine months later, I was promoted to the plumbing department. This role was strictly based on commissions and selling installation and service warranties. Again, I had to learn the products and find new ways to connect with customers. There were mistakes made along the way, and I had to learn how to address issues and challenges to create a great experience for people. As my communication skills strengthened, I learned how to sell installation and service warranties with almost every product. This put me on the radar of the senior leaders in the store. Five months later, my manager asked if I wanted to make a huge transition and move into the shark tank—the television department. Second to appliances, the television department was the prized jewel of the store. Most of the people in the TV department were full-time employees. This was their career. Some of the staff had spent years in this one area. I jumped at the opportunity to take on the challenge and learn from seasoned salespeople.

I stepped into the role three months before the holiday season. I had to ramp up quickly to get ready for Black Friday and Christmas. I was only nineteen at the time, and the company was taking a risk in putting such a young person with experienced salesmen. Some of my colleagues wanted to see me fail. They didn't want some kid taking away from their commission sales. It didn't take me too long to figure this out, but I tried to stay humble and respectful. I was inquisitive and asked questions. I picked up information quickly and didn't have to be told things twice. Two of my colleagues took me under their wing and taught me about all the products. There were small TVs, projection and flat-screen models, HDTVs, VCRs, DVD players, and computers. Then there was learning about the different service plans and extended warranties. This was where most employees made their money. If you sold certain flat-screen HDTV models with an extended warranty, you could take home five hundred dollars in commission!

I also closely observed how each of my colleagues interacted with customers. There was an art to building relationships and selling. Some customers only wanted to interact with their specific salesperson. This was intriguing to me. We were all given business cards. We were all given opportunities to connect with first-time shoppers. We all learned about new products as they came into the store. The playing field was even. However, the best salesmen in the department differentiated themselves. They established rapport and connected with people. They were charismatic. There was an essence about them that resonated with customers. They were great listeners. They were engaging and entertaining to interact with. They took time to remember small details about people. And they were great at selling. One of my colleagues could take a customer looking for a twenty-four-inch TV and have them walk out the door with a sixty-inch flat-screen HDTV with a five-year extended warranty. It was amazing to see these people work.

At the same time, I learned what not to do in a customer sales interaction. You couldn't be too pushy and force products and solutions down a buyer's throat. You couldn't come across as an arrogant know-it-all. You couldn't rush people. You had to be patient and invest in the relationships. You had to avoid coming across as a salesman. It sounded counterintuitive, but people needed to feel like they came to the decision to buy the product you were trying to sell on their own.

After eight or nine months, I started to keep a ledger with all my customers' information. This helped me track people and remember small details about their lives. I remembered the names of wives and children. I learned about their hobbies and interests. I also upgraded my wardrobe. I was always in a suit and made sure I was the best dressed in the department. Many of my colleagues didn't pay attention to these details, yet I noticed that these things began to have a tremendously positive effect on what I sold. I started to move up the sales ranks and became a top performer. The most important factor that contributed to my advancement was how I built rapport with people. Sales became a secondary driver for me. I knew that if I invested in the lives of customers, I would get repeat business. I made sure to treat every interaction as if the customer was the most important priority even if they were only buying ten-dollar wires for a TV antenna.

As a consultant and business psychologist today, I am always selling myself. I'm always working toward building and strengthening my brand. I credit my success today to the lessons I learned in the TV department at Sears. There, I learned one of the most important lessons in my life: It's not about what you're selling. It's about the experience you create for people. If you invest in establishing rapport and getting to know others, they will trust you, they will listen to your advice, and they will be loyal, repeat customers of whatever products or services you are selling.

The interactions between sales employees and customers can have a tremendous impact on revenue sales, customer spending patterns, and consumer perceptions of an organization. From a theoretical perspective, rapport building is thought to increase feelings of perceived control in a relationship, leading to greater levels of customer satisfaction. It also leads to high levels of loyalty to the brand or product being sold. In retail, for example, rapport has been found one of the major determinants in the long-term success of customer-employee relationships.[19] Studies have found that rapport building in commercial settings serves as a foundation for customer engagement, service quality, and word-of-mouth communications about a retailer. The personal connections that salespeople make with their customers inspire confidence and lead to repeat business over time.

A variety of strategies and techniques for building rapport in sales environments have been researched over the last forty years. Four unique areas have been found to lead to the highest degree of customer satisfaction and increase in spending: attentive behaviors, imitative behaviors, courteous behaviors, and common grounding behaviors. Some research suggests that simply being attentive to customer needs drives revenue sales. Predictors of attentiveness include eye contact, physical proximity, back-channel responses (e.g., head nods and "mm-hmms"), and empathetic listening. Attentive behavior can also be exhibited through motor mimicry—that is, when one person displays communicative behavior appropriate to the situation or similar to the person with whom they are interacting.

Rapport is also often cultivated by imitating the behaviors of others. In general, this imitation involves matching the behaviors or voice patterns of the other person. Such matching can take place in a variety of areas, including posture, voice tone, type of language, pace of speech, gestures, breathing patterns, or facial expressions. Furthermore, social psychology literature suggests that emotions displayed by two people are often matched through imitation, mimicry, and interpersonal facial expressions.[20] In a sales context, a neuro-linguistic programming approach calls for salespeople to observe verbal and nonverbal cues and react accordingly to develop higher levels of rapport. Such imitative behaviors are useful in interactions with customers because people tend to gravitate toward and become more comfortable around those similar to themselves.

Courteous behaviors also serve as a positive method for cultivating rapport. For example, in a study of grocery cashiers, researchers have found that courteousness helps an employee form a quick bond with the customer and creates the necessary rapport for a positive customer service interaction.[21] Courteous behaviors often include simple actions that make encounters enjoyable for others. For sales employees, those actions might entail smiling, using congenial greetings, engaging in polite behavior, showing concern for the customer's welfare, remembering the customer's name, or thanking the customer for their patronage.

In personal selling literature, scholars suggest that people experience meaningful interactions when they have similar backgrounds, characteristics, tastes, and lifestyles.[22] Common grounding occurs when a sales employee attempts to discover areas of similarity or mutual interest with the customer. For example, office scanning, in which salespeople look around a customer's office for common ground topics (e.g., evidence of mutual hobbies or similar interests), is one strategy salespeople use to build common ground with their customers. Employee behavior that attempts to identify areas of similarity is also applicable in retail contexts, especially if employees and customers have an opportunity to engage in varying degrees of conversation unrelated to the sales transaction (e.g., small talk).

Rapport building is also important in building interpersonal trust and obtaining commitment from customers. The relationships that salespeople establish with customers operate on a continuum that often starts with rapport. One research model that has been used for decades to study salesperson-customer relationships identifies five phases of the relationship: awareness, exploration, buildup, maturity, and decline.[23] It is in the exploration phase that sales representatives attempt to build trust with the customer. For a customer to have trust in a sales rep, the customer must believe in the employee's integrity and reliability. This is a critical and fragile stage in the relationship. The salesperson's goal during the exploration stage should be to reduce uncertainty in the customer's mind. During this phase, the customer is exploring his or her needs and the employee's capability to meet those needs. When determining the capability to meet those needs, lack of established rapport and trust may cause customers to challenge an employee's claims by raising objections. When salespeople address objections in a manner that satisfies the customer and builds trust, they help move the relationship beyond the exploration stage.

For a sales representative, enjoyable interactions and personal connections with customers are essential for success. Rapport indicates customers' feelings about their relationship with the employee. Increasing levels of rapport build a deeper sense of loyalty in customers and inspire more information disclosure from them. Once rapport with a customer has been established, it can have a positive effect on multiple aspects of the sales process. For example, rapport provides a state of grace for service problems after the sale. Research has also found that rapport building increases customers' post-sale satisfaction and repurchase intentions. It also reduces negative word of mouth between customers.[24] The power of rapport building between sales employees and customers creates greater experiences for both parties. It is a vital component of building and maintaining the relationship over time.

PUTTING IT INTO PRACTICE

Establishing rapport is the foundation of any great relationship. Having something in common with another person instantly builds a connection that emphasizes our shared humanity. Building rapport is essential for effective interpersonal communication in a variety of settings. In this chapter, I've outlined its importance across many different fields (e.g., medicine, selection and job interviewing, law enforcement, and sales/customer service). It plays a critical role in how any relationship progresses, personally or professionally. So how can we build rapport with people? What tools and techniques are used to make sure that initial connection matters? How can you develop the skills needed to build great rapport with people? Here are several critical techniques for building rapport with others.

Make a Good First Impression

Making a good first impression is essential for building rapport with people. We all know the age-old saying "dress to impress," which matters most when you're meeting people for the first time. The key is to understand your environment and the people with whom you are interacting. For example, dressing for a business meeting is very different from dressing for a first date. Tailor your outfit and appearance to the demands of the situation. It is also powerful to learn and use names. This was one of the most challenging things for me to do early in my career. I would meet a room full of leaders and forget their names right after they told me! Remembering people's names and saying them back is a courteous way to show you're interested and paying attention. Another simple skill is being polite and engaging. Smile at people, and be open. You'll be surprised how many people forget to smile, which quickly puts a bad taste in people's minds.

I cannot stress the importance of making and maintaining eye contact. Use eye contact to build credibility, convey trust, and accent your points at important parts of the conversation. Look the person directly in the eyes as much as possible. At the very least, you want to be looking the other person in the eye the entire time he or she is speaking. If you are going to look elsewhere at any time during the conversation, do it while you are talking. Even then, keep straying eyes to a minimum. If you don't, it can show people you've become distracted or have lost interest in the discussion. You'll notice that if you're talking to someone and looking around, they'll start looking around too. In the best-case scenario, the only time to break eye contact is when the other person draws your attention to something else, or vice versa. Direct eye contact during a conversation will help build all the positive feelings that you're looking to create. They will let people know if you are interested or disinterested, if you really care or couldn't care less, and whether you're paying attention or off in another world. Pay attention to the messages you send with your eyes as well as the messages others send with theirs. If you make the most of eye contact, you'll find you will connect better with people.

Posture and body language are critical to making a strong first impression. Simple things like standing tall and keeping your shoulders back show confidence and poise. The way you use your body can draw a person in or push them away. Make sure to lean into conversations when you first meet people. Use your hands and other nonverbal gestures to show genuine interest in the other person. Equally important as using your own body language is observing the actions and behaviors of others. Are they drawn into the conversation? Are their nonverbal gestures indicating they are enjoying the interaction? Do they seem interested in speaking to you based not only on what they are saying but also on what they are doing? Reading subtle cues can help you make the best possible first impression.

Draw the Person into the Conversation

Rapport building happens easily when you make the other person feel valued and appreciated. You have to be available to ask questions that draw the other person out. There are tons of different questions you can use to get a person engaged in a conversation. You can ask about hobbies and interests, sports, life history, family, entertainment, fashion, food, or music. I've even found it fun to ask people about the things I geek out on (e.g., Marvel movies and *Star Wars*). The right questions at the right time in the conversation can be light and playful. In most situations, people have their guards up when they interact with someone new. Asking questions and listening attentively shows the other person that you are genuinely interested in getting to know them. It's also important to be gentle and pleasant. I cannot tell you the countless times I've stepped into conversations where people have big egos or need to prove their value or worth. If you are too aggressive, harsh, or direct, it will turn people away. Communicating a positive attitude, showing your enthusiasm, and being flexible with the conversation create a stronger connection.

Find Common Ground

Over the years, I've found that being authentic, genuine, and transparent when I meet new people is a powerful way to build a strong connection. I learned this years ago when I first met some of my close friends and colleagues. What were they going to think of me? How could I put my best foot forward? What if I said the wrong thing? How much should I tell them about myself? I'm sure they felt similarly, but several of them were so authentic when we met that it caused me to open up and share more about my life. They were great at finding common ground and showing empathy. Empathy is powerful. We'll discuss it in more detail in our next chapter. For now, it is important to highlight that understanding an individual's situation and taking a moment to see the world from their perspective shows that you really are interested in getting to know them. Asking open-ended questions can encourage others to open up to you, allowing you to show them empathy and compassion.

To find common ground, you need to choose the best communication method. Experts in the field of communication and interpersonal relationships have found that people rely predominantly on one of three sensory modes: visual ("I see what you mean"), auditory ("I hear what you're saying"), or kinesthetic ("It feels to me like..."). The dominant processing mode affects how an individual reacts to various types of communication. The Visual-Auditory-Kinesthetic (VAK) model suggests that although people use all three methods, each of us has a natural preference for one of the three in how we give, receive, and process information. This is said to be largely genetically determined, but it also develops over time as we grow. Even a basic understanding of the different modes can help you connect to another person more effectively. Acknowledging these different ways of processing information is important because if we know how an individual is representing their world at a particular time, we can develop better rapport with them. Understanding a person's preferred mode enables you to tailor the way you talk to them so you can find common ground more easily.

Mirroring is another technique for finding common ground. People are naturally more comfortable around those who seem the same as themselves. When you mirror, you're purposely behaving similarly to the other individual. The goal is for the other person to sense or feel the similarity without recognizing the intention and to become more open to the conversation. If done properly, people feel more connected to you, and mirroring creates an environment where people connect on a deeper level. It's important to note that mirroring isn't mimicking. Mimicking can be insulting and immediately transparent to the other person. For mirroring to work, it has to be a genuine, honest attempt to understand someone's frame of reference. That means you need to pay attention and try to subtly match the body language, posture, traits, and moods of the person with whom you are interacting. Some of the best leaders I have worked with understand this powerful technique and use it regularly to find common ground with others.

Make it Fun

Nothing connects two people more than humor and laughter. Telling a joke, making one smile, and learning to laugh at yourself help immensely when establishing rapport. I've found that being playful and humorous in the right way at the right time can greatly impact how people perceive me. However, remember that making one laugh is not the same as laughing at someone. You also need to be able to gauge the other person's appetite for humor given the context of the situation. Telling a joke at a party is different from telling one in a business meeting. To avoid making mistakes, there are four areas you should consider:

1. Object (Who or what is the target of the humor, and will they be hurt by it?)
2. Strength (What strength of emotion will the joke arouse, and is that appropriate in the situation?)
3. People (Who is the audience, and who might be offended?)
4. Occasion (Is this the right time and place for a joke?)

Just as it is important to know how to tell a joke, it is also important to know how to respond to one. You can kill a conversation quickly by not responding in the right way to a joke from another person. I always try to determine someone's level of playfulness when I first meet them. Some people are so uptight and serious that it can be hard to get them to smile or laugh. If you can break the ice in the right way, it is great to laugh with someone. A bonding connection takes place over humor.

Giving compliments is another way to engage others and bring them into a fun conversation. This may seem like just another way to be friendly, but it deserves its own recognition in building rapport. If something catches your eye and there is a way to give a compliment about it, that can be a great way to make a connection. In my executive coaching work with leaders, I encourage them to focus on two areas when giving compliments. First, be specific with what you're sharing. Saying you like a person's outfit is nice. Being specific about what you like about their outfit will go a longer way. Second and more importantly, be sincere. Compliments that are surface level or don't have much meaning to the person will get brushed off quickly. If you admire something about the person with whom you are interacting, share it with them in a genuine and authentic way. You'll be surprised how important this can be later on in the relationship.

Proficiency in rapport building takes commitment and practice. I've been working on honing and perfecting it for the last twenty years, and I still have long ways to go. What has worked best for me, however, is not only practicing but also observing the behavior of others. Observe how people interact with one another in restaurants, social settings, business meetings, parties, shopping situations, etc. Look, listen, and learn. Once you've learned how to create rapport, the next step toward building life-changing relationships is understanding others. This skill also takes time and can only begin to occur if rapport has been established.

[1] J. L. Jackson, J. Chamberlin, and K. Kroenke, "Predictors of Patient Satisfaction," *Social Science Medicine* 52, no. 4 (2001): 609–620.

[2] H. L. Shepherd, M. H. N. Tattersall, and P. N. Button, "Physician-Identified Factors Affecting Patient Participation in Reaching Treatment Decisions," *Journal of Clinical Oncology* 26, no. 10 (2008): 1,724–1,731.

[3] B. N. Dang, R. A. Westbrook, C. M. Hartman, and T. P. Giordano, "Retaining HIV Patients in Care: The Role of Initial Patient Care Experiences," *AIDS Behavior* 20, no. 10 (2016): 2,477–2,487.

[4] R. M. Epstein and R. L. Street, "Patient-Centered Communication in Cancer Care: Promoting Healing and Reducing Suffering," *Bethesda National Cancer Institute, NIH Publication*, no. 07-6225.

[5] J. R. Serwint and L. Rutherford, "Sharing Bad News with Patients," *Contemporary Pediatrics* 17 (2000): 45–66.

[6] G. L. Krahn, A. Hallum, and C. Kime, "Are There Good Ways to Give 'Bad News'?" *Pediatrics* 91 (1993): 578–582.

[7] R. E. Frieder, C. H. Van Iddekinge, and P. H. Raymark, "How Quickly Do Interviewers Make Decisions? An Examination of Interviewers' Decision-Making Time across Applicants," *Journal of Occupational and Organizational Psychology* 46 (2015): 616–638.

[8] A. I. Huffcutt, C. H. Van Iddekinge, and P. L. Roth, "Understanding Applicant Behavior in Employment Interviews: A Theoretical Model of Interviewee Performance," *Human Resources Management Review* 21 (2011): 353–367.

[9] N. Ambady and R. Rosenthal, "Thin Slices of Expressive Behavior as Predictors of Interpersonal Consequences: A Meta-Analysis," *Psychological Bulletin* 111 (1992): 256–274.

[10] J. R. Curhan and A. Pentland, "Thin Slices of Negotiation: Predicting Outcomes from Conversational Dynamics within the First Five Minutes," *Journal of Applied Psychology* 92 (2007): 802–811.

[11] D. A. Levy, B. E. Collins, and P. R. Nail, "A New Model of Interpersonal Influence Characteristics," *Journal of Social Behavior & Personality* 13 (1998): 715–733.

[12] M. R. Barrick, S. L. Dustin, T. L. Giluk, G. L. Stewart, J. A. Shaffer, and B. W. Swider, "Candidate Characteristics Driving Initial Impressions during Rapport Building: Implication for Employment Interview Validity," *Journal of Occupational and Organizational Psychology* 85 (2012): 330–352.

[13] R. P. Fisher, R. E. Geiselman, and D. S. Raymond, "Critical Analysis of Police Interviewing Techniques," *Journal of Police Science and Administration* 15 (1987): 177–185.

[14] C. Dando, R. Wilcock, and R. Milne, "The Cognitive Interview: Inexperienced Police Officers' Perceptions of Their Witness/Victim Interviewing Practices," *Legal and Criminological Psychology* 13 (2008): 59–70.

[15] G. M. Davies, H. L. Westcott, and N. Horan, "The Impact of Questioning Style on the Content of Investigative Interviews with Suspected Child Sexual Abuse Victims," *Psychology, Crime & Law* 6 (2000): 81–97.

[16] J. P. Vallano, J. R. Evans, N. Schreiber-Compo, and J. M. Kieckhaefer, "Rapport Building during Witness and Suspect Interviews: A Survey of Law Enforcement," *Journal of Police and Criminal Psychology* 27 (2014): 305–321.

[17] C. E. Kelly, J. C. Miller, A. D. Redlich, and S. M. Kleinman, "A Taxonomy of Interrogation Methods," *Psychology, Public Policy, and Law* 19 (2013): 165–178.

[18] I. Herschkowitz, *Children's Testimony: A Handbook of Psychological Research and Forensic Practice*, eds. M. E. Lamb, D. L. La Rooy, L. C. Malloy, and C. Katz (Chichester, England: Wiley-Blackwell, 2001), 109–128.

[19] K. S. Campbell, L. Davis, and L. Skinner, "Rapport Management during the Exploration Phase of the Salesperson-Customer Relationship," *Journal of Personal Selling and Sales Management* 26 (2006): 359–370.

[20] P. A. Anderson and L. K. Guerrero, "Principles of Communication and Emotion in Social Interaction," in *Handbook of Communication and Emotion*, eds. P. A. Anderson and L. K. Guerrero (San Diego, California: Academic Press, 1998), 49–96.

[21] W. S. Ford and C. N. Etienne, "Can I Help You? A Framework for Interdisciplinary Research on Customer Service Encounters," *Management Communication Quarterly* 7 (1994): 414–441.

[22] G. A. Churchill, R. H. Collins, and W. A. Strang, "Should Retail Salespeople Be Similar to Their Customers?" *Journal of Retailing* 51 (1975): 29–44.

[23] R. F. Dwyer, P. H. Schurr, S. Oh, "Developing Buyer-Seller Relationships," *Journal of Marketing* 52, no. 4 (1987): 11–27.

[24] T. DeWitt and M. K. Brady, "Rethinking Service Recovery Strategies," *Journal of Service Research* 6, no. 2 (2003): 193–207.

UNDERSTANDING OTHERS

Walk with me for a while, my friend—you in my
shoes, I in yours—and then let us talk."
—Richelle E. Goodrich

Building strong relationships is a process. It doesn't happen overnight.
Give-and-take must occur between two people. You have to invest
time, energy, and commitment to make a relationship grow, whether
the relationship is between a parent and a child, a boss and a direct
report, two friends, or a husband and his wife. Understanding others
is a critical component of relational intelligence because it allows a
person to identify the things that are most important to another individual. It enables people to learn about the backgrounds and experiences of others and how this shapes their views of the world. The
foundation for understanding others comes from a strong sense of
self-awareness and emotional intelligence. You need to understand
your own feelings and emotions and how they impact others. You
also need to understand the feelings and emotions of others and how
to respond to these appropriately. Without noticing how people are
responding and reacting in each moment, you will miss opportunities to better understand where they are coming from.

Active listening plays an enormous role in how we understand
and connect with people. Active listening is an acquired skill. Most
people inherently want to share their own perspectives. I've worked
with many clients who need to practice this skill more frequently. To
listen effectively, you have to listen with the intention of genuinely
understanding the thoughts and perspectives of others. It's about taking in information, not trying to change someone's point of view.
You cannot be led by a personal agenda or a preconceived idea of

where you want the conversation to go. As an organizational psychologist and leadership advisor, active listening plays a huge role in executive coaching work with my clients. Great coaches seek first to understand before they look to influence people and drive behavior change.

Understanding others is also about being curious and inquisitive. You have to ask questions that draw information out of others. For over twenty years, I have practiced this in the work my firm does around executive assessments. The executive assessment process is a rigorous approach to learning about the talents and capabilities of leaders and whether they will be a good fit for an organization's culture. The key component of a strong executive assessment process is the behavioral interview. This interview typically lasts two to three hours and explores a candidate's personal leadership journey. A great leadership advisor is able to solicit information from the candidate by asking them questions that draw on their history and life experiences. The information they share enables the psychologist to make highly nuanced behavioral insights about their strengths, potential blind spots, and derailer risks.

To effectively conduct a behavioral interview, the leadership advisor has to know how to ask probing questions. For example, the goal is not just to learn where a candidate grew up, though that may be the first question. The goal is to probe deeper into areas that give the consultant a stronger understanding of the leader. I'll typically ask questions like, "What role did your father and mother play in your personal growth and development?" "What values and beliefs did they instill in you at an early age?" "Which role models and mentors shaped your perspective of leadership in high school or college?" "How did your relationships with your siblings impact how you view the world?" The power of questions in a behavioral interview is in how you probe around surface-level answers. In the same way, effective relationship builders know how to ask probing questions. They are open-minded and truly want to understand another person's perspectives.

Learning about other people gives us a glimpse into their lives. It's about showing empathy and relatability. You also have to be vulnerable and share some things about yourself. It has to be a give-and-take dynamic when you're starting to learn about and understand another person. There is an art to doing it effectively. It takes practice and time to strengthen this skill. Some of the best leaders I have worked with are constantly finding new ways to learn about people. They're willing to admit what they don't know and show an appetite for acquiring new knowledge. Such knowledge allows them to more deeply understand their people and teams.

Emotional Intelligence as the Foundation for Understanding Others

I've always had a passion for the concept of emotional intelligence (EI). As I mentioned in the introduction, learning about EI started my conceptualization of how it played a role in influencing others and building life-changing relationships. In graduate school, I took a deep dive into truly understanding EI, learning how it was used to grasp one's emotions and those of others, seeking the connection EI had with empathy, and investigating how it was used to effectively lead others. Since the publication of Daniel Goleman's book *Emotional Intelligence: Why It Can Matter More Than IQ* in 1995, the concept has generated unparalleled interest in both the general public and the scientific fields.[1] EI became a topic of rapid interest for researchers and academicians when I was completing my doctoral degree. It was also considered one of the hottest buzzwords in corporate America at that time and still garners high interest over twenty-five years later.

The concept of EI was introduced for the first time by Peter Salovey and John D. Mayer in 1990. They defined it as "a form of intelligence that [involved] the ability to understand and monitor one's own and others' feelings and emotions, to discriminate among them, and to use this information to guide one's thinking and actions."[2] But although EI was studied before Goleman's book, he made the term popular. As I started to learn more about the subject, I quickly realized there were many different versions of what EI actually meant. Goleman laid out a powerful case that stated that factors such as self-awareness, self-management, social awareness, and relationship management determine personal and professional success. At the same time, another researcher, Reuven Bar-On, introduced the concept of EQ, which he defined "as an array of non-cognitive capabilities, competencies, and skills that [influenced] one's ability to succeed in coping with environmental demands and pressures."[3] These three different theories have attempted to describe the skills, traits, and abilities associated with EI.

The Mayer-Salovey-Caruso ability model of EI focuses on four areas that enable people to understand and use emotions. The first area, emotional perception, they define as the ability to be self-aware of emotions and express emotions and emotional needs accurately to others. This is the area that has the most impact on understanding others. Without an awareness of your feelings and emotions, it is very difficult to engage and interact effectively with others. The second area, emotional assimilation, is the ability to distinguish among different emotions a person is feeling and to identify those that are influencing certain thought processes. When building relationships with others, it is critical that you can assimilate how you are feeling based on what another person is sharing with you. Are they making you feel frustrated or angry? Are they eliciting positive emotions from you? Can you identify what you are feeling based on what they are saying?

The third area, emotional understanding, is the ability to understand complex emotions and identify transitions from one emotion to another. This plays a role in how you understand what people are trying to convey when you are interacting with them. Are they communicating good or bad information based on the subtle nuances in their feelings and emotions? Can you pick up on transitions from frustration to satisfaction and from sadness to joy? The final area, emotional management, is the ability to stay open to both pleasant and unpleasant feelings. It allows you to reflectively connect or detach from an emotion and regulate emotions in both yourself and others. This plays a critical role in how we connect with and learn about people. Those who have the ability to use emotional management skills to guide a conversation create the greatest positive connection with others.

Goleman's competency model defines EI as a set of abilities that motivates one to survive in the face of frustrations, control impulses and delay gratification, manage one's moods and keep distress from having an impact on one's ability to think, and show empathy toward others.[4] His model also comprises four constructs that look at EI from a perspective different from that of Mayer, Salovey, and Caruso. Self-awareness is defined as the ability to identify one's emotions and recognize their impact. Self-management involves controlling one's emotions and impulses to adapt to changing circumstances. Social awareness consists of the ability to sense, understand, and react to others' emotions while comprehending social networks. And relationship management focuses on the ability to inspire, influence, and develop others while managing conflict.

While studying Goleman's model in graduate school, I found it difficult to wrap my head around his conceptualization of EI. Did it focus on awareness of one's specific feelings and emotions or self-awareness more broadly? He often interchanged the two frequently. Did self-management extend behind managing one's emotions? For example, a person could effectively manage anger or frustration in a conversation but could have impulse control issues in other areas (e.g., spending or eating). Social awareness was a puzzling bucket as well. Having a good understanding of your own emotions and those of others did not guarantee that you could read a room, navigate organizational politics, or build effective networks. I was most confused with his final area: relationship management. Inspiring people involves many more skills beyond EI. Influence comes with building trust and embracing diversity. Conflict management skills are not just about EI but about knowing how to deescalate interpersonal problems when they surface. This involves taking time to learn about situations, people, and the context through which conflict arises. These skills extend way beyond having good EI.

Bar-On's mixed model of EI was even more interesting than Mayer et al.'s and Goleman's frameworks. His model of EI focused on the concept of mixed intelligence, which consisted of cognitive ability and aspects of personality, health, and well-being. His definition of EI included vast dimensions, including emotional self-awareness, assertiveness, self-regard, self-actualization, empathy, social responsibility, problem-solving, reality testing, stress tolerance, and impulse control. He believed that the combination of these skills, related to one's emotions and cognitive intelligence, equally contribute to a person's general intelligence and potential success in life. As I spent more time studying his conceptual model, I found it hard to distinguish it from concepts in other areas of psychology. His view of EI seemed to be an umbrella term, under which you could throw almost every psychological trait or skill.

For the purposes of understanding others as part of relational intelligence, I view the Mayer-Salovey-Caruso ability model as the best way to define and describe EI. In simplest terms, EI refers to the ability to recognize and regulate emotions in ourselves and others. We have to be able to perceive emotions if we are to truly understand other people and how they engage and interact with us. We need to assimilate emotional information if we are to distinguish the "what" someone is saying from the "how" they are saying it. We need to understand the differences between certain emotions if we are to capture the essence of someone's attempted communication. Most importantly, we need to effectively manage emotions, those in ourselves and others, to connect on a deep level with others. EI is a powerful tool in helping us understand others. However, it is only one piece of the puzzle. Getting to know someone in the context of a relationship and understanding them contains many other factors.

THE POWER OF ACTIVE LISTENING

I've always been amazed by people who are good active listeners. I learned this at an early age through some of the family dynamics in my home. My mother was a great active listener. It didn't matter what I was trying to communicate and share with her. She always listened attentively and let me express my thoughts before she interjected with counsel or advice. As a special education teacher for fifth- and sixth-grade students, active listening was a skill she developed over time. She taught me that listening was one of the most import-ant elements in developing relationships with students, as it showed respect for them. It also made genuine dialogue possible, as students were more articulate with the support of a good listener. This was even more important with timid or shy students, who had difficulty finding words to express themselves and talking things out.

One can argue that teachers are not counselors and that class time is too precious to be spent on listening. While this may contain an element of truth, without genuine listening and taking time to understand students, it is impossible to establish meaningful rela-tionships. I witnessed my mom do this firsthand with some of the most difficult and challenging pupils. Mom was always giving special attention to those who needed extra love, care, and support. She had a knack for identifying where kids were coming from and took the time to learn about their stories. Many of her students came from broken homes. Verbal and physical abuse was the norm in their households, so she provided an atmosphere in her classroom where children could feel safe and secure.

It is often said that good listening can be therapeutic and can heal people who are deeply troubled by negative emotions and feel-ings. Great teachers don't talk before they listen. They pay atten-tion to their students. An active approach to understanding others requires accepting and respecting others' opinions and, at times, probing problems by showing an eagerness to learn more. Although I saw this with my mother, I often had difficulty seeing this with my own elementary school teachers. In many situations, when students come to a teacher, the teacher often feels compelled to suggest solu-tions to tackle the problem, which deprives students of opportunities to express themselves fully. Researchers have found that active listen-ing is more productive by reflecting to students what has been heard and assuring them it has been heard correctly.[5] It is a mutual effort to ensure that communication is carried out genuinely and with trust, acceptance, and the exchange of true feelings. During active listen-ing, students are confident that what they say is not only heard but also fully understood, which makes them feel secure enough to reveal deep emotions and feelings to the teacher. Active listening helps students fully express and explore underlying issues they may be facing.

What I learned from my mother was that good active listening as part of a focus on understanding others was the foundation for transforming a classroom into a learning environment where students embraced a spirit of acceptance, respect, and security. The quality of student-teacher relationships often determines whether students' needs are met and affects their attitudes and classroom behavior. Great teachers aim to create a classroom climate that represents an effective blend of warmth, care, tolerance, respect, acceptance, and competent teaching. My mother's students loved being in her classroom. Her warm and friendly demeanor engendered trust and support. Amazingly, years after students had been in my mother's class, they would come back to the school just to visit her. My mother has tons of letters from people ten and twenty years later about the influence and impact she had on them at a young age. It's a testament to how she took time to build relationships with her students.

Active listening is also widely assumed to be essential in well-functioning, intimate relationships. Attentive listening in relationships, particularly during moments of self-disclosure, is essential for sustaining intimacy and providing adequate support. When understanding others, active listening can be conceptualized as having three main elements. First, the listener shows interest in the speaker's message through nonverbal behaviors such as back channeling. Back channeling includes brief acknowledgments (e.g., "mm-hmm" and "yeah") showing the listener is following the conversation. Second, active listening includes paraphrasing the partner's message without evaluations or judgment. The third element of active listening is comprised of open questions that encourage the speaker to further elaborate on personal thoughts and feelings.[6]

Research in the field of family psychology has found that the basic features of attentive listening have several functions in the context of emotional disclosures of stressful events. First, active listening is necessary and inevitable if one wants to understand a partner's stressful experience and its meaning for the disclosing partner. For example, a husband's perception of his wife's communicated attitudes, feelings, and behaviors could be more accurate if he listens to his wife attentively. According to the systemic transactional model in relationships between couples, the supporting partner must first perceive and decode the stressed partner's signs of stress in order to understand the significance of the stressful event or situation.[7] This requires attentive listening, which, in turn, is needed to adapt to the situation and provide adequate coping mechanisms that meet the needs of their partner.

Second, listening attentively and understanding the disclosing partner's stress also have a positive effect on that partner. Social scientists have found that active listeners are perceived as more understanding, responsive, and supportive by disclosing partners.[8] For example, when a husband is perceived to be more understanding and responsive, his wife will feel more intimate and satisfied after disclosing a stressful event or situation. Third and most importantly, active listening encourages more self-disclosure. When a partner listens attentively, the speaker is more prone to talk without fear of criticism or negative judgments. This adds depth and detail to conversations. Although much of this research has been conducted with couples and stressful life events, the process through which two people engage with each other is applicable to all relationships. When one person is actively listening, taking the time to understand another, the person being listened to can be more open, share additional details, and feel they are being heard.

Mindfulness also plays a critical role in actively listening and understanding others. Mindfulness is the basic human ability to be fully present, aware of where we are and what we're doing, and not overly reactive or overwhelmed by what's going on around us. It is a quality that every person possesses to a certain degree. Those who can tap into it more frequently through practice and repetition are more grounded and present in various circumstances. It also helps one be more aware of thoughts and feelings without distraction or judgment.

Research has found many benefits to mindfulness practices. Mindfulness improves emotional well-being.[9] Being mindful makes it easier to savor pleasures in life as they occur. It helps you become fully engaged in activities and the environment around you.[10] It improves mental and physical health. Mindfulness can help relieve stress, treat heart disease, lower blood pressure, reduce chronic pain, and improve sleep. More importantly, it enables us to connect on a deeper level with people by being present and in the moment. Being mindful directly influences the ability to regulate, control, and manage our emotions and how we respond to people. It has been linked to active listening, empathy, and compassion with romantic partners, patients and therapists in clinical settings, and in working relationships.[11]

Both active listening and mindfulness focus on the importance of attention and present orientation. Because active listening consists of three important processes—cognitive processes (i.e., attending, understanding, or interpreting messages), affective processes (i.e., being motivated and energized to attend to another person), and behavioral processes (i.e., verbally and nonverbally signaling that a message has been received and understood)—it is easy to see how mindfulness plays such a critical role in our ability to be attentive to others. Because they conceptually overlap, mindful attending encourages the listener to orient themselves to the other person and to stay present in the moment. Additionally, facets of mindful attending, such as aware acting, observing, and describing, have been found to be predictive of active listening because these facets are closely aligned with the sensing, processing, and responding components that make up listening.[12]

CURIOSITY AS BREEDING GROUND FOR UNDERSTANDING OTHERS

When I first entered graduate school, I was excited to meet and connect with new people. I moved from New Jersey to Tampa, Florida, for my doctoral program, and I was eager to learn about my fellow colleagues and the professors at our university. At one of our first social mixers, I met the people in my cohort as well as some older students and professors. Graduate school was a funny place. Most students wanted to brag and bloviate about their accomplishments. The older students had to let us know that we were the first years and that there was a pecking order for how things took place in the program. I remember walking around the party and listening to all the professors discuss their areas of expertise, the awards they had won, the articles they had published in obscure research journals I had never heard about, and the great work their graduate assistants were conducting. The older students operated in the same way. It was almost as if people were trying to prove themselves and their value to the newcomers.

Then there was Kelly. Kelly was different from the normal graduate student. You saw her right away because she was one of the tallest people in the room. She was also stunningly beautiful. Prior to graduate school, she had been a model for several years and was used to the attention of others. However, she didn't have to prove her worth to anyone. She didn't talk about her accomplishments. She didn't go on about her knowledge or expertise. She worked her way around the room and genuinely showed interest in others. I was making a drink by the bar when she came up to me to introduce herself. The first thing she said to me was, "Boy, these parties are lame, aren't they?" It made me laugh. She then asked what I enjoyed doing in my spare time. I had been on a health kick since I moved to Tampa, so I mentioned that I enjoyed cooking. Kelly's eyes widened as she probed for details: "What's the most exotic dish you've made?" "What makes a great chef?" "What else in your life are you passionate about?" Kelly continued to ask questions to learn about my hobbies and interests. She was curious and inquisitive. It wasn't an act or some show. She was genuinely interested in learning more about me. This resonated with me because she wasn't trying to get anything out of the conversation. She had an appetite for learning about people and their backgrounds and experiences. I found out later that she was one of the smartest people in the room. She had the highest GRE placement score in the entire program and was on a full-ride presidential scholarship. Although these were impressive accomplishments, it was her curiosity about the world around that was appealing to me.

Everyone experiences moments when they are interested or curious. Where people differ is in the frequency, intensity, length, and scope of these experiences. Curious people tend to recognize and pursue knowledge and new experiences. They possess an open and receptive attitude toward targets of their attention. They show a greater willingness to manage the novelty and uncertainty that arise when they meet new people. To the extent that people engage in these behaviors regularly, curiosity contributes to exploration, discovery, growth, and development.

According to the self-expansion model of relationships,[13] a primary reason for humans doing much of what they do is to increase knowledge and experiences concerning themselves, other people, and the world around them. One of the best ways to accomplish these ends is to enter into close relationships with others. When someone is willing to listen to and integrate what another person is sharing, this process is characterized as self-expansion and has strong positive effects for both the person and the relationship. When we develop relationships that offer self-expansion opportunities, we become closer to others. Several studies have shown that greater self-expansion leads to greater relationship satisfaction and commitment.[14] During relationship formation, considerable tension exists as two people manage heightened novelty and uncertainty. A lack of curiosity and intolerance for uncertainty will have a negative effect on how the relationship develops. Curious people show a strong tendency to engage in tension-producing situations that offer self-expansion opportunities. When profoundly aware and curious, a person is able to be responsive to the information shared by others. This strengthens bonds and opens the door for more growth in relationships.

Situations differ in their potential rewards for a curious person. For example, let's look at two common situations for an initial encounter between two unacquainted strangers. In one situation, the two people facilitate intimacy by listening to, reciprocating, and building on self-disclosures. Information shared helps each person get to know and value the other. This creates the groundwork for a positive relationship to form. In the other situation, people engage in small talk with relatively few personal disclosure opportunities.

Although small talk will break the ice, these initial interactions often end before disclosure can occur. That's because most people do not find small talk interesting and tend to withdraw or disengage from a conversation quickly. Curious people, on the other hand, are intentional about altering the content of a conversation by redirection, playfulness, or self-disclosure. Because they have an appetite for learning about others, they will ask probing questions to find areas of similarity or learn new information.

Research in the field of organizational psychology has found various benefits to curiosity in business settings. In the short-term, curiosity is used to seek out, explore, and immerse oneself in situations with potential for new information or experiences. In the longer term, consistently acting on curious feelings serves to expand knowledge, build intellectual and creative capabilities, and strengthen relationships.[15] A curious person is responsive to different social dynamics, networking needs, and politics in organizations. They can adapt more effectively to organizational changes. They are more intrigued than frustrated when trying to understand and appreciate the unique value of new colleagues. They're also flexible enough to adapt strategies and plans to unfamiliar cultures in sophisticated global markets.[16] In research on working adults, curiosity has been positively associated with idea generation, job performance, interpersonal relationships, and commitment to organizations. To improve their work performance, curious employees are more apt to proactively seek feedback, ask open-ended questions during integration and meeting new people, and effectively cope with ambivalent feedback from leaders in senior management.

Social scientists have found several elements of curiosity. First, there is a general fascination with new information and experiences and the intrinsic desire to resolve an information gap. Second, curiosity is typically contingent on two automatic, rapid judgments. The more obvious judgment is whether a person believes there is potential for novelty in a situation or interaction with another person. If sufficient novelty potential is present, a person's attention is more likely to be captured and held. The less obvious judgment is that a person must also believe they possess the adequate mental faculties to cope with feelings or emotions that arise from engaging in new, complex, uncertain, or unfamiliar situations. For a person to engage curiosity, they must believe there is sufficient novelty potential and that they can cope with or manage this novelty. Third, humans are social creatures, and the degree to which a person feels a sense of belonging has a large influence on how fulfilled they feel when interacting and learning about others. Most people are intrigued by and gravitate toward others for a host of social benefits (e.g., comfort, excitement, commiseration, and connection). The socially curious person is open to a diversity of opinions and yearns to understand others more completely.

Curiosity has also been found to facilitate personal growth and development as we build relationships. For example, curiosity in social interactions tends to broaden one's attention to information about people and topics of conversation, which increases a person's desire to have more interactions with others. An accumulation of interactions with the same person who continually produces flow-like absorption and a desire to learn more about their perspectives and experiences lead to a more enduring relationship over time. Personality traits such as openness to experience and agreeableness increase the likelihood that people will have positive interpersonal interactions. Likewise, personality traits that increase sensitivity to rewarding features of social interactions can lead to the development of stronger relationships. People who interact with highly curious individuals are more likely to feel closer to them and find them more attractive than less curious people. We feel good when others listen, respond, and demonstrate interest in what we say and who we are.

WALKING A MILE IN MY SHOES: EMPATHY MATTERS

Empathy lies at the heart of social communication. It shapes our lives by motivating people to connect on a deep level with others. Over the course of my life, I've come across people who display empathy in different ways. In my consulting practice, some of the best leaders I work with know how to understand where others are coming from. They take time to see things from other people's perspectives. In my social life, I've gravitated toward people who know how to share the emotional experiences of others. Some of my closest friends don't just understand me from a cognitive perspective. They can connect with my affective states and create positive shared experiences. However, I've seen the greatest display of empathy in the relationship I have with some of my family members. My sister takes empathy to a whole different level. She's a medical doctor, and the empathy she shows is best characterized by warmth, compassion, and a genuine concern for others.

At her core, my sister comes across as a curious and inquisitive person. When she meets people for the first time, she asks probing questions and wants to learn about and understand them. As an organizational psychologist, I do similar work with my clients when we are conducting executive assessments. It is pleasantly surprising to see someone with a physician's background and training utilize similar skills. My sister has this unique ability to find common ground with people no matter the subject of conversation. She is great at recognizing other people's emotions and understanding their perspectives. She also knows how to develop deep emotional connections with people.

Empathy can be defined as a natural tendency to share and understand the emotional experiences of others. It is believed to elicit an approach orientation toward others in need and facilitate prosocial behavior.[17] Empathy plays an essential role in the development and maintenance of long-term relationships. It is a foundational component in understanding and connecting with others. One of the main reasons for this is that empathy forms a key aspect of emotional support, which is a strong correlate of relationship satisfaction. Having someone understand our feelings helps us become more aware of those feelings, thereby enabling us to more fully become who we really are. For example, in romantic relationships, feeling understood by someone has been found to be related to self-esteem and to feeling satisfied with one's partner independently of feeling accepted.[18]

Carl Rogers, one of the founders of the humanistic approach in psychology, was one of the first to conduct an in-depth analysis of empathy. He described empathy as the listener's effort to hear another person deeply, accurately, and nonjudgmentally.[19] He believed empathy involved skillful reflective listening that clarified and amplified the person's own experience and meaning. It is about entering the private perceptual world of another person. It includes being sensitive moment to moment to the changing felt emotions they express. It is about communicating your sense of who they are and what's most important to them. Since his early work on the subject, psychologists across many disciplines have explored empathy's effects on interpersonal dynamics and relationship formation.

Today, empathy is widely believed to be an umbrella term. Most researchers consider empathy a multidimensional construct, mainly including three areas: cognitive empathy, affective empathy, and empathic concern. Cognitive empathy describes how people recognize others' emotions and understand their perspectives. It involves having an awareness of another person's thoughts, feelings, beliefs, and intentions. Many of the leaders I work with display this with their direct reports. Maria, a senior executive in the financial services industry, is great at showing empathy toward her people. When new people join her team, she takes time to get to know them personally. She asks probing questions to get at underlying issues about how they are wired and what's most important to them. She finds ways to tap into their true talents and capabilities. Her people often refer to her as a mama bear, a testament to her ability to make people feel warm, welcome, and part of the team.

Affective empathy refers to autonomic and vicarious emotional responses to others' emotions. It is often used interchangeably with emotional contagion—that is, the ability to mimic the physiological and behavioral experiences of another person's emotional experience and, thus, experience the same emotions. One of my closest friends, Mark, a professor of psychology at a prestigious university, is skilled at connecting on a deep level with others. It is one of the reasons we have been friends since graduate school. Mark has the unique ability to feel and express what others are experiencing. I witnessed this firsthand early on in our relationship. I was in a deep depression and didn't know if I wanted to complete my doctoral degree. I remember coming home that summer not knowing if I would return to school in the fall. Mark went out of his way to spend time with me and just talk about life. He empathized with where I was coming from and my emotional state. We had deep heart-to-hearts where he listened; shared how I was feeling; and offered guidance, counsel, and support. Without his encouragement, I would have never completed my doctoral program.

Empathic concern can be defined as an emotional response of compassion and concern upon witnessing someone else in need. It has been suggested that empathic concern reflects the deeply rooted drive of parental nurturance, as it has evolved in humans to help offspring survive. Were humans not interested in protecting, helping, and nurturing their vulnerable young, our species would have died out quickly. I've seen genuine empathic concern from many of the pastors and faith-based organizations with which my firm works. Jonathan, a senior pastor of a large church in New Jersey, is a great example of someone who has empathic concern for others. He places such a strong emphasis on building close relationships with his parishioners that empathetic tendencies filter down into many of the activities of his church. From making first-time guests feel welcome to outreach and volunteer work in the community, he embodies compassionate love and care for all around him.

For years, neuroscientists have been trying to improve our knowledge on the neural basis of a wide range of human behaviors, like empathy, attachment, and connectivity. The social brain hypothesis states that our brains have expanded so much over the course of evolution because of the challenges involved in living in complex social groups.[20] In fact, empathy is one of the most important factors for our ability to survive and adapt to our environments. The metaphor of the human brain as a social organ that can be empathic and compassionate is supported by findings in neurodevelopment and attachment theory. Research in these fields suggests that our brain develops in the context of relationships and that brains regulate one another during moment-to-moment interactions.[21] The establishment of human bonds and interactions is essential for human survival, which explains why relationship building is particularly powerful and salient. Our understanding of others can only be fully realized if we display empathy toward people. Without empathy, the strong bonds that form long-term relationships cannot take place.

PUTTING IT INTO PRACTICE

Understanding others is the second critical skill in building life-changing relationships. People who have strong emotional intelligence, are good active listeners, have a curious and inquisitive mindset, and are genuinely empathetic toward people form the strongest bonds with others. You have to be willing to put in work to learn about and understand people. We all have some innate ability to show an interest in getting to know others. From marriage to relationships with extended family and friends, our ability to understand others impacts how we connect with people in our personal lives. From colleagues and coworkers to customers and external key stakeholders, understanding others plays a role in how we build businesses and lead organizations. When coaching clients, there are many training and development tools that I use to help leaders learn how to cultivate a deeper understanding of their people. Here are four things you should focus on if you want to grow in this area.

Develop Your Emotional Intelligence

EQ is a skill all people should learn. Our ability to understand our own emotions and others is critical to success in our personal and professional lives. The first step to strengthening your emotional intelligence is to take an EQ assessment. There are three ways to do this. The first approach takes the form of a self-report. These tests are similar to personality tests, like the Myers-Briggs and the Enneagram. The Bar-On Emotional Quotient Inventory (EQ-i) is one of the best self-report measures of emotional intelligence for people sixteen years and over.[22] It was developed as a measure of emotionally competent behavior that provided an estimate of one's emotional and social skills. The EQ-i is not meant to be a measure of personality traits or cognitive capacity but a measure of one's ability to be successful in dealing with environmental demands and pressures. It is a good tool if you want to get a quick take on where your EQ skills stand today.

The second approach involves informant measures, like how others perceive you. These types of assessments are typically conducted in one of two ways. Goleman's Emotional Competence Inventory (ECI) is a multi-rater 360 survey tool that provides ratings on a series of behavior indicators of EQ.[23] It is most often used in organizational settings, as it enables a leader to get rater feedback from different stakeholders (e.g., direct reports, peers, and upper management). The second approach, which we use at our firm, is through 360 stakeholder interviews. Similar to a 360 feedback survey tool, we gather feedback from a number of different people who work with a leader. The difference is that we do interviews instead of using a survey. This allows us to get at real examples and situations where a person has demonstrated EQ in how they work with others.

The third approach involves ability or performance measures. The most well-known ability measure is the Mayer-Salovey-Caruso Emotional Intelligence Test (MSCEIT).[24] Here, a person has to work on a number of different problems or tasks while keeping EI in mind during workflow activities. During the test, people are evaluated against the four areas I outlined earlier in this chapter (emotional perception, emotional assimilation, emotional understanding, and managing emotions). In my opinion, the MSCEIT is the best assessment tool for learning about your emotional intelligence, because it focuses on critical dimensions for understanding, using, and managing emotions. No matter what type of EQ assessment you use, it is important to get a baseline understanding of where you stand today so you can figure out how to make improvements and grow.

Once you have an idea of your EQ, it is important to put together a plan for how you can improve it. There are many books and resources for developing EQ. In the business world, one of the books I recommend is Goleman's *The Emotionally Intelligent Workplace*. It is a great resource for understanding how to build teams and cultures on a foundation of strong EQ. Another option I highly recommend is working with an executive coach. Executive coaching is a great way to develop deeper self-awareness and an understanding of your strengths and areas of opportunity. Good coaches will take the results of an EQ assessment and help you build a personal development plan that will drive the behavioral changes you want to make. When finding an executive coach, make sure you work with someone who has expertise in emotional intelligence. We have resources on our website that can help you identify and select the right coach: www. bandelliandassociates.com.

Practice Active Listening

Active listening is an acquired skill. Most people have some propensity for it, but great relationship builders make a habit of listening to others. I've learned that the best way to get better at active listening is to practice it in different settings. For example, when you're with your family, make an effort to spend quality time and give special attention to your spouse and children. Ask them about their days. Listen to their challenges and issues without jumping in to try to solve problems. Put down your phone and set aside other distractions so you can be present with them in the moment. You'll be amazed at how personal relationships will flourish and grow if you spend time on them.

In our work lives, there are several ways to practice active listening. The first is in the work we do with direct reports and their teams. I always encourage my clients to find time each month to consistently meet with each of their direct reports. These meetings are different from typical project status updates. They are meetings where the leader's job is just to focus on their direct report's growth and development. It is a time where they can be a resource to those beneath them. This is one of the best places to practice active listening. The meeting content is generally driven by the person's direct report, so there is no predetermined agenda to cover. This enables the leader to just listen and provide guidance and support.

The second way to practice active listening is through the relationships people have with colleagues or peers. Active listening is critical in these settings because most organizational initiatives require a strong degree of partnership between different departments or business units. Good leaders seek to understand their colleagues before they get points across. They go into meetings with a desire to learn before sharing opinions or beliefs. They ask questions to get at underlying issues and concerns. They are good at hearing people out. Some of the best senior executives I work with have a knack for listening more than they speak. They take everyone's input into account before making decisions. Make sure you practice this with your coworkers. People need to feel that you are working toward collective organizational outcomes. It's not just about your personal goals and objectives.

The third way to practice active listening is through relationships with clients or customers. In my work, I've built my practice around how I listen to my clients' needs. I am never prescriptive in the feedback I provide. I don't act like the psychologist or expert in the room. I want people to see me as a key thought partner and trusted advisor. To do this, you have to be great at active listening. Sometimes, it's the subtle things people say that can enable you to build a strong connection with them. You have to be listening for those things. If you're doing most of the talking, it won't happen. I've also found that silence can be a great asset in how you initially build a relationship. Most people cringe when there is silence on a call or in a meeting. I've learned to capitalize on these moments to give others a chance to think and reflect. Most of us are constantly on the go and don't take time for reflection. Make sure you give people the space to think and reflect as you listen and gather information from them.

Seek Out Feedback

I've touched on this several times already. We all grow by getting feedback from others. This doesn't have to involve a fancy 360 assessment or some EQ test. You can request feedback just by reaching out and asking others to share opinions with you. It takes humility to ask for feedback. You have to be willing to work on the areas people share with you. One of my clients in the telecommunications industry collects feedback from his team on a quarterly basis.

He brings his team together in a room and draws three columns on a whiteboard. Column one focuses on what his people like about him. What is he doing well? Column two is about the things he does that drive people nuts. Where can he get better? Column three focuses on ways he can be more supportive. What are others not getting from him that prevents them from reaching their full potential? He sets the columns up, then leaves the room. While he is gone, the team works together to provide feedback in each column. Everything must remain anonymous and confidential. He doesn't want to know who says what. When he gets back in the room, the team takes him through the feedback. They work together to rank the most important areas in each column. This gives him a blueprint for where he needs to improve. His ability to actively listen and understand others in these settings is what makes the exercise so important to the team. People are honest, open, and transparent because he has created an environment where he listens and is receptive to their inputs. His team loves doing this exercise, and he is consistent in doing it every three to four months. It has served as the foundation for a culture where people are open and receptive to receiving feedback from one another. I encourage you to do the same with your people and teams.

On a more personal level, it's similarly important to know how we are showing up for others. One of the keys to a great relationship is being open to listening and understanding your partner. If you haven't practiced this before, it's easy to get started. Sit down with your spouse or loved one and discuss your relationship. Ask for their input and opinion. Show a desire to learn and grow. Let them know you want to be better for them and the relationship. You only grow if you know where you can develop and improve. Some of the best relationships in my life came out stronger after a heart-to-heart, where people were open and honest with me. It's one of the greatest things you can do for the people around you.

Observe Others

If you want to learn how to better understand the people around you, it's critical to find role models who demonstrate this behavior. Early in my career, I had the opportunity to work with several different mentors. One of them was Marissa, a senior consultant at a firm I was a part of for many years. Marissa was a great people person. She knew how to connect with others on a deep level. The first time I met her was at an all-employee annual retreat. I attended her breakout session on executive women in leadership. She was chairing a panel of senior executives who were discussing the influence women had in senior leadership roles. The panel discussed things like empathy, diversity and inclusion, networking, and understanding how to navigate organizational politics. What I found most interesting was how Marissa brought each panelist into the conversation. She was skilled at asking a question, then shaping the conversation to get input and information from the four women she was interviewing. Her ability to connect with her panelists by listening attentively made for an engaging and entertaining discussion.

The next day, at lunch, Marissa discussed the work she had been leading for our firm and the research we were conducting. Our meeting was highly informative. However, the thing that stood out the most was how she invested in getting to know me. She took time to learn about my background and experiences. She asked about the research I was conducting, and we discussed possible partnerships we could do together in the future. That day was the start of a great professional relationship. Over the next five years, I had opportunities to work with Marissa on several different things. She invited me to work on several of her client engagements. We did some research together. We got to partner on assessment and executive coaching work. Through each of these different experiences, I got a front-row seat to how she interacted and built relationships with others.

By observing the way she built relationships, I learned three important lessons. First, you have to be genuine and authentic when connecting with others. Marissa was down-to-earth and easy to get along with. She made people smile when they were around her. Second, she was a great active listener. She had good emotional intelligence and could empathize with the experience of others. Third and most importantly, she understood the power of diversity. We'll talk about this in great detail in our next chapter. For now, it is important to note that she embraced people's differences. She valued seeking out and learning from people who were not like her. She believed it helped make her a better consultant to her clients and a stronger leader to the people in her firm. You have to find people like this in your life if you want to grow and get better at relationships.

Look for ways to observe others. Do it at work with colleagues. Observe people in your extended family. Watch people at social events when you're out with friends. I've learned so many different lessons about people from making a point to stop and take in the world around me. You might credit this tendency to my being a psychologist, but anyone can do it. All you have to do is make a concerted effort to study people. If you want to go a step further, find a good mentor, therapist, or coach. Mentors invest in helping us grow. They are great to work with because they help us see things to which we haven't been exposed. We can learn a lot from their wisdom and experience. Therapists are great resources as well. They can help us explore parts of ourselves that make us do some of the things we do. A good therapist also offers a unique perspective because they are not living in the situation with you. The same can be said of a good coach. These types of people are great external thought partners who can help you think and process through situations, events, and people.

Whatever you do, make sure you find people from whom you can learn. I cannot emphasize enough the importance of observing others' behaviors. We learn so much from how the people closest to us interact with the world around them. There's power in what we pick up from others. Surround yourself with people who are skilled at understanding others. It's the gateway to embracing individual differences, developing trust, and cultivating influence.

---

[1] D. Goleman, *Emotional Intelligence: Why It Can Matter More Than IQ* (New York, Bantam Books).

[2] P. Salovey and J. D. Mayer, "Emotional Intelligence," *Imagination, Cognition, and Personality* 9 (1990): 185–200.

[3] R. Bar-On, *Bar-On Emotional Quotient Inventory: Technical Manual* (Toronto: Multi-Health Systems).

[4] D. Goleman, *Working with Emotional Intelligence* (New York: Bantam Books, 1998).

[5] T. Gordon, *Teacher Effectiveness Training* (New York: Wyden Books, 1974).

6   C. R. Rogers, *Client-Centered Therapy: Its Current Practice, Implications, and Theory* (Boston, Massachusetts: Houghton Mifflin, 1951).

7   G. Bodenmann, "A Systemic-Transactional Conceptualization of Stress in Coping Couples," *Swiss Journal of Psychology* 54 (1995): 34–49.

8   D. D. Cahn and L. R. Frey, "Listeners' Perceived Verbal and Nonverbal Behaviors Associated with Communicators' Perceived Understanding and Misunderstanding," *Perceptual and Motor Skills* 74 (1992): 1,059–1,064.

9   S. R. Bishop, M. Lau, S. Shapiro, L. Carlson, N. D. Anderson, and J. Camody, "Mindfulness: A Proposed Operational Definition," *Clinical Psychology, Science and Practice* 11 (2004): 230–241.

10 S. L. Bowling and R. A. Baer, "Relationships between Mindfulness, Self-Control, and Psychological Functioning," *Personality and Individual Differences* 52 (2012): 411–415.

11 B. R. Burleson, "The Experience and Effects of Emotional Support: What the Study of Cultural and Gender Differences Can Tell Us about Close Relationships, Emotion, and Interpersonal Communication," *Personal Relationships* 10 (2003): 1–23.

12 J. Ciarrochi and T. B. Kashdan, *Mindfulness, Acceptance, and Positive Psychology: The Seven Foundations of Well-Being* (Oakland, California: Context Press, 2013).

13 A. Aron and E. N. Aron, "Self-Expansion Motivation and Including Other in the Self," in *Handbook of Personal Relationships*, 2nd ed., vol. 1, eds. W. Ickles and S. Duck (London: Wiley, 1997), 251–270.

14 A. Aron, E. Melinat, E. N. Aron, R. Vallone, and R. Bator, "The Experimental Generation of Interpersonal Closeness: A Procedure and Some Preliminary Findings," *Personality and Social Psychology Bulletin* 23 (1997): 363–377.

15 S. von Stumm, B. Hell, and T. Chamorro-Premuzic, "The Hungry Mind: Intellectual Curiosity Is the Third Pillar of Academic Performance," *Perspectives on Psychological Science* 6 (2011): 574–588.

16 J. C. Neubert, J. Mainert, A. Kretzschmar, and S. Greiff, "The Assessment of 21st Century Skills in Industrial-Organizational Psychology: Complex and Collaborative Problem-Solving," *Industrial and Organizational Psychology* 8 (2015): 238–268.

17 E. Stocks, D. A. Lishner, and S. K. Decker, "Altruism or Psychological Escape: Why Does Empathy Promote Prosocial Behavior?" *European Journal of Social Psychology* 39 (2009): 649–665.

18 D. Cramer, "Facilitativeness, Conflict, Demand for Approval, Self-Esteem, and Satisfaction with Romantic Relationships," *Journal of Psychology* 137 (2003): 85–98.

19 C. R. Rodgers, "Empathic: An Unappreciated Way of Being," *The Counseling Psychologist* 5 (1975): 2–10.

20 R. I. M. Dunbar, "The Social Brain Meets Neuroimaging," *Trends in Cognitive Sciences* 6 (2012): 101–102.

[21] J. P. Lorderbaum, J. D. Newman, A. R. Horwitz, J. R. Dubno, R. B. Lydiard, and M. B. Hamner, "A Potential Role for Thalamo Cingulate Circuitry in Human Maternal Behavior," *Biological Psychiatry* 51 (2002): 431–445.

[22] R. Bar-On, "Bar-On Emotional Quotient Inventory (EQ-I): Technical Manual (Toronto, Canada: Multi-Health Systems, 2002).

[23] D. Goleman, R. E. Boyatiz, and K. S. Rhee, "Clustering Competence in Emotional Intelligence: Insights from the Emotional Competence Inventory," in *Handbook of Emotional Intelligence*, eds. R. Bar-On and J. D. A. Parker (San Francisco: Jossey-Bass, 2000), 343–362.

[24] J. D. Mayer, P. Salovey, and D. R. Caruso, *Mayer-Salovey-Caruso Emotional Intelligence Test (MSCEIT) User's Manual* (Toronto, Canada: MHS Publishers, 2002).

EMBRACING INDIVIDUAL DIFFERENCES

A person has not started living until they can rise
above the narrow confines of their individualistic
concerns to the broader concerns of all humanity.
—Martin Luther King Jr.

If we desire to build deep relationships with others, we must understand the power of embracing individual differences. Our differences are what make each of us unique. They separate us from the masses and speak to the backgrounds, histories, and personal experiences that shape who we are. Research across many different fields has found that people who are skilled at accepting the differences (e.g., age, gender, race and ethnicity, sexual orientation, religious beliefs, education, and culture) of other people possess higher levels of social skills and are more effective communicators.[1] When we show genuine respect and decency to others, particularly those with ideologies different from our own, relationships flourish and grow. You cannot build sustainable, long-term relationships with a variety of people unless you have this skill.

At its most foundational level, embracing individual differences is about race and ethnicity. If we do not have an appreciation for the racial and ethnic diversity of the people around us, we live with a closed-minded perspective. In the workplace, diversity and inclusion programs have proliferated in the last ten to fifteen years. Researchers have found consistent evidence that a diverse workplace positively affects people's job performances, team effectiveness, organizational commitment, interpersonal communication, job satisfaction, and

53

employee morale.[2] Organizations with a diverse workforce also receive more internal and external benefits than those that do not promote the value of workplace inclusion. When companies leverage the power of diversity internally, people and teams have higher levels of innovation and creativity, realistic decision-making, and enhanced problem-solving. External benefits resulting from a diverse workforce include access to minority markets for new clients and customers and many opportunities to recruit talented employees from different cultural, ethnic, and minority groups. Embracing racial and ethnic individual differences is a necessary skill that is required for effective communication and the development of lasting working relationships.

Gender also plays a critical role when embracing and accepting individual differences. It has been over thirty years since the metaphor of the "glass ceiling" was coined to describe the often subtle but very real barriers women face as they try to climb the corporate ladder. In my consulting practice, some of the best senior executives I've worked with have been women. Many of these women have higher levels of EQ and empathy. On top of this, they invest in their personal relationships with their people, which leads to stronger team dynamics, higher work productivity, and commitment to the organization. In our personal relationships, understanding our own gender dynamics and making space for others can strengthen the bond between people. It contributes to feelings of love and acceptance as we build relationships and can lead to more satisfying partnerships and friendships in the long term.

In addition to race and gender becoming topics of workplace attention, the attitudes, norms, and laws regarding sexual orientation have been undergoing a worldwide revolution. Namely, over the last two decades, lesbian, gay, bisexual, transgender, questioning, and other (LGBTQ+) identities have gained increased attention and have rapidly shifted from taboo to politically contested to accepted in many contexts. These changes have numerous practical implications for relationships in our personal and professional lives. For example, in organizational contexts, companies are increasingly taking steps to attract, retain, support, and effectively manage LGBTQ+ employees.

Employers have taken sides on issues related to sexual orientation to signal progressive values to a wide range of stakeholders. They have also enacted HR practices to promote sexual orientation diversity and prevent discrimination.[3] The leaders I work with who are more open and accepting of differences in sexual orientation have connected the best with many of their people. They create an environment where people feel safe and can be vulnerable with one another. They also tap into some of the creativity and innovation that comes from diversity of thought between LGBTQ+ leaders and their colleagues.

Faith, religion, and spiritual practices also play a role in how we embrace individual differences. I come from a family that has diverse spiritual practices. People on my father's side of the family are Muslims. Their devout faith impacts how they interact with people and the world around them. I am a Christian. Christianity is the foundation and bedrock of all that I do. From the work of my firm to my involvement in the community, I live out my faith in how I treat others. Cousins on my mother's side of the family are Jewish. Having all three of these major world religions in my extended family has given me an understanding and true appreciation for the humanity in all of us. Cultural differences are also linked to our faith and spiritual practices. Some of the greatest cultural lessons I have learned in my life have come from interactions with my Arab cousins. At the same time, the Italians in my family have helped shape my beliefs on the importance and value of family. If we cannot embrace the spiritual and cultural differences of the people around us, we operate from a limited perspective. This can prevent us from connecting deeply with others and forging bonds to sustain long-term relationships.

Leaders of my firm have begun conducting research on what we call the "decency factor." Our work stems from the proliferation of corporate diversity and inclusion programs organizations have adopted over the last twenty years. There is a certain degree of tolerance, mutual understanding, and acceptance of people's differences that is needed if companies are going to thrive. We all know the "golden rule," but the decency factor goes a step deeper. It implies that we must not only show empathy and understanding of others but that we must also have a genuine desire to care for others' needs and concerns. To show common decency to other people means wanting something positive for them while ensuring that everyone feels respected and valued. The decency factor manifests itself in everyday interactions with colleagues and coworkers. It implies a focus on doing right by putting the needs of others before ourselves. When this occurs, it opens the door for people to be authentic and vulnerable. Showing vulnerability is hard for many people. Pride and arrogance can often block us from sharing who we really are. However, if we truly want to build thriving relationships, sharing our vulnerabilities is a critical driving factor for intimate connection.

IT'S THE CONTENT OF OUR CHARACTER, NOT THE COLOR OF OUR SKIN, THAT MATTERS

My first real exposure to racism was when I was in elementary school. Most of my classmates were White. They were predominantly Irish and Italian. Then there was me and Alonzo. Alonzo was one of three Black kids in our whole school. I was one of the few Arabs. I became close friends with Alonzo because of our love for basketball. We both idolized Michael Jordan, as most kids did in the late 1980s and early 1990s. Because my parents got divorced when I was five, I was used to being around kids who were different from me. When I was with my mother during the week, most of my friends were White. On weekends, I would be with my father, and he would take me to his mosque. Most of my friends there were Arabs or Blacks. It was normal for me to be around kids who didn't look like me, kids who spoke different languages and had different customs and beliefs. It wasn't until the fifth grade that I was given a rude awakening about hatred and racism.

I remember walking into class on the first day of the school year and seeing a group of boys at the back of the classroom. My friends Tommy and Jonathan were in the group, so I ran over to say hello. Before I could get halfway across the room, the new kid who just moved into town, Kevin, started calling me nigger lips. He shouted at me, "Hey, nigger lips! Don't come over here. We don't want you around us!" I had never heard someone call me that before. I didn't even know what it meant. I remember feeling sad that two of my closest friends just stood by and watched as Kevin taunted me. This type of behavior went on for months.

The hatred finally reached its crescendo later that year during the gym period. We were picking teams for soccer with Charley and Michael as team captains. Charley's first pick was Kevin. This was the norm, as he was one of the most athletic kids in our grade. As we started going through picks, Kevin had a sly comment for everyone. When it was Michael's turn to pick, he chose Alonzo. Kevin screamed out, "Glad we didn't get the nigger!" Alonzo shot his head around and gave a death glare at Kevin. "What did you just say?" he said. "You heard me, boy!" Kevin blurted out. Before I could blink, Alonzo bolted across the gym, jumped on Kevin, and started punching him ferociously in the face. Then all the boys started jumping and fighting. The gym teachers ran over to break it up. It was too late, though. Alonzo had broken Kevin's nose, and there was blood everywhere.

Later that night, I asked my mother why Alonzo got so mad. It was our first conversation about racism. I'll never forget the important lessons she taught me about people. She talked about how some people were ignorant and were raised in families where hatred was encouraged and instilled. We discussed how all people were created equally and how I always needed to be respectful to others regardless of the color of their skin. She also taught me to appreciate the beauty in all people, that there were always things we could learn from those who were different from us.

Notable cases of unarmed Black people (e.g., George Floyd, Breonna Taylor, and Ahmaud Arbery) being murdered by police changed the course of the United States in 2020. This made an impact on every aspect of American life—from politics to sports to media and entertainment. Even in the midst of a global pandemic and a historical presidential election, Black Lives Matter (BLM) became the year's center stage focus. The uptick in support for and focus on BLM produced a tangible cultural shift most prominently exhibited through months of sustained protests with record-breaking turnouts. The public discourse on race, which too often centered on the racism of the past, dating back to slavery, shone a scrutinizing spotlight on the present-day racism affecting our nation at all levels.

As a result of the events of 2020, media documentation and news coverage increasingly has brought to light the ways Black people are disproportionately the victims of racial bias across many areas in our country. Despite this new work, Black people have been sounding the alarm for generations. Racism goes back further than the 1964 Title VII of the Civil Rights Act, which prohibits discrimination on the basis of race, color, and ethnicity. A litany of studies across a wide array of disciplines, including psychology, sociology, medicine, and public health, has established the pervasiveness of systematic racism and its negative effects on people and the relationships between different groups in our country.[4]

Critical Race Theory (CRT) is a crucial model for understanding systemic racism. CRT tenets make explicit how embedded racism is in all of American society and the manner in which supposedly race-neutral institutions, systems, policies, and practices maintain White supremacy.[5] CRT highlights that there are four components to systemic racism in our country. First, racism is ordinary and ubiquitous rather than isolated in certain circumstances. Second, racism is hard to remedy because objectivity and meritocracy claims camouflage the power and privilege of White people. Third, race is socially constructed and manipulated. And fourth, the experiential knowledge of racism by Black people is legitimate and appropriate. Naming the harm created by constructing Whiteness as the embodiment of normalcy while condemning Black people to a place of inferiority is vital to understanding the genesis of group and race-based hierarchies within our society.

When considering the ways that Black lives matter, it is important to highlight broader historical and macro-level contexts and their interrelatedness for people to grasp the ubiquity of the systemic racism highlighted by CRT. Research has shown that White people are significantly less likely than Black people to perceive individual and systemic racism, which is partly accounted for by their relative ignorance of documented racism in the past.[6] In the context of relationship formation, this has a tremendous effect on the types of people with whom we surround ourselves. Ignorance of the experiences of other races and ethnicities limits people's ability to connect with others.

In organizational contexts, race and ethnicity have often been the foundational elements of diversity and inclusion programs. At its core, the concept of diversity is based on individual acceptance and respect. It is an understanding that people are unique and different. Researchers in the field of industrial-organizational psychology have developed a number of theories to study race and ethnicity in business contexts. Most of these theories come from a micro-theoretical perspective and attempt to explain behavior from an individual level. These theories have often been used to introduce or justify hypotheses that have focused on negative outcomes or predictions as a result of differences in race and ethnicity. Three important findings have stemmed from most of this work. First, humans judge one another on surface-level characteristics in the absence of additional information. Second, group membership based on these characteristics implies true similarities or differences between people, which then creates the formation of in-group and out-group distinctions. Lastly, these judgments ultimately result in outcomes that may have negative effects on minority or out-group members (e.g., lack of mentors, stalled careers, and lower performance evaluations). These factors are often most noticeable in the way relationships tend to form between different groups.

As diversity and inclusion programs continue to thrive and grow, social scientists have focused on what is called the value-in-diversity perspective, which argues that a diverse workforce is generally beneficial for business. Proponents of this perspective claim that diversity pays and represents a compelling interest—an interest that meets customers' needs, enriches one's understanding of the marketplace, and improves the quality of products or services offered by companies.[7] Moreover, racial and ethnic diversity enriches the workplace by broadening employee perspectives, increasing innovation, strengthening the effectiveness of teams, and improving cooperation. All these factors can only take place if strong relationships are formed between coworkers.

Although diversity programs have existed in organizations for the last two decades, the treatment of Black people by police officers in 2020 had a tremendous impact on the way leaders deal with diversity. Companies started developing purpose statements that represented how they viewed equality and the treatment of people from different races, ethnicities, and cultures in their organizations. For example, one of my clients in the financial services industry did a complete revamp of their strategic objectives for the next three years. They put together an executive committee that was responsible for building out a diversity purpose statement that would be directly linked to their strategic goals and priorities. They shared this work with the board and got buy-in and alignment with their executive leadership team. The purpose work now tied into the objectives of the organization across all functions and business units.

Another client in the retail industry instituted a mandate to hire more ethnically diverse leaders in their senior vice president ranks and higher. They partnered with my firm to map out key leadership competencies that would help prepare their organization for the ever-evolving needs of their leaders now and into the future. A third client in the telecommunications industry had their chief human resources officer and her team develop a diversity program that extended beyond typical inclusion initiatives. They focused on teaching employees how to respect and embrace the differences between employees. They instituted cross-functional teams with leaders from various races and ethnic backgrounds to incubate ideas on how to drive innovations for the organization. Leaders with strong relational intelligence understand the power of diversity as it pertains to people from different races and ethnic backgrounds. They take these differences between their employees and use them to improve the impact and effectiveness of their teams.

BREAKING THROUGH THE GLASS CEILING

I'm always amazed by many of the powerful and influential senior executive women with whom I work. These women have grace and poise to their leadership. They are direct and no-nonsense in their approach to managing people but have empathy and compassion I do not see in their male counterparts. This enables them to connect with their people and build strong, solid relationships. One of the most impactful leaders with whom I've worked is Alyssa, a chief operating officer (COO) for a Fortune 500 financial services company. I've been her executive coach for the last five years, and it has been one of the most interesting and engaging client programs on which I have ever worked.

When I first met Alyssa, she had recently joined the organization, and I was supporting her with onboarding and integration. When she joined the company, she had been given responsibility over corporate strategy, technology, operations, branding and communication, strategic sourcing, and customer solutions. Her CEO gave her the mandate to focus on three areas. First, she was to lead a full enterprise transformation for the firm. Second, her teams were responsible for onboarding new businesses into the organization and making sure operations were able to integrate the new businesses successfully. Lastly, she was to improve the firm's branding and communications strategy.

Upon stepping into the role, Alyssa spent the first six months getting to know her people and teams and the culture of the organization. She made several changes to her leadership team and brought in strong, diverse talent to support the key initiatives she was responsible for leading. She placed a particular emphasis on bringing women and minorities into the organization to drive diversity of thought and innovation. Once she assembled the right talent on her leadership team, she brought the group together to outline her vision for the future. She solicited input and counsel from her direct reports to align the team on key strategic priorities. They also established three cultural pillars for how her organization was to operate moving forward. The pillars focused on developing people, innovating with big ideas, and striving for excellence. I admired how, as a leader, she prioritized instilling trust and collaboration with her people. I saw her direct reports inspired by her leadership. They were committed to the mission and empowered to deliver in their roles.

As we began our coaching work, Alyssa had just begun spending time on the technology organization. Her teams upgraded their entire IT function—they brought in third-party vendors to support the onboarding of new businesses, and they created a joint venture partnership with a group that would take on most of the day-to-day technology and IT responsibilities. Within eighteen months, the technology team had completed a significant number of large, strategic initiatives while improving security, managing operational risk and stability, and lowering their operating costs. Her teams continued to excel at delivering their goals and objectives. Yet as Alyssa continued to make changes to her organization, she started to get strong resistance and pushback from her three largest internal customers. The leaders of the three key business units in the firm began complaining that she was driving too much change without getting their buy-in and approval. This caused friction between her teams and leaders in the business units.

As our coaching work continued, her CEO wanted us to work on two areas. First, he wanted Alyssa to cultivate stronger relationships with her peers on the executive leadership team. Second, he wanted Alyssa and her teams to get more exposure to the business. He felt that if Alyssa got out into the business more, she would have a better understanding of how to support her internal customers. As Alyssa and I discussed how to incorporate these areas into our coaching work, she told me how the challenges with her peers had developed over time. Alyssa believed she was given the mandate to innovate and drive change for the firm but that her peers were accustomed to tradition and the status quo. They did not want to evolve and accept the changes needed. This caused most of the issues between her organization and the business units. This is a classic issue I see with many of my clients. A leader is asked to join the organization and drive change, but many of their colleagues want things to stay the same. To dive deeper into the issues, I recommended we conduct a 360-degree assessment to determine what themes were emerging across the organization about her leadership. Alyssa thought this was a great idea, as she had then been with the company for two years and had received little feedback from others. We put a 360 participant list together that included her direct reports, peers, external business partners, and senior leadership. We ran the list by the CHRO for his alignment with the participants, and I began conducting my interviews.

As I analyzed all the interview data, three themes emerged. First, Alyssa's people loved working for her. They saw her as a breath of fresh air, bringing about changes the organization needed to thrive in the future. They also found her to be an inspirational leader. Alyssa got her team focused on the vision, gave them the autonomy to perform their job responsibilities, and provided support whenever they needed it. Second, her peers, most of whom had long tenures with the organization, wanted full power to run their businesses. They believed it was their responsibility to oversee all aspects of their operations and technology teams. Any corporate functions needed to deliver what they wanted and give them full authority to make the decisions that would improve how they ran their businesses. They also saw little value in making changes. Things had worked well for many years, and they were comfortable with the status quo. Lastly, Alyssa's CEO had a laid-back and laissez-faire leadership style. He rarely stepped in to address conflicts with his direct reports, which gave the business unit leaders freedom to challenge most of the programs Alyssa wanted to implement for the firm. This created a perfect storm. Alyssa had teams that wanted to innovate and drive change, but she had peers who didn't think they needed the changes and a CEO who didn't step in to support her efforts. When I shared the feedback with Alyssa, she wasn't surprised.

Now Alyssa was a confident and courageous senior executive. She had no problem challenging the perspectives of others and fought for what she believed would strengthen the firm's operations. Her courage was one of the greatest strengths she brought to the firm. Her direct and candid leadership style brought clarity to challenges the company faced. However, we had to change the perception that she did what she felt the company needed without getting buy-in and support from her peers, so we focused on two developmental goals for our coaching. First, she needed to strengthen her relationships with all her peers. Second, she needed to get out into the business and learn what the teams needed from her organization to be successful.

What I admired most about Alyssa was how she took the feedback to heart and worked on driving greater alignment with her colleagues. Over the next year, Alyssa strengthened her partnerships with her peers. She listened more and spoke less. She went out of her way to ensure the three business unit leaders were aligned with the changes her organization needed to make. She got out into the business and learned how her teams could better support the work of their colleagues. Our coaching work focused on strengthening her relational intelligence so she could positively influence and impact her peers. This changed the perception that she only cared about driving change and leading the enterprise's transformation efforts. It made her come across as more engaging and collaborative.

In the end, Alyssa and her teams were able to deliver on all the key strategic initiatives for the organization. The enterprise transformation was completed ahead of schedule. The firm had successfully onboarded and integrated important new businesses. Their branding and communication efforts continued to increase while the firm spent less. Through the use of innovative social media and data analytics solutions, the firm became well-positioned to thrive in the future. Alyssa's ability to take feedback, reflect on her leadership, and make the appropriate behavioral changes made her successful. By focusing on developing deeper relationships with her peers, she was able to move the business forward. She became an influential senior executive not only because of her intellect and strategic thinking capabilities but also because she was able to adapt to her surroundings to drive change.

In the last twenty years, women have made remarkable headway in the workplace and have risen to the ranks of key management positions. Although many researchers have written about the advancement of women into these types of roles, there continues to be evidence of the glass ceiling. This refers to the barrier that appears invisible but is strong enough to hold women back from top-level jobs merely because they are women rather than because they lack job-relevant skills, education, or experience. Different theoretical perspectives compete for explanations for the glass ceiling. Classic research suggests that organizations minimize risk by restricting entry to people who are different.[8] Person-centered theories have examined differences in skills, abilities, and attitudes between men and women. These include differences in human capital investments in education, training, and experience as well as attitudinal differences, whereby women are less likely to ask for advancement, are ambivalent about success, and fear taking risks.[9]

The pipeline perspective holds that more women in middle management will continue to push women into the executive ranks. This argument is driven by the looming retirement of an old-fashioned generation of male executives and the belief that younger women have great role models to emulate. Related to examinations of the pipeline perspective is growing research on young women's attitudes toward executive work and the glass ceiling. Contemporary young women have been found to be more agentic and with higher self-esteem than past generations.[10] They are also aware of discrimination but believe it to have lessened due to legislation, social progress, and high-profile female success stories.

While most research on women and leadership focuses on the barriers that limit women's upward mobility in organizations, a growing body of research has explored the conditions under which the barriers are overcome. The "glass cliff," as it is called, suggests that women are more likely than men to be promoted in companies that are struggling, in crisis, or at risk of failing. Several factors contribute to why women leaders are more likely to be promoted into high-risk senior executive positions. First, women may face less competition from men for these positions, as highly qualified male candidates may view these positions as too risky or otherwise undesirable.[11] Women, on the other hand, may be more amenable to accepting such positions out of fear that a comparable opportunity may not materialize in the future. Second, there is evidence that the requisite competencies of leaders may be context-specific and vary depending on the health of a company.[12] Specifically, stereotypically feminine attributes, including emotional sensitivity, strong interpersonal skills, morale-building capabilities, and a collaborative leadership style, may be more valued during times of crisis. Such qualities may also make female candidates more attractive when decision-makers perceive a job to be particularly challenging or high-risk. Lastly, a crisis or high-risk situation may motivate decision-makers to promote nontraditional leaders, including women, to signal to key stakeholders that a company is headed in a bold new direction.[13]

Although a growing body of research has found empirical support for the glass cliff theory, I have found in my consulting practice that female leaders have an enormous positive impact on organizations that are thriving. Many of the senior executive women I coach bring a mix of skills (e.g., empathy, alignment, and commitment) to the table that often their male counterparts have not fully developed. I've also found my female clients to bring a greater diversity of thought to their people and teams. They are more accepting of individual differences and tend to build teams made up of different types of people. This creates cultures where employees value idea sharing, collaboration, and the pursuit of shared goals and performance outcomes. Research has also found that female leaders are associated with greater innovation and profitability, broader consumer outreach, and stronger records of corporate social responsibility.[14] It is no surprise, then, that embracing individual differences is a critical skill women use to build lasting professional relationships. If more of their male colleagues did the same, there would be a greater focus on the diversity of thought and appreciation for the talents and capabilities women bring to the table.

The Impact of the LGBTQ+ Movement in the Workplace

Some of the best leadership advisory consultants I've worked with have been lesbian or gay. Earlier in my career, I was exposed to several lesbian leaders who were impactful in a firm where I worked. They taught me many things about connecting on a deep level with different leaders and creating authentic partnerships with clients. I've also had the chance to work with a number of gay men, and my experiences have been the same. One man, in particular, is my colleague

Matthew, with whom I've worked and known for ten years. Matthew has exceptional relational intelligence. He can quickly establish rapport with leaders from different minority groups and takes the time to truly learn how their stories have shaped who they are as people and leaders. Matthew's professional journey has been a testament to his ability to embrace individual differences and understand people on a deep level. To understand how he builds relationships and influences his clients in such a powerful way, you have to understand his personal story.

Matthew grew up in the suburbs of Denver in the 1970s, where gay bashing was a common occurrence. This was at a period in our country's history where violence toward gays happened regularly. For Matthew, his earliest recollections of knowing he was "different" started in the second grade. He was head over heels for one of his best friends and knew it was similar to the way girls felt about boys. Yet he kept these feelings at bay as he progressed through elementary school and on into high school. He learned how to mask his sexuality and became a master at blending in with his straight friends. In high school, he did all the typical things a teenager did. He had girlfriends. He went to prom. He was active and social. He had many groups of friends and was popular. He was into music and the performing arts. At the same time, he struggled inwardly with the feelings and emotions he was experiencing. It wasn't until after he graduated from high school that he started to explore his sexuality in greater detail.

One of his best friends was an exchange student from Sweden. Before heading to college, Matthew took a year off and traveled in Europe with his friend. This was the first time he could be open, honest, and free. He didn't have to hide who he was, and he remembers the experience as very liberating. He no longer had to struggle with feeling awkward and insecure. Upon returning to the US, he started college at NYU. He began seeing a therapist, and they worked on how he would come out to his family and close friends. This was during the AIDS crisis, where the stereotype was that if you were gay, you would die. This ideology prevented him from coming out to his family for a while. When he eventually did, it brought peace to his world.

Professionally, it took Matthew years to authentically own who he was as a consultant. He would hold back with clients and colleagues, as there were still heavy stereotypes and biases against LGBTQ+ people into the early 2000s. It was difficult for him to discuss his personal life with people at work. He never talked about dating, what he did on the weekends, and whom he spent time with for fear of how he would be perceived. Many of his male clients had a history of internalized homophobia that prevented them from understanding gay men. Although it took many years for him to feel comfortable with being authentic around clients and coworkers, Matthew developed a deep understanding of how to connect with those who felt "other." This enabled him to have strong empathy for the experiences of Blacks, Hispanics, Asians, women, and other members of the LGBTQ+ community.

Today, Matthew is one of the best leadership advisors and executive coaches with whom I've worked. Through the power of being authentic about his sexuality, he is able to very quickly get to a deep, real, and long-lasting connection with his clients. The people with whom he works are impacted in a great way because Matthew meets them where they are and is genuine and open. Clients often tell me that Matthew "gets in the boat" with them and is able to partner with them for the journey. These quick connections and lasting professional partnerships stem from his ability to embrace individual differences and promote the acceptance of who people really are. I've learned how to be a more empathic and authentic leader in my own work given what I've learned from him.

It's been nearly thirty years since the Society for Human Resource Management (SHRM) made what was for the time a bold move: including sexual orientation in its nondiscrimination statement. While SHRM was not the first organization to take this initiative, it was an action that created great controversy.[15] Since then, almost all Fortune 500 companies have adopted such statements, and most companies now offer domestic partner benefits. In the late 2000s, sexual orientation was said to be the "last acceptable bias" in organizations. While many people understood that racial and ethnic stereotypes were off-limits, people still had negative views toward gay or lesbian employees. However, as the war for talent increased substantially over the last ten to fifteen years, active promotion of LGBTQ+ inclusiveness has been found to have many positive effects on organizations. Research has shown that inclusion is related to higher levels of creativity and innovation, stronger mentoring and leadership development initiatives, and greater organizational commitment.[16]

In the workplace, a company's approach to diversity is highly related to worker morale. Research has found that workers who rate their organization's philosophy and commitment to diversity higher are more satisfied with their companies, are more likely to report they would stay longer, and are more likely to recommend their companies to others. These high ratings extend beyond typical diversity initiatives aimed at gender, race, or ethnicity. A greater focus on sexual orientation in organizations' diversity practices often leads to better work performance and enhances career progression, team cohesion, retention, and cross-functional collaboration.[17] Sexual orientation many be unique among other elements of diversity in that it can be readily hidden, or closeted, often due to the stigma of homosexuality. When LGBTQ+ employees feel comfortable disclosing their sexual orientation, it has been shown to predict greater job satisfaction and to lower job anxiety and role ambiguity.

Many LGBTQ+ leaders suggest that embracing individual differences starts with a company's culture. The support of top management to create an environment of inclusivity enables people to feel a sense of freedom in sharing their opinions and beliefs. The words and actions of the senior executives become imprinted on the company and serve to guide the words and actions of people across the organization. I've seen this dynamic manifest itself in many of my clients across different industries. As an example, one of our firm's retail clients came to us recently for help in developing a diversity and inclusion program geared toward broadening their employees' understanding of diverse populations. The company already had many initiatives to support sexual orientation diversity. They had adopted nondiscrimination policies, offered health benefits to employees' same-sex domestic partners, and endorsed employee resource groups. The training program they wanted to partner with us to develop would expand upon the ways they were educating employees about diverse populations to further reduce discriminatory behaviors.

At the onset of the engagement, we knew we wanted to build something different from our typical diversity and inclusion programs. I met with the CEO to discuss key desirable outcomes the company was looking to get from our work. We talked about greater acceptance of differences across minority groups, but the emphasis was on preventing biases and stereotypes between different employee populations. Once we had a clear understanding of the direction we wanted to take, I pulled together a small think tank that would serve as major ambassadors of the program. This group of ten leaders came from different demographic groups across the company. We had every major diverse population represented in the sponsorship group. We then began to develop core content to be used in a two-day training off-site around diversity. The topics of focus for the off-site included race/ethnicity, age, gender, and sexual orientation. Each area of the training was to be delivered by leaders from that subpopulation. This setup would allow for all areas to be well-represented by leaders from that specific group throughout the training.

A mentoring and coaching component was also necessary to drive sustainable change at all levels of the organization. First, we needed to determine how many participants would be in our pilot program. We selected twenty leaders across all areas of the business. Next, we took time to identify the right mentors for the program. Our mentors had to represent each of the diverse populations so people could be paired with the right senior leaders. We chose mentors based on how different they were from our participants. For example, we paired a Black male mentor with a White female program participant, a lesbian mentor with a straight male participant, or a gay mentor with an Asian female participant. This forced people in the program to work side-by-side with someone who was different from them.

On top of this, we had the mentor-mentee pairings set personal goals together. According to the science of goal-setting theory, goals have two major functions. They are the basis for motivation, and they direct people's behavior. Goals are intentions that guide behavior and influence people's actions through several mechanisms: (a) goals direct attention and effort toward goal-relevant behaviors; (b) goals affect persistence, as people tend to prolong efforts toward challenging objectives; and (c) goals affect behavior indirectly by leading to the arousal, discovery, and use of task-relevant knowledge and strategies.[18] Research has shown that self-set goals are particularly effective for enhancing diversity training effectiveness. A powerful effect takes place when personal goals are set so what people learn in training can be transferred back into their work after the program concludes. Additionally, relational cultural theory suggests that mentors are a source of influence because they provide an opportunity for assistance, feedback, and psychosocial support.[19] Consistent with relational cultural theory, research has found that mentors are a source of formal influence and that mentees do rely on mentors for guidance and support. We knew this would be important for the program to maintain the continued support of key stakeholders in senior management. It would demonstrate the importance of diversity at the highest levels of leadership in the organization.

After the pilot program, we found three important takeaways. First, all the mentors played a large role in getting the participants to sustain the behaviors they learned in the training. Specifically, each leader went back to their part of the business and served as a role model for advocacy and support in embracing individual differences. Second, the lesbian and gay mentors were found to have the most impact during the program. Their empathy and compassion for the participants were on display throughout the initiative. They also had the innate ability to connect deeply with the participants during the off-site and in one-on-one settings. Third and most importantly, the participants walked away from the program with long-term relationships with their mentors. The program served as just a starting point for getting people to identify with and accept the differences of their colleagues.

The program would not have been as successful without the efforts of the gay and lesbian mentors and trainers. They went above and beyond the leaders from some of the other diverse populations and really committed to supporting the changes that needed to be implemented across the enterprise. This taught me a powerful lesson about the value of embracing sexual orientation in the workplace. When leaders embrace these aspects of others' lives, they are able to have greater empathy and connection with people. We made the diversity training program a staple in the company's inclusion initiatives. It made the organization a better, more positive place to work. Employees across the company had the freedom and autonomy to express themselves and truly appreciated the things that made people different.

Cross-Cultural Factors and Spirituality in Embracing Individual Differences

Early in my career, I had the opportunity to work with many multinational clients. This exposed me to leaders from different cultural backgrounds and experiences. One particular leader was Sergio, a president and general manager for a medical devices company. I met Sergio about fifteen years into his career when he was looking to make a job transition from a larger health care provider to a smaller company. From the instant we met, we had strong chemistry and rapport. I did an executive assessment on Sergio for the president and general manager role overseeing the company's European region. Throughout our interview, his drive, high energy, and passion resonated with me tremendously. Within five minutes of sitting with Sergio, anyone could tell how motivated and inspired he was to succeed. He also had a great understanding of how to lead people from different cultures. His previous roles had involved oversight in regions of South America where he got to interact with and lead people from Brazil, Chile, Argentina, Peru, and Colombia. Based on his background and leadership experiences, I thought he would be a great fit to lead the European part of the business.

Sergio was offered the role, and shortly thereafter, I began his executive integration coaching. We ended up working together for two years, and I can honestly say, I have never seen another executive with more passion and drive. We sometimes joked that he never slept! He was always on a plane, heading to one of the nine countries under his leadership. He would do whatever was necessary to win. This resonated with his people. It didn't matter if they were in Italy, Germany, Spain, Greece, the UK, or elsewhere. He found ways to connect with and inspire all his team members. What I started to notice very quickly was that Sergio took time to build distinct relationships with each of his country managers. He didn't have a one-size-fits-all approach to how he interacted with different leaders. He took time to learn about their market, the types of people they served, and how to inspire commitment at an individual and team level.

A year into his role, we launched a culture survey for his entire organization. I got to travel to all nine countries and meet with the leaders from the respective regions. It was the first time I got to interact with leaders from so many different countries. There were universal commonalities that made for successful leadership. Each country manager had to set a vision and drive alignment. They had to take time to create expectations and hold people accountable. They had to invest in their people and grow individual capabilities. And they had to create a good team climate and organizational culture for their regions. What I found fascinating was how each of them did these things by using their cultural understandings of the people in their countries. For example, the way the Germans led their teams was very different from how the Italian leaders did. The managers in the UK had to navigate differences between people in England, Scotland, and Wales. The leaders in Spain operated their business differently from those in Portugal or Greece. But even though they all led their teams differently, Sergio knew how to garner buy-in and commitment from each country's leader.

My most memorable experience with Sergio was when he invited me to present the results of the organizational culture survey at his annual all-employee sales meeting in Monte Carlo. I got to present to over one thousand employees the results of the survey and its implications for the business the following year. First, I took the entire organization through the group-level results and how they related to the vision Sergio had set for the European region. We then had break out groups by country so that each country manager could go through the results with their teams. This gave people an opportunity to compare their country-level cultural success factors to results for the overall region. People walked away from this experience with a deep understanding of the cultural pillars Sergio was trying to drive for the business overall, but they also understood what this meant for the people in their countries.

Sergio wrapped up the meeting by outlining their goals and objectives for the following year. By the end of his presentation, I could tell that all the employees were committed to the overarching mission and vision for their business. Sergio rallied his troops behind a compelling and inspiring future state. He found things that were important to all of them but gave his leaders the freedom to own a vision for their unique teams. I learned three valuable lessons from this experience. First, culture plays a critical role in how leaders build relationships. Had Sergio not taken the time to connect deeply with each of his leaders and learn about their people and teams, he would never have gotten people to follow his vision. His ability to move from country to country and adapt and adjust his approach was what drove his success. Second, cultural identity is of paramount importance when leaders are influencing the actions and behaviors of others. People need to feel that their customs and beliefs are valued and respected if they are going to deliver results. Lastly and most importantly, cultural diversity brings out the best in employees. When leaders understand and embrace the cultural differences that exist between people, they are able to forge lasting relationships. It didn't matter what country his people were from. Sergio found ways to connect with them on an individual level. He leveraged his understanding of their backgrounds and values to inspire commitment to the team's purpose and mission.

Cultural identity can be defined as a person's individual image of the cultural features that characterize their group and of the reflection of these features in their self-representation.[20] Cultural identity represents the individual-level reflection of culture as it is constructed by each of us. It addresses our sense of ourselves as cultural beings. It can be seen as a person's road map of how the group guides personal behaviors. The first aspect of cultural identity is a person's construction of the group, which can vary across people in that group. Although two people may define membership in a group basically the same, each can describe the group's cultural features quite differently. For example, two people may identify as being Egyptian, but their views of being Egyptian and what it means for them personally may not be the same. One might be an Egyptian living in New York, whereas the other might actually live in Egypt. They may share similar ethnic identification but have dissimilar experiences and ways of looking at the world.

The second aspect of cultural identity is the individual's feelings about the cultural features ascribed to the group. Two people may agree in their depiction of a reference group that they share, but these images may carry quite different weight. For example, two Americans may view the US culture as characterized by having liberal views on sexuality. One may feel positively about it while the other has negative thoughts and feelings associated with the subject. The third and most important aspect of cultural identity is a person's view of where, how, and to what degree the group culture is reflected in their view of themselves. Using the previous example, the person who has positive feelings about US culture sees themselves as having liberal values and believes this reflects their enculturation as an American. The person with negative feelings about these values may have conservative beliefs that reflect their personal preferences. A third person may perceive similar features in US culture but not associate positive or negative feelings to characteristics of themselves. Cultural identity has implications for how people socialize and interact with one another. Just because people come from the same cultural heritage does not mean they will view it in the same way. This, in turn, can impact how they connect with and build relationships with others. Having a greater appreciation for these subtle differences can improve our understanding of others and how we adapt to the differences between peoples.

Cultural diversity is defined as the representation, in one social system, of people with distinctly different group affiliations of cultural significance.[21] The major tenet in this framework is that because social groups vary in their preferred patterns of values, beliefs, norms, styles, and behaviors (e.g., their cultural features), our membership in these social groups distinguishes us not only in name but also in our views of the world, our construction of meaning, and our behavioral and attitudinal preferences. This definition emphasizes that all of us are, in an essential sense, cultural beings shaped by and oriented in the world by the cultures of the groups to which we belong. Embracing individual differences at a cultural level is critical to people's success in an ever-evolving global landscape. When people can appreciate the differences that exist at a cultural level, relationship building thrives and extends beyond race, gender, and sexual orientation. Nuances tie all these factors together and create the context through which relationships can flourish.

In organizational contexts, a culturally diverse company encompasses many different cultural backgrounds. Because cultural backgrounds are mainly characterized by people's values, they are deeply engrained in the self-concepts we have as human beings. Cultural backgrounds have a strong impact on our behaviors and how we connect with others. When differences in value systems are accepted and embraced, research has found links to higher levels of work satisfaction and organizational commitment.[22] I've seen this in many of my global clients. The teams that are made up of culturally diverse leaders have a greater impact on driving the business forward.

Culturally different employees feel more included in their organization when diversity is a valued characteristic of their team. Instead of being perceived as problematic, when cultural diversity is perceived as an advantage for the organization, it enables people to see the best in others. To enhance identification with diversity, a company must develop an intercultural group climate in which diversity becomes characteristic of the organization. Diversity must be perceived as a positive feature for bringing people together. In addition, differences should be open to discussion, appreciated, and taken into account. While this might seem obvious, many organizations fail to do it. They tend to emphasize similarities among employees by downplaying the relevance of cultural differences for the organization in the interest of improving community spirit. This, however, limits people's ability to use diversity of thought to improve organizational outcomes.

Related to cultural differences are spiritual practices. The meaning of the term *spirituality* is often misunderstood and can have negative connotations for many people. Spirituality is often seen in the same context as organized religion—with particular beliefs, moral rules, and traditions. Spirituality, however, is not formal, structured, or organized. Organized religion has more of an external focus, whereas spirituality involves a person looking inward and is therefore accessible to everyone, whether religious or not. Spirituality is often assumed to be a dimension of the human being that is shared by all people. It has been related to things like self-actualization, self-fulfillment, authenticity, meaning and purpose, and intrinsic motivation.[23] The starting place for spiritual diversity is not in finding common ground or unity but in embracing differences and encouraging cooperation and mutual understanding. If unity is achieved, it is reached through a process of open dialogue and sharing of ideas.

With increased globalization, spiritual diversity is becoming an essential part of the workforce. Spiritual identity is tied to an array of important workplace outcomes. People's workplace decisions and contributions can be informed by and enhanced with a clear connection between occupation and spiritual values and behaviors. Spirituality contains dimensions related to meaning and purpose in life. It's tied to people's missions and callings. It focuses on wholeness and connectedness. The notion of the authentic self is a key aspect of spiritual diversity. It refers to the desire to express one's internal self through actions to the external world. To be authentic, people must experience congruence between internal values and external expressions. When building relationships, embracing and accepting different spiritual practices and beliefs leads to stronger partnerships between people. Similar to the other areas I've discussed in this chapter, culture and spirituality play a critical role in our expression of the world. Valuing these differences enhances our ability to have meaningful, deep connections with others.

WHAT'S YOUR DECENCY QUOTIENT?

Early in my career, I worked with a number of leaders who were struggling in their ability to influence and impact others. These executives had difficulties building sustainable relationships to maximize the performance of their employees. I remember one leader with whom I worked in the retail industry. Tommy was a district manager for a big box electronic retailer. Prior to working for his company, he was an NYC police officer in Staten Island. Given his background as a cop, he was used to interacting with people in a certain way. Fear and intimidation were regular aspects of his job. He felt he had to impose his will on most situations to get the best possible outcomes.

After retiring from the police force, Tommy made a transition to retail sales. He came in as an assistant store manager and quickly started to drive results. He brought great structure, discipline, and process to his store. Senior leadership saw him as responsible and dedicated to hitting monthly sales quotas. Within eighteen months, he was promoted to a general store manager. As GM, he developed a reputation for being a tough, no-nonsense type of leader. Tommy's people worked their tails off because they didn't want to disappoint him. They saw the way he conducted business, and many of his people emulated him. This worked well for a small store environment with thirty to forty employees.

Tommy's store quickly rose to being a top performer in his district. Through highly structured processes and procedures, he managed his store like a military sergeant. People had to get in line with his leadership approach, or they found themselves out the door. While this worked for some of his assistant managers, there was heavy turnover at the lower levels of his store. But despite the high turnover rate, Tommy continued to lead the only way he knew how. Given that his store had successfully exceeded revenue targets for three consecutive years, Tommy was promoted to a district manager, overseeing a totally different part of the company's broader region. He went from the NY metro area to a larger district in Upstate New York. As we all know, the cultures and lifestyles of New Yorkers are very different from other parts of the country. The hard-nosed, pick-myself-up-by-the-bootstraps hustle mentality doesn't always culturally fit elsewhere. Upon assuming the new role, Tommy quickly imposed his will on the whole district. He put strict processes and rules in place and expected all fourteen of his store managers to get with the program.

Tommy quickly became known as the stereotypical "bull in the China shop." Employees feared his store visits. On these visitations, he was harsh, cold, and overly aggressive with the staff. He put people down and called out employees in front of customers. This created tension throughout his district. After an investigation by HR into his leadership practices, I was asked to step in and coach him to turn things around. If he wasn't able to make the right behavior changes and get buy-in and commitment from his people, he was going to be let go.

I remember flying up to Syracuse, where his district office was, for our first conversation. The firm where I worked at the time had a reputation for being ineffective with leaders from this region. These East Coast leaders found consultants and business psychologists a joke. It wasn't uncommon for consultants to move through this area of the company like a revolving door. No traction could be made with these leaders. So I knew the cards were stacked against me before we even started the engagement. I had a leader who was defensive about needing help even though he knew the stakes were high. I had a client who didn't value working with leadership advisors.

As I walked into his office for the first time, I immediately knew I had to build a trusting relationship with Tommy for him to take any of my counsel and advice, so I instantly put my relational intelligence framework to work. I made our first meeting entirely about him and his leadership journey. I took time to establish rapport and make him feel comfortable with me. I paid attention to his verbal and nonverbal behaviors throughout our time together. He was guarded for the first thirty minutes but then began to lighten up when he realized I was there to help him and not judge. After a three-hour discussion, I was able to create a safe environment, where he felt comfortable sharing his true self knowing that I was there to support him.

We started our process off by doing a 360 assessment. I went around to all fourteen of his stores and interviewed the GMs and their teams. I assured them that the feedback was all anonymous and confidential. This put people at ease, and they started to open up about how Tommy treated people. What struck me the most wasn't his leadership approach but how he struggled to show common decency to others. People feared Tommy because he criticized and put folks down. He belittled people when he visited stores. What he thought was tough love really made an impact on people's spirits. When I shared the feedback with Tommy, he was blown away. He felt horrible that people saw him as an unrelenting tyrant. I empathized with him and told him we could turn things around if he made some simple changes in his behavior.

As a result of the 360, we put a simple coaching plan together. First, we focused on treating employees with greater respect and support. Tommy had to engage and build relationships, not direct and demand performance. If he put time into treating people with decency, they would respond positively. Second, we made sure he took the time to coach and develop his people. I had him hold monthly one-on-one meetings with each of his direct reports to talk about their goals and future ambitions, not the needs of the business. Lastly, I had Tommy change the types of things he said to people. If he wanted to inspire and galvanize leaders across the district, he first had to win their hearts and minds.

After several months of implementing these behaviors, we started to see positive changes. Tommy showed greater care and empathy for his people. He instituted monthly team events where employees got together and had time to connect and celebrate their successes. He showed compassion toward people and adjusted his approach according to different stakeholders. I saw people get excited when he entered stores because he would encourage and point out positives rather than negatives. In the end, Tommy was able to turn things around. His teams were more committed to his vision and strategy for the district. They exceeded their performance goals and moved into the top tier of the company's region. It was how he treated people that mattered the most for this change. People now enjoyed working for Tommy because he put others first.

The decency quotient (DQ) has been defined as having empathy for employees and genuinely caring for their physical and emotional well-being. DQ means wanting something positive for everyone in one's workplace and ensuring that everyone feels valued and respected. Ajay Banga, the former CEO of Mastercard, was one of the first leaders to discuss DQ in a talk for students at Duke University's Fuqua School of Business. He highlighted that if leaders could bring their decency quotient to work every day, people would enjoy being there and doing the right thing. When stressing the importance of DQ, Banga noted three qualities all good leaders had: urgency, curiosity, and competitiveness. However, Banga believes that when a person brings basic human decency to each one of these qualities, you get the difference between a good leader and a great one capable of actually changing things for the better.

Human resilience is important now more than ever before given the many challenges we have gone through with the COVID-19 pandemic and social justice in 2020. Decency is the guiding principle that supports that resilience. Our ability to flex and pivot as problems arise, to focus on what we can control, and to still find moments of levity and joy depends on a baseline level of well-being. The burden of building that resilience can't sit solely on the shoulders of the individual. Organizations have a crucial role to play in this effort. After all, employees are the engines of every company's success. They drive creativity and innovation and are the guardians of quality and service. If leaders take good care of their employees, employees will be able to care for their families, friends, and businesses better. In essence, helping employees thrive helps communities and companies thrive as well.

When you give people the opportunity to bring their hearts and minds to work, supporting them every step of the way, you create a culture of decency that extends beyond the walls of your business. This is how leaders turn crisis into creativity and hope into a future reality where people are supporting one another. But decency doesn't just come from the CEOs of the world. It really is as easy as putting your hand at another's back and giving them a lift with whatever you can offer. Sometimes, that is as simple as offering a listening ear. I've highlighted several times how diverse teams are more innovative. However, there is one caveat. Everyone on a diverse team must feel like they are on the team. In other words, each member must bring their true and authentic self to the table to work toward a common goal. People won't do that if they don't feel genuinely supported and valued, and when that's the case, a team can quickly become dysfunctional.

If a company is serious about decency in its leaders, they must be intentional about screening for decency in the hiring process. By the time most people start their careers, their values and moral compass have largely formed. That means you can't leave hiring for decency to chance. Our firm is challenging companies to be intentional about factoring decency into the qualities they actively assess. For example, at Mastercard, they assess DQ through a robust interview process involving many people in the company who share a culture in which decency is valued and prized. Duke University has also been leading the charge in admitting students with high DQ. They feel it's essential to admit people who share their values and beliefs. Their application essay questions are designed to get at a candidate's values. One of their prompts is simply having candidates write down twenty-five random facts about themselves. Collectively, those facts reveal so much about a person. They also look for decency in their interview process. The result has been a community of future leaders who support, nurture, and learn from one another during their time at Duke.

A growing number of CEOs are searching for ways to show that they care about more than boosting profits and stock prices. In late August 2020, the heads of the world's biggest businesses signed a new statement of purpose, saying they would lead their companies to benefit customers, employees, suppliers, and the community. Some of the commitments included (a) delivering value to all their customers, (b) investing in their employees, (c) supporting the communities where they worked, and (d) protecting the environment by embracing sustainable practices across their businesses. Tone was set at the top—with how people treated one another; ethics, integrity, values, and compassion; and doing the right thing by customers, employees, and the community.

Leaders demonstrate (and employees emulate) what is acceptable, rewarded, and fostered and, therefore, what leads to promotion within the organization. Make no mistake, setting the tone of an organization is an important responsibility of leadership, and it includes demonstrating decency. If people can become intentional about decency, it can become the healing force our world so badly needs. It can be a model for how people who are very different come together to work with common purpose. It can demonstrate respect and caring that transcends difference and polarization. It can solve some of the world's toughest problems by uniting people to find the right solutions.

PUTTING IT INTO PRACTICE

Embracing individual differences is the third skill of relational intelligence. People who are able to promote the acceptance of their differences with others build great relationships. This goes beyond developing an understanding of people who are different from us. It is about cultivating an appreciation for different races and ethnicities. It is about understanding the similarities and differences between genders. It is about showing empathy and compassion for people regardless of their sexual orientation. It is about embracing the cross-cultural factors and spiritual practices that influence how people interact with the world around them. It is about decency and treating people the way you want to be treated. From our personal relationships to our professional ones, being open to people's individual values and beliefs is critical to developing long-term, sustainable relationships. So what's the key to learning to embrace individual differences? Our outlook on peoples' differences starts with our upbringing and how we are raised. It continues to grow in high school and college. It becomes fully developed as we step into our careers. Regardless of where you are today, here are two ways to improve this invaluable skill.

Pursue Diversity of Thought

If you are to develop the skill of embracing individual differences, your primary goal should be to pursue diversity of thought. It is not just enough to connect with people from different backgrounds, customs, and beliefs. You must actively get around people who will make you think differently. I did this for the first time when I was in college. I did a study abroad program in England during my sophomore year. Prior to the trip, I had never really stepped outside the environment where I grew up. I was accustomed to being around Americans and was only exposed to different people through the relationships my mother and father had with their friends. Living in England was the first time I interacted with people from different cultures. The study abroad program was unique in that I got to take classes Monday through Thursday and then got to travel Friday through Sunday every week. I visited France, Ireland, Italy, Germany, Spain, Portugal, Scotland, and Wales. The people I met exposed me to new things. They challenged the way I looked at the world. It forced me to step out of my comfort zone. I walked away from that experience with a greater appreciation for how others thought, what made them tick, and how to build relationships across international boundaries.

In the work at our firm, we regularly encourage clients to build leadership development programs that expose their leaders to new and different ideas. Several years ago, we had the opportunity to work with a Fortune 100 consumer products company to help them build a high-potential talent program. The company wanted to develop its next-generation leaders, and we needed to put in place systems that could be replicated each year. To build a strong high-potential talent program, several areas must be included in the design. First, there needed to be an assessment component to help leaders learn about their strengths and areas of opportunity. We developed a process that included personality tests, leadership interviews, and a 360-degree assessment. This gave the program participants insight into how they showed up as leaders.

Next, we had each leader put together an individual development plan (IDP). The IDPs had three to four goals the program participant wanted to work on over the next six to eight months. We encouraged leaders to pick stretch goals that would challenge their thinking. The third component of a strong high-potential program was to develop a core curriculum of topics that would help prepare leaders for future roles with larger scale, scope, and responsibility. We had senior leaders work with us to develop content that would get their employees to operate differently. We created training modules around creativity and innovation, diversity and inclusion, and enterprise leadership. Senior leaders from the company helped deliver the training for this part of the program. We selected leaders from all areas of the business so participants could be exposed to various parts of the organization. Having diverse leaders involved in the program was one of the most important factors for getting people to begin to step outside their comfort zones.

The fourth component of the program was to assign mentors to each of the participants. Our mentors played an important role because they exposed the program participants to different styles of leadership. This encouraged cross-functional collaboration and got people to focus on areas where they typically did not spend time. The last part of the program and perhaps the most important one for creating diversity of thought was having the participants work on action learning projects. Action learning was a way to bring leaders together to work on special assignments for the business. There were three action learning projects, which focused on different challenges facing the organization. Leaders were put in teams of ten to fifteen people to come together and figure out how to address different problems. This pushed people to interact with others and find ways to work together as a diverse team. The program was a great success because it challenged leaders to grow by encouraging them to think in new ways.

Whether it is in your personal life or professionally, surround yourself with different types of people. We learn best when we are forced to think outside our comfort zones. I've found this to be inspiring and personally gratifying in my own life. When I've been exposed to different ways of thinking, I can see the world through the eyes of others. I encourage you to do the same. You'll be surprised at how much it impacts the way you build relationships.

Focus on Authenticity

If you want to get better at embracing individual differences, you first have to get comfortable with yourself. Self-comfort comes from deep reflection and self-discovery. Authenticity is the gateway to appreciating and accepting who you are and how you relate to the world. If you are not authentic with yourself, you will not be able to be authentic with others. In my own life, I've learned this over time. For many years, I considered my consulting work to be my professional life. It was my career—what I did for a living. This didn't change how I approached people, but it did limit my ability to be truly available to the clients I supported.

Three years ago, I started working with a senior executive in the media and entertainment industry. Christina was an open book. She was genuine, transparent, and honest with everyone she encountered. When we first started working together, I went into a consulting mode to get to know her and her leadership style. In our first session, she was so honest and real that it challenged the way I chose how open I would be with people. She got me to take off my mask and let my guard down. It was pleasantly surprising because I was the one who usually played such a role with others! So I started being more authentic around her. Our conversations evolved from business topics to personal ones as we developed a friendship over the last few years. Her authenticity wasn't just shared with me. I saw her offer it to all her people and teams.

When we conducted a 360 assessment with leaders across her organization, her authentic approach was validated by others. People saw her as a leader who genuinely cared for the well-being and psychological safety of others. She built deep, personal relationships with all her direct reports. Her authenticity had an impact on how she engaged her peers and senior management as well. People found it refreshing to be around her and to partner on work together. Her approach also had a great impact on the way people viewed their own work. They were more energized and committed to the organization. Her people would go through walls for her because she put them first.

Taking the lessons I learned from this coaching assignment, I started being more open and authentic with all my clients. The results were amazing! I've connected in such deeper and more meaningful ways with people in the last three years than I have in my entire career, and it's not hard work. We all have our little quirks and idiosyncrasies. You just need to be willing to be vulnerable and to open yourself up to others. That's hard for a lot of people. People wear masks all the time. We have our work self, the self we present to family and friends, and the self we share with our neighbors and the people in our communities. When you have the courage to take off the mask and engage with people in the same way across the areas of your life, you'll see tremendous growth. You'll own who you are, and in turn, you'll be able to embrace people in new and different ways.

So get honest with yourself. Look in the mirror and value who you are as a person. Fully embrace all aspects of your life. Then go out and connect with the world. Start in small and simple ways. You can do this by working on your personal and professional life. Our work-life balance is critical to true fulfillment. When you can be the same in both areas, you'll find greater peace. It will also help you connect deeply with others. Embracing individual differences serves as a gateway to moving from surface-level relationships to lasting, meaningful partnerships with others. It also opens the door for developing trust—an essential factor for building life-changing relationships. We'll explore this in depth in the next chapter.

---

[1] G. Robinson and K. Dechant, "Building a Business Case for Diversity," *Academy of Management Executive* 11 (1997): 21–31.

[2] C. C. Chen and E. Van Velsor, "New Directions for Research and Practice in Diversity Leadership," *Leadership Quarterly* 7, no. 2 (1996): 285–302.

[3] N. E. Day and P. G. Greene, "A Case for Sexual Orientation Diversity Management in Small and Large Organizations," *Human Resources Management* 47, no. 3 (2008): 637–654.

4   R. Clark, N. B. Anderson, V. R. Clark, and D. R. Williams, "Racism as a Stressor for African Americans: A Biopsychosocial Model," *American Psychologist* 54, no. 10 (1999): 805–816.

5   K. Crenshaw, N. Gotanda, G. Peller, and K. Thomas, eds., *Critical Race Theory: The Key Writings That Form the Movement* (New York: New Press, 1995).

6   J. Nelson, G. Adams, and P. Salter, "The Marley Hypothesis: Denial of Racism Reflects Ignorance of History," *Psychological Science* 24, no. 2 (2013): 213–218.

7   T. Cox and L. B. Ruby, *Developing Competency to Manage Diversity* (San Francisco: Berrett-Koehler Publishing, 1997).

8   R. M. Kanter, *Men and Women of the Corporation* (New York: Basic Books, 1977).

9   A. M. Morrison, R. P. White, E. Van Velsor, and C. F. Leadership, *Breaking the Glass Ceiling: Can Women Reach the Top of America's Largest Corporations?* (Reading, Massachusetts: Addison-Wesley, 1992).

10 L. Schweitzer, E. S. Ng, S. Lyons, and L. Kuron, "Exploring the Career Pipeline: Gender Differences in Pre-Career Expectations," *Industrial Relations* 66 (2011): 422–444.

11 M. K. Ryan and S. A. Haslam, "The Glass Cliff: Evidence That Women Are Over-Represented in Precarious Leadership Positions," *Academy of Management Review* 32, no. 2 (2007): 549–572.

12 A. H. Eagly and S. J. Karau, "Role Congruity Theory of Prejudice toward Female Leaders," *Psychological Review* 109 (2002): 573–598.

13 R. Khurana, *Searching for a Corporate Savior: The Irrational Quest for Charismatic CEOs* (Princeton, New Jersey: Princeton University Press, 2002).

14 C. Glass, A. Cook, and A. Ingersoll, "Do Women Leaders Promote Sustainability? Analyzing the Effect of Corporate Governance Composition on Environmental Performance," *Business Strategy and the Environment* 70 (2015): 702–728.

15 M. R. Losey, "Is Sexual Orientation an Issue in the Workplace," *HRNews* 12 (1993): 16–17.

16 R. Florida, *The Rise of the Creative Class* (New York: Basic Books, 2002).

17 M. J. Tejeda, "Nondiscrimination Policies and Sexual Identity Disclosure: Do They Make a Difference in Employee Outcomes?" *Employee Responsibilities and Rights* 18, no. 1 (2006): 45–59.

18 E. A. Locke and G. P. Latham, *A Theory of Goal Setting and Task Performance* (Englewood Cliffs, New Jersey: Prentice Hall Publishing, 1990).

19 J. K. Fletcher and B. R. Ragins, "Stone Centre Relational Cultural Theory: A Window on Relational Mentoring," in *The Handbook of Mentoring at Work: Research, Theory, and Practice*, eds. B. R. Ragins and K. E. Kram (Thousand Oaks, California: Sage Press, 2007), 373–399.

20 B. M. Ferdman, "Literacy and Cultural Identity," *Harvard Educational Review* 60 (1990): 181–204.

21 T. Cox Jr., *Cultural Diversity in Organizations: Theory, Research, and Practice* (San Francisco, California: Berrett-Koehler Publishing, 1993).

22 B. M. Meglino, E. C. Ravlin, and C. L. Adkins, "A Work Values Approach to Corporate Culture: A Field Test of the Value Congruence Process and Its Relationships to Individual Outcomes," *Journal of Applied Psychology* 74 (1989): 424–432.

23 N. Bhindi and P. Duignan, "Leadership for a New Century: Authenticity, Intentionality, Spirituality, and Sensibility," *Educational Management and Administration* 25 (1997): 174–180.

DEVELOPING TRUST

Trust is the glue of life. It's the most essential ingredient
in effective communication. It's the foundational
principle that holds all relationships.
—Stephen R. Covey

When building effective relationships, trust is of paramount importance. With trust, people can count on one another in both good
and bad times. Without it, relationships do not prosper and flourish.
When it is damaged or destroyed, relationships, whether personal
or professional, end quickly. I've seen this time and time again with
many clients. Often, my team is brought in as a last resort when leaders have damaged relationships with their colleagues and coworkers.
In some of these instances, the trust can be repaired. It takes honesty,
self-awareness, reflection, and commitment to drive true behavior
change. In other instances, the trust has been damaged so severely
that relationships cannot be restored.

I recently worked with a senior executive in the insurance
industry who had wreaked havoc across his organization. Alex was
brought into the company to innovate and revolutionize how the
firm used data and analytics to better serve their customers. He had a
reputation in the market as a brilliant strategist in building and putting in place systemic and sustainable analytics departments. When
he came into the company, his manager gave him full autonomy and
authority to create a service offering leaders across the firm could use.
Alex quickly took his marching orders and began to execute his top
priorities.

Challenges started to arise quickly in how he partnered with
others. He would come into meetings and one-on-one sessions with

colleagues and dictate how data and analytics would support their businesses. He had forty- to fifty-page slide decks about his approach and methodology and always had to be the smartest person in the room. Leaders across the business felt he was not willing to listen and take into account their requests or feedback. He had a way of doing things, and people needed to "get with the program." You can imagine how people across the firm reacted to his approach. I got the call about eight months into his tenure. His manager said that Alex was having difficulty getting buy-in and alignment from his most senior stakeholders. The trust between his department and the business units had suffered dramatically because of his approach to interacting with others.

As I do with most coaching engagements when we kick things off, I recommended a 360-degree assessment to dive deeper into Alex's main issues and challenges. I spoke to about fifteen of his colleagues across all areas of the company. The feedback was not good. Alex's direct reports did not feel that they were getting the proper guidance and support on how to help the business unit leaders. His peers in corporate functions found him to be aggressive and abrasive. Different people shared several examples about how he would storm out of rooms if others didn't agree with his position or point of view. His internal customers didn't believe he took the time to understand their businesses or to listen to their needs.

The most damaging feedback was from the president of the division Alex was supporting. During our conversation, he shared a story about when Alex presented to his senior leadership team the progress analytics had made in supporting the business. Alex went on for twenty-five minutes about the strategy and approach but never stopped to ask any questions. He could not read the room and see that people were completely disengaged. After this went on for a while, the president got up and told him to stop because he wasn't listening to the team. Alex proceeded to argue with him for five minutes that they weren't listening to his vision. This event was the final straw in many people's minds. Many colleagues told me that he had burned too many bridges.

When I sat down to give him the feedback, he didn't look surprised or concerned. He told me they didn't understand what he was trying to build for the company. He was brought in for a reason, and they were too accustomed to the status quo. There was no acknowledgment of all the damage he had done. After giving him the feedback, we scheduled our development planning session for two weeks later. He canceled the meeting the night before without any reason or excuse. Two days later, I received a call from his manager that Alex was being let go. The trust he had damaged could not be repaired or restored.

Trust builds over time. It starts with self-awareness and acknowledging and accepting who you are as a person. If you cannot be truthful with yourself, you will never be able to do it with others. As you move from your inner world to your external environment, trust becomes more about living a life of honesty and integrity. You have to be open and transparent with others if you're going to build trusting relationships. Making deposits into what I call the "bank account of trust" is critical. This involves being consistent and showing stability to others. Small withdrawals can be tolerated only if a substantial number of deposits have been made. People need to count on you to keep your word if you're going to have a positive impact on their lives. The best relationships are built on trust. When people have this intimate connection, they can start to influence one another in positive and meaningful ways.

KNOWING THYSELF: THE MIRROR TEST

We cannot be truthful and develop trust with others if we cannot be true with ourselves. I've learned this the hard way in my own life. It took me close to ten years to come to terms with my bipolar disorder. As I mentioned in the chapter on establishing rapport, I was diagnosed for the first time in 2007. This was during a challenging and difficult time in graduate school. The diagnosis came as a shock to my system. It made me question who I was and what my life would be like with this disorder. My pride couldn't handle the thought of being damaged or inferior, so I rejected the diagnosis outright. The doctors were all wrong. I rationalized that I just had a nervous breakdown because of the stress of my doctoral program. Within three months of the diagnosis, I stopped taking my medications. I stopped going to therapy. I was going to dust that period of my life off my shoulders and press forward.

At the time, my care team (e.g., close family, psychiatrist, and therapist) told me to take a year off graduate school and get my life back in balance. I refused to do that. After a short summer break, I rushed back to Tampa to complete my degree. The next three months were agonizing. I had to prepare for and take my program's comprehensive exams. The exams were the series of tests doctoral students must complete at the end of their program in order to graduate. I was still in the throngs of a major depressive episode and had to study six to eight hours a day for a solid month before the exam. I was alone in a small apartment with no support. If you've ever been depressed, you will know that at times, you cannot think straight, let alone try to read, comprehend, or memorize anything. I had fifteen to twenty books I needed to process and internalize. Looking back now, I don't know how I did it. I wouldn't advise anyone struggling with bipolar disorder to do what I did that year.

By sheer luck, I passed the exam after three months of grueling pain and suffering. When I got the final completion letter, it was a huge sigh of relief. I took the next month off and did absolutely nothing. At the same time, I prepared to start a three-month interview process for the firm I was looking to join. As the depression subsided, I was able to focus and prioritize things better. I landed a job with the firm for which I wanted to work and started my career. However, there still was no acknowledgment or self-honesty about the bipolar diagnosis. I forgot about it for several years. During that time, though, my life was a whirlwind. I was working fifty- to sixty-hour weeks, training for my first full marathon, and still finding time to party and drink with friends. This went on for several years. People couldn't keep up with me. The hypomania that came with bipolar disorder was on full display. The extremes in behavior were mostly positive during that period. Marathon training and dieting seemed like healthy addictions. My work was all-consuming as I started to gain credibility and notoriety across my firm.

Shortly after I completed my last marathon, my actions and behaviors took a turn for the worse. I started spending time with the wrong crowd. Several of my Wall Street clients started taking me out to dinners and events to celebrate their successes and accomplishments. If you've seen *The Wolf of Wall Street*, you will know where this story is going. I had been exposed to drugs earlier in my life. They were always around in college. My fraternity brothers got high on a regular basis. Yet I never found any of that interesting. At that time, I was on a mission to complete my studies and become a business psychologist. However, when I was with my clients, things became different. What was wrong with letting loose and having some fun? At one of these private events at a nightclub, I was introduced to cocaine. I thought nothing of it when I tried it for the first time. The high was exhilarating.

Over the next six months, what started as a once-in-a-while occasion with clients became a weekly habit with friends. I told myself it was my day off. I deserved to treat myself. My career was thriving. I was in a long-term relationship and had plans to get married. Nothing could have been better at that time! The cocaine addiction slowly started to take control of my whole life. I'll talk more about this later in this chapter, but for now, know that not coming to terms with my bipolar disorder led me down a dark path. It wasn't until my stint in rehab that I finally accepted my disease. You may not have a mental health disorder or substance abuse addiction, but everyone has some dysfunction in their lives. You have to identify it and understand the role it plays in your life. Without doing so, you can never develop honest, open, and transparent relationships with others. I talked about authenticity in the last chapter. You can't be your true, authentic self if you don't take a deep dive into who you are as a person. We all wear masks. Many of us compartmentalize parts of our lives to meet the needs of different stakeholders. Self-trust starts with how you live your life on a consistent basis. It's about developing self-esteem and confidence and accepting all aspects of ourselves.

The self-knowledge required to build trust with others not only helps promote strong relationships, but it also has value toward one's own self-actualization. Abraham Maslow, the pioneering American psychologist best known for creating the hierarchy of needs, was one of the first to study the concept of self-actualization. Self-actualization is the need for personal growth and discovery that is present throughout an individual's life. Maslow's hierarchy of needs framework is made up of a five-tier model of needs, which is often depicted as hierarchical levels within a pyramid. From the bottom to the top, the needs are physiological (e.g., foot and water), safety (e.g., shelter and job security), belongingness (e.g., human connections and friendships), esteem (e.g., prestige and achievement), and self-actualization (e.g., achieving one's full potential).[1] Needs lower in the hierarchy must be satisfied before people can attend to needs higher up. Self-actualization is considered the area on which we must consistently focus to reach our full potential.

To reach our full potential, we have to get to a point where we trust who we are and how we interact with the world around us. According to Maslow, a person is always growing and never remains static. In self-actualization, a person comes to find a meaning to life that is important to them. Many of the characteristics of self-actualizers come from cultivating a deeper understanding of themselves. They accept how they are wired with all their strengths and blemishes. They are able to look at their life objectively and draw relevant and pragmatic conclusions. They perceive reality efficiently and can tolerate uncertainty. They are capable of a deep appreciation for basic life experiences. They have strong morals, values, and ethical standards.[2] Learning to trust yourself plays a critical role in the self-actualization journey. Without trust, we cannot get outside ourselves to connect with others. With it, we can develop trust in dynamic relationships.

Building dynamic relationships isn't only about having a deep understanding of who we are and having trust in ourselves. Although that's a starting point, you have to go a step further. It becomes about how you live your life. Are you an honest, open, and transparent person? Do you have strong values, morals, and integrity? Are you a trustworthy person? Can people count on you? The mirror test, as I call it, is being able to stand in front of a mirror and be honest with yourself about who you are as a person. Are you able to identify what you are passionate about and what may frustrate you? Can you discern the things that are important in your life and those that are not as relevant? When working with clients to develop a deeper understanding of themselves, we take them through our leadership experience process. Our approach draws from multiple data sources to help an individual get an accurate picture of the type of person they are. There are three components that make up our leadership experience assessment process. First, we have people complete a personality inventory that gets at an individual's strengths, derailers, and personal values and beliefs. This gives us the baseline for how they are wired as a person.

Second, we conduct our leadership experience interview. This interview is a three-hour in-depth discussion about a leader's personal journey. We cover numerous topics during the conversation. We talk about a person's upbringing and the early childhood events that started to shape their understanding of the world around them. This is critically important to unlock the events that have made an impact on how they view themselves today. We discuss their educational experiences and social life in high school and college. This gives us insights into how they built early life relationships and acquired knowledge and information. Next, we have people take us through their entire career history. We talk about each of their job roles and the organizations for which they have worked over their career. This allows us to understand their experiences managing and leading teams, partnering with others, and solving problems and business challenges.

Lastly, we conduct 360 stakeholder interviews to understand how other people perceive the individual we are working with. Once we have data from all these sources, we put together an aggregate report that outlines the findings from our leadership experience process. Our deliverables provide a person with a depth of insight into who they are, how they interact with others, and the type of leader they tend to be. When we present the findings to a person, we tell them the narrative of their life. The process is eye-opening for many people.

You may not need to go through an in-depth psychological assessment process to learn deeply about yourself, but you can find ways to better understand the impact and influence that you have on others. I'll talk about some resources and tools that are available to start this journey at the end of this chapter. For now, the gateway to developing trust with others is first understanding and truly trusting yourself. When we trust who we are as a person, we unlock our ability to empathize and develop an understanding of others. Trust enables us to embrace and value individual differences. It opens the door for dynamic relationships to start to take shape across all areas of our lives.

DEPOSITS AND WITHDRAWALS: THE BANK ACCOUNT OF TRUST

My first few years of college were an exciting period of my life. The university I attended had a five-year accelerated degree program in industrial-organizational psychology, where you could earn your bachelor's and master's degrees at the same time. At that point, I knew I wanted to be a business psychologist, so I applied for the program in the second semester of my sophomore year. The application process was intense. I had to complete several essays about why I wanted to choose this career. I also had to go through an in-depth interview process with several of the professors of the psychology department. I had already started building a relationship with Dr. Thompson, the chair of the department, in my freshman year, which helped with the interviews. After a few months of waiting, I received notification that I had been accepted into the program. On top of this, I was offered a teaching fellowship and would work directly with Dr. Thompson. He became my first mentor.

Working as his graduate assistant, I learned many things. I learned a lot about the field of I-O psychology. I learned how to teach a college-level course. I learned how to navigate relationships with different leaders across the university. All these things were important to my development. However, I learned the most through the one-on-one conversations we would have at the start of each day. We would get together early in the morning before classes started and just talk about life. Many of the conversations focused on my future. Did I want to start my career after completing my master's degree? What type of work did I want to do after college? Did I want to teach at a university? Did I want to secure an internal role within an organization? Did I want to work as an external management consultant? Did I want to get my doctorate in I-O psychology?

Dr. Thompson always had two graduate students who worked for him during the school year. My first colleague was my friend Mark, whom I had known since high school. We met each other while selling TVs at Sears. Our prior history enabled us to have a greater partnership together. Mark was two years ahead of me in the program, and I learned so much from him. I learned about putting people first and sharing in the successes of others. I learned about the value of trust and how important it was when working with others. I always saw Mark go out of his way to do favors and help support people. He never expected anything in return for his actions. This resonated with so many different people. For over a year, I had a front-row seat to watch someone make deposits into other people's lives on a consistent basis. He was genuine, honest, and transparent with people.

After Mark graduated, Dr. Thompson selected a new graduate assistant, who would be working with me for two years. Jonathan was a charming and witty guy. He easily established rapport with Dr. Thompson and influenced him to make the hiring decision. Yet when I met Jonathan for the first time, something didn't sit right with me. He was too assertive and aggressive in wanting to learn all the ins and outs of the department. He asked questions and was curious, but there always seemed to be an ulterior motive behind his actions. I started observing how he built relationships with the men and women throughout the department. He quickly befriended one of our female colleagues, and within a few weeks, they were dating. That ended quickly after he had sex with her. He also started manipulating others in the department. I saw him use information to pit people against one another. He was highly competitive and thrived off seeing others struggle.

He lived in a zero-sum game. As long as he ended up on top as the winner, life was good. If others succeeded, he would tell jokes about them to diminish their efforts. I watched firsthand how he got people to trust him and then used that trust for his personal advantage. He tried to do this to me several times, but I wouldn't have it. I always kept him at arm's length because of how he treated others. By the end of his first year in the program, he had damaged and destroyed the trust of all his colleagues. People didn't want to work with him. They didn't trust him. As word started getting back to Dr. Thompson, he was shocked to hear how manipulative Jonathan was with people. Dr. Thompson never saw any of this behavior, as Jonathan was skilled at hiding his intentions. After an investigation was conducted into his behaviors, Jonathan was fired from the department. It was a powerful lesson about the importance of trust and about how quickly it could be destroyed.

The emotional trust account is where we must continually make deposits if we want trust to develop and relationships to flourish. The concept of reciprocity—the practice of exchange with others for mutual benefit—is a part of this puzzle, but trust has to go a step further. It must come from intentional generosity. Generosity is a sacrifice we make for others when we want relationships to prosper. It is about planting seeds consistently, which take time to grow. Your deposits must have meaning to the other person. They have to show your commitment to the relationship and your desire to support another's emotional well-being. Selfishness is often one of the biggest deterrents to trust. It leads to more withdrawals made, which can ultimately deplete the account and destroy a relationship. If we are to make the right deposits and avoid detrimental withdrawals, it is first critical to understand the different components of trust.

Many writers—mainly from the disciplines of sociology, psychology, and economics—have put forward different definitions of trust. Early definitions conceptualize trust as the general belief in the goodness of others.[3] Some have proposed that trust occurs when a person expects an event to occur and the expectation leads to certain types of behavior.[4] Negative consequences are drawn when the expectation is not met, and positive ones occur when expectations are confirmed. Others have defined trust as an expectancy held by an individual or group that the word, promise, or written statement of another individual or group can be relied upon.[5] Common to these and other definitions of trust is an expectancy that one person will behave in a predetermined manner. These expectancies may be due to the characteristics of the person being trusted (e.g., similar values, ethics, and beliefs), the forces in a given situation (e.g., social or cultural norms), or the disposition of the person who is doing the trusting. Trust is needed only in situations where there is uncertainty about the actions that will be undertaken by others and when these actions are of consequence to those involved.

Yet trust is more than just expectancies about others' actions. The predictability of a person's actions does not necessarily imply trustworthiness. A person who may be counted on to do whatever is most self-serving may be called predictable but will not likely be someone trusted by others. Similarly, people can cooperate with others they do not trust, but this cooperation may result from coercion or threat, not from any expectancy based on the reliability of that person. For trust to take place, a person must be willing to be vulnerable, and the willingness to be vulnerable is based on expectancies about the motives of others in the relationship and on the belief that these motives are adequate protection against self-serving behavior.

Researchers have found that predictability (e.g., subjective probability of a person's actions), dependability (e.g., trust placed in the person rather than in that person's actions), and faith (e.g., trust for all situations that may be encountered in the future) are the key indicators of trust.[6] Trust evaluations are also composed of perceptions of the ability, benevolence, and integrity of the person being trusted. Ability is the skills and characteristics that enable a person to have influence within some area of expertise. Benevolence is the extent to which the person being trusted is believed to want to do good to the person doing the trusting. Integrity involves the person doing the trusting to perceive that the other person adheres to a set of principles that the trustor finds acceptable.[7]

Trust has been argued to provide relationships without the need for continual proof of legitimate intentions of others. In economics, trust has been described as "central to all transactions" between two people.[8] Sociologists and social psychologists maintain that the absence of trust will make the everyday lives that we take for granted "simply not possible." Research by industrial psychologists on relationships between organizations has found that trust is essential for the survival of alliances and technological collaborations.[9] Within a company, interpersonal trust between team members has been identified as a critical element in facilitating day-to-day functioning. Trust helps people and teams accomplish shared goals and objectives, and it creates the foundation for cultivating influence.

In the early stages of a relationship, most people assume that others are trustworthy. They suspend the belief that others' values may be different from their own. This does not mean that a person is gullible. A gullible person is one who, in the absence of any kind of information, takes another person's trustworthiness on faith and assumes the risk of being exploited. Trusting another person and assuming they share our values are often preferred to initial distrust. Trust is an easier option for people to process, and for this reason, there is a strong incentive to being in a relationship with it. This is not to say that people do not use their own values to decide whether to trust others. Assuming that distrust is not present in the early stages of a relationship, the experience of future trust will be determined by the content of continued behavior exchanges between two people. If trust is to be built over time, two people must be able to exchange and share the feelings and thoughts that structure the relationship. Successful behavioral exchanges are accompanied by positive moods and emotions, which help cement the experience of trust and set the stage for deeper connections and stronger relationships.

Conditional trust is usually sufficient to facilitate a wide range of social interactions. It is consistent with the idea that one of the bases for trust is knowledge or positive expectations of others. Unconditional trust starts when a person abandons the pretense of suspending belief, because shared values now structure the relationship and have become the primary vehicle through which two people experience trust. With unconditional trust, each person's trustworthiness is assured based on confidence in the other's values, which is backed up by evidence derived from repeated interactions. When unconditional trust is present, relationships become significant and often involve a sense of mutual identification. For this reason, unconditional trust is something we all should strive for to build dynamic, long-term relationships.

Trust dissolves quickly when people engage in behaviors that do not line up with the established expectations of others. Assuming that trust starts at a conditional level, any subsequent discrepant behavior exchanges or violations of mutually agreed upon expectations will cause trust to be reduced and put the relationship in jeopardy. If trust has become unconditional, the dissolution process is far more complex. When unconditional trust exists, the relationship is infused with meaning and positive affect. Short-term behavioral lapses by one person are likely to be forgiven by the other. However, a perceived violation that puts trust to the test is the key contingency in severed relationships. Sometimes, the sheer magnitude of the discrepant behavior can be so enormous that it precipitates an immediate collapse of trust. The injured person is assured that discrepant values exist, attitudes become unfavorable, and negative emotions signal the end of the trust relationship. This is most often the case in intimate relationships when infidelity occurs. Common expressions like, "That was the last straw," capture how a person feels when trust has been severely damaged. It doesn't matter what types of deposits or the amount that a once-trusted person makes after such collapse has taken place. When trust is lost, relationships end quickly.

UNDERLYING ASPECTS OF TRUST BUILDING

The financial crisis of 2008 hit many US companies hard. The economic landscape was hit the worst in the finance and insurance sector. Many companies collapsed and had to close their doors. Luckily, my client's company was given an opportunity to rebound and rebuild. Although they were given the chance to turn things around, Rebecca, their CEO, had a tall order in front of her. The company had to rebuild trust with its employees and its external environment. If they could not regain trust, the company was sure to fail. To do this, she needed to restructure and redesign the entire organization and make sure the right leaders were in the right roles to get through the turnaround. It was around this time that Rebecca reached out to my firm to inquire about our process for leadership development assessments. She had gone through a leadership development process earlier in her career and thought this would be a great first step to giving her top thirty leaders the insights they needed to make the changes required for future success.

When we first met with Rebecca, she had a specific framework in mind for how she wanted the assessment process to go. We needed to build a leadership competency model that would reflect where the company was headed—its future state, not the current circumstances. She wanted leaders to be open about their reports and their feedback and to use this process as a mechanism for driving the changes needed at all levels of the organization. She was fully committed to seeing this development process through from start to finish. Based on her request, my firm crafted a series of assessment protocols to get her people the input and feedback they needed. We used a multimethod assessment approach involving a three-hour in-depth leadership interview, the use of online critical thinking tests and leadership personality instruments, interview-based 360-degree feedback, and external resume benchmarking and job profiling. The combination of these assessment tools enabled us to get accurate and detailed information about each leader. We then used this data to compare each leader to the leadership competency framework we developed for the future state of the organization.

From start to finish, the assessment and feedback process took close to eight months to complete. It was by no means a smooth process at various points throughout the engagement. Many of her top leaders did not feel the need for a leadership assessment at such a pivotal junction in the company's history. Others did not want to go through a 360-degree feedback process and definitely did not want to share the results of the assessment with Rebecca or one another. But despite these obstacles, Rebecca remained steadfast and determined to have her entire leadership team go through the assessment and feedback process. She felt it was critical to their growth and ability to learn about themselves so they could start to rebuild trust with their people. Rebecca understood the importance of commitment to developing trust. She had the fortitude to stay the course and make tough decisions for the benefit of the enterprise. She made sure that her team persevered through this process despite operating in a high-stress and complex economic environment.

Feedback can do one of two things to a leader: The leader may reject the assessment and get defensive with a consultant. This is not a strong starting point for behavior change. In other instances, a light goes on, and leaders take the feedback to heart. They use it to make improvements and strive to be better. Luckily for my firm, once all the leaders received their feedback, many responded positively. They found the exercise and the insights and feedback derived from the process to be immensely helpful. It enabled them to look at their personal impact and that of their teams. It built a sense of trust and camaraderie between leaders as they began to restructure and redesign the organization. It created the environment for a strong rebound and rebuilding of the company beyond the economic crisis.

Not only was the feedback process helpful to Rebecca and her top thirty leaders, but it also initiated a focus on leadership and organizational effectiveness throughout their company. Once the top thirty leaders were given feedback, they wanted to offer this opportunity to many of their direct reports. We began working to drive positive leadership change across various areas of the business. Additionally, through Rebecca's commitment to driving true leadership impact and change, the organization partnered with my firm to design key leadership competencies that would have an impact across functional boundaries and at various levels of leadership. We took the leadership framework that was used for the top thirty leadership assessments and cascaded this down to the SVP, VP, and director levels. As time progressed, we began to see the leadership changes start to take place across the business. Leaders at all levels were more open to feedback from one another and from external stakeholders. Trust began to be rebuilt across the organization. We were witnessing a true leadership turnaround, and it all began with Rebecca's commitment to rebuilding trust.

Rebecca understood the importance of commitment and its vital role in building trust. She knew how to strive for a critical goal despite obstacles, setbacks, and challenges. She challenged her people to be greater and invited them to take part in a story of evolution and change. She prioritized leadership effectiveness as a critical growth factor to get her organization through the turnaround. This fostered clarity of purpose for her people and helped them navigate times of doubt and uncertainty. Rebecca persisted despite the circumstances. She had the necessary focus and concentration to push her team through a difficult period and achieve their desired outcomes.

In our personal relationships, one of the quickest ways to erode trust is by not following through on commitments. I've seen this occur with families. It happens all the time in romantic relationships. Dropped commitments also have a negative impact on friendships. If you want to build dynamic relationships, commitment has to be part of the puzzle. When we honor our commitments, people have faith we will do so again in the future. People can rely on us in good times and bad. There is a sense of comfort and peace that comes when we know that others will keep their commitments. When commitment is consistently broken, people distrust the actions and behaviors of others. They start to second-guess others' intentions and question the value and importance of the relationship.

Consistency is another factor that plays a role in building trust with others. Consistency is about character, courage, and integrity. It's about walking the talk. I've seen it demonstrated in the best fashion in many professional athletes. LeBron James, Peyton Manning, Derek Jeter, and Tom Brady are just a few examples of people who demonstrate consistency day in and day out. They walk the talk. They understand that setting a positive example for others speaks louder than words. I've had the pleasure of getting to know some sports psychologists who worked with Kobe Bryant. We all saw the game-winning shots, the five championships, the numerous all-star appearances. What we did not see was the work he put in to accomplish those great feats. Kobe was consistently the first one in the gym at 5:00 a.m. He would work on his shot over and over again, sometimes shooting until he hit fifty to sixty shots in a row. He did this from all over the court. Next, he would work on his dribbling and ballhandling skills. After that, he would be in the weight room for two hours. This was all before any of his teammates even showed up at the practice facility! He led by example in practice, pushed his teammates as if they were playing in a live game, and constantly strived to make everyone better. This built trust with people. They could count on him when the stakes were high. They always knew he was going to give his best efforts. It inspired others to do the same.

When it comes to consistency, our character is of utmost importance. Our background and upbringing matter. Childhood is where we develop character traits that will have an impact on us for the rest of our lives. Some of the most effective leaders with whom I have worked have stories from their past that have shaped who they are today. It's the simple things parents should teach their children—manners at the dinner table, asking for things politely, and saying please and thank you. It's the role of mentors and role models to encourage and support children as they grow. These early life lessons begin to shape our character. They shape how we will interact with the world later in life. They can help us foster an environment of trust with different stakeholders.

Many of our character traits are formed by modeling the behaviors of others at a very young age. This starts with parents but extends to the broader family circle; to friends and acquaintances during formative school years; and to coaches, teachers, and role models later in high school. I've seen it time and time again with many of the executives with whom I work. Most of them can recall a person or experience from their childhood that has left a strong impression on them. I hear stories like, "My father's work ethic helped shape how I approach my work today," "My dance instructor taught me the importance of focus and never giving up," "My mother showed people respect and compassion. I learned to do the same with others," "My high school coach taught me what it meant to have discipline and commitment," and "My grandfather taught me about looking for the best in people."

Our character sets the stage for how we will interact with others, for how we will treat people, and for how we will build long-term relationships. People who use their upbringing and early life experiences to shape strong characters—those who are marked by honesty, fairness, and respect for people—have the greatest influence. This is because character determines how we will navigate both good and bad times. A person who is honest will always place a strong emphasis on building and sustaining trusting relationships. Our character serves as a foundation for the impact we will have on others.

People who are consistent tend to have the courage to stand behind their convictions. They stand up for what they believe and see things through until the end. Courage is developed with practice. It does not happen overnight. Life circumstances dictate how well we develop this skill. We have all heard the saying that life is 10 percent what happens to you and 90 percent how you handle it. Courage falls in the 90 percent range. I've seen people develop courage in some of the most difficult and trying conditions. I've also seen some of our clients struggle with demonstrating courage and the lack of it damaging relationships.

One of my clients in the retail sector demonstrated courage under fire. His business had enjoyed three consecutive years of increased revenues and profits. During this time, he focused on growing his leadership team, strengthening the capabilities of his direct reports, and putting in place a strong high-potential leadership development program. Going into year four, the economic landscape started to shift. At the end of their first quarter, he saw sales drop by 20 percent. The overall trend for the year was not looking promising. Given this news, my client had two choices staring him in the face. On the one hand, he could cut selling, general, and administrative (SG&A) expenses and focus on driving revenue with an intense execution. On the other hand, he could continue the work on developing his team and the people below his direct reports and reinforce their focus on sales execution at the store levels. The easy thing to do would have been to drop all the work investing into his team and the broader organization. Expenses needed to be cut, and leadership development programs were typically the first thing to get cut.

However, my client took a firm stance on his belief that leadership development made his people better. It helped them drive customer service and sales force excellence at the store levels. He chose to keep the programs going that helped prepare people for the future. We stuck with the high-potential program. We kept the team effectiveness work with his leadership team. They missed revenue targets in two quarters that year but saw the back half of the year have a strong surge. To this day, my client looks at that period as a moment that tested his courage and commitment to his people. He had the courage to stick to what he believed was right even though contextual and situational factors told him to take a different course.

There is a powerful relationship between courage and character. A strong background and upbringing helps solidify behaviors that create great relationships. Once a person's character takes shape, the choices and decisions they regularly exercise typically involve courage. It takes courage to do the right things when the wrong things are easier to do. It takes courage to stand behind one's values and beliefs and be willing to challenge colleagues when they are not doing the same. It takes courage to lead through difficult times when the people around you want to give up and quit. When a person is consistent in demonstrating courage, they begin to serve as a positive role model for others. Trust is easier to build from there.

Our attitudes also impact how we build trust with others. Attitude is shaped by integrity. People with high integrity understand the importance it plays on how they relate to others. Like character, people develop integrity based on early life experiences. They are taught—by parents, family, friends, or other early-life role models— how to respect people, how to treat people, and how to carry themselves in the public arena. Some of the most effective leaders with whom I've worked operate from a foundation of high integrity. They tend to be motivated by more than personal gain or achievement. They promote the greater good of their organizations. They inspire trust through both words and actions. They communicate good and bad news to colleagues in a straightforward and honest manner.

When integrity is missing, problems quickly arise. I can remember this happening for a client with whom I worked in the energy industry. He approached most of his interactions with a win-lose mindset. He was highly competitive with people and always had to come out ahead. This often caused him to treat people as means to an end rather than as colleagues. Early in his career, this was not much of a problem, as he was an individual contributor and could focus more on his duties and responsibilities. However, once he got into management, things started to fall apart. His tendency to treat people disrespectfully and to always have to get his way caused a lot of friction with his direct reports. It also damaged the trust of his cross-functional peers.

When I started coaching him, there were some pretty significant gaps in his leadership. However, before we could get into any of his behaviors, we needed to identify what mattered most to him: his core values and beliefs. I needed to know where the self-interest originated. Did he come from a family with a lot of brothers and sisters where competition was valued? Did he go through early life experiences that made him develop a strong sense of self-entitlement? What were his core values? Did he value power, security, or influence? We had to uncover his guiding principles in order to have a framework through which we could drive behavior change.

After our first few coaching meetings, it became clear where his values and beliefs originated. As an adolescent, he was a top athlete in track and field. He was a two-hundred-meter and four-hundred-meter runner. Everything involved in his training was based on competing with others. He looked at other track athletes as foes he had to beat. He was also one of three boys growing up. Both of his brothers were older than him. He regularly put pressure on himself to do and be better than his older siblings. Then he brought this mindset into relationships in high school and college. It quickly became clear throughout his life that he was rewarded for winning. His belief system was formed around striving to be his best and to outperform those around him. Once we identified his core beliefs, we began to work on changing some of his guiding principles. He no longer had to lead with a winner-takes-all mentality. We started shifting the attention to team effectiveness. He began to see that to win meant his team being successful. It meant that he had to start taking time to build solid relationships with others. He had to start thinking about the thoughts and feelings of colleagues and lead with greater integrity. Integrity is so important when it comes to developing trust with others. When we put people first and demonstrate consistent behaviors each day, we set the stage for building great relationships.

WHEN TRUST IS DAMAGED AND DESTROYED

When I started using cocaine, I thought nothing of it. At the time, I was two years into a committed, long-term relationship with my ex-wife, Stacey. The first two years of our relationship were amazing. We had so many shared interests. We both had completed our doctorate degrees from prestigious universities. We both had a passion for health and physical activity. We trusted each other. Trust was the bedrock of our relationship. Stacey knew she could count on me through thick and thin, and I felt the same about her. We both let our guards down, as unconditional trust was established.

Six months before we got engaged and moved in together, I used cocaine for the first time. I was down on Wall Street with some of my clients. They were celebrating a big end-of-the-year event for their firm. It was Christmastime. I remember the brisk, cold air outside before entering the party that night. When I was offered it, I had already been drinking and was in great spirits. The feeling of inhaling a line burned the first time, but the high that followed a few minutes later was exhilarating. I only did a few lines that night, but the seed had been planted. A few weeks later, I was home with some friends, watching basketball, late on a Saturday night. One of my close friends introduced me to Jeremy, who had a reputation for being a party guy. He had brought cocaine with him, and we all did some lines together while drinking beers and watching the game. At the end of the night, I exchanged numbers with Jeremy. It was one of the worst mistakes I had ever made in my life.

Over the next several months, I typically worked sixty-hour workweeks. I saw Stacey two to three times a week for date nights. I had one night every week when I hung out with the fellas. These nights were always with the same three or four guys. Jeremy was the pack leader. We snorted our cocaine, talked about life for hours, and went to strip clubs. That was the pattern each and every week. I kept this from Stacey, as I knew she would be appalled that I was doing drugs and going to strip clubs. She never asked because she completely trusted me. This worked when we were living separately. I kept my life in nice little compartments.

Stacey and I got engaged later that summer. By that time, the cocaine habit had started to take a hold of me. I was doing it two times a week. Most often, it was just me and Jeremy. He would come to my place on the weekends, when it was just the two of us, and we would get high together. Shortly after we got engaged, Stacey and I moved in together. We were starting our life. We were planning our wedding. It was an exciting time in our lives! At the same time, I still made sure I had two nights a week when I hung out with Jeremy. I would go to his place since Stacey and I were living together. The lies started to get worse. If I told her I was going to his place on a Sunday afternoon to watch football, it ended up being a whole day event. I would come home at ten or eleven o'clock at night still high and lie straight to her face. I told her I had a few drinks and was a bit tipsy. Because she still trusted me unconditionally, she didn't think anything of it.

A few months later, I started using it three to four times a week. I would wait until she left for work, call out of work myself, and do cocaine all day with Jeremy. We worked a schedule around her schedule. Whenever I had time alone, I was able to get high. As the addiction got worse, the lies continued to grow. I started canceling plans and stopped showing up for dates and times we were supposed to spend together. For example, if I was to meet Stacey for dinner in the city after she got out of work, I would text her an hour before we were supposed to meet and tell her I got stuck with work. If we had planned a day together on the weekend, I would tell her I was going to visit my parents or had a last-minute change in my schedule.

After over a year, I was using it almost every day. Stacey started questioning what I was doing and who I was with. She knew something was off but couldn't put her finger on it. She simply thought I was overwhelmed with work or was suffering from depression. I knew things were falling apart but couldn't stop using. The worse was that I didn't even try to fix it. I let things slip away over the next six to eight months. Our wedding was disastrous. I started using early in the morning that day and hid it throughout the entire event. By that time, Stacey didn't even want to be in the same room with me.

My addiction got even worse the following year. I wanted to stop using so badly but couldn't. It didn't matter how much I tried; things just continued to get worse. A month before the end-of-year holidays, Stacey took a trip to Las Vegas for a convention with her job. She was gone for a week. I did cocaine every day she was gone. I almost overdosed. The morning after I made up my mind to check myself into rehab, I called her to tell her the truth. It was a crushing blow to her. She was speechless and told me right away that she was leaving me. The woman I thought I would spend the rest of my life with was gone. We tried to work on our relationship for a year after that. I did all I could to try to restore trust. However, permanent damage had been done. Stacey couldn't trust me any longer. She was constantly second-guessing what I was doing when we were apart. This taught me a painful lesson about destroyed trust. Once you break unconditional trust, an emotional vacuum is created. When we finally got divorced, I was devastated. I knew things would never change in her mind, and that was what crushed me the most. As I look back now, I understand that trust can never be violated that strongly. When such violation happens, people lose all confidence in who we are and how we feel about the relationship. As you think about your own life, remember to honor the trust and commitment you create with others. It is the only way a relationship can flourish and grow.

PUTTING IT INTO PRACTICE

Developing trust is the fourth skill of relational intelligence. Trust is the glue that takes a relationship to its deepest levels of connection and intimacy. For trust to impact the quality of our relationships, we first need to understand who we are as people. Being true to yourself is the first step to learning how to build trust with others. We have to get clear on our values and beliefs and the impact they have on our lives. Knowing ourselves sets the stage for building trust with others. When it comes to our relationships, trust takes shape over time. It is built by the deposits we make into the lives of those we want to impact. This must come from a place of intentional generosity. We have to put our pride and ego aside when it comes to putting others first. Commitment and consistency help us do this. Keeping our commitments helps others believe we will always honor our word. Being consistent in how we show up for people enables us to impact their lives. Consistency sets the stage for cultivating influence and helping others become the best versions of themselves. The most powerful thing with trust is making sure we never break it. Although small infractions can take place, we must avoid major ones. If we do not, our relationships will end quickly. So what's the best way to build trust with others? Although it takes time, it is not as difficult as people often believe. Here are the three areas you must focus on to build strong, trusting relationships.

Learn About Who You Are

It is each of our responsibility to understand how we are wired and what makes us tick. Although our values and beliefs start to form early in life, we have to continue to develop them over time. There are many ways we can do this. First, we can examine what we were taught by our parents and extended families. We learned by what our parents or guardians taught us and the behaviors they consistently modeled. This could be good or bad depending on the environment. Friends, teachers, and other role models had an impact on us during schooling years. For me, this impact was through friendships I developed with basketball coaches and teammates. I learned about discipline, dedication, teamwork, and leadership from the people with whom I surrounded myself. I also learned from teachers I respected in high school. They encouraged my growth in literature, mathematics, and psychology. The balance between sports and academics cemented in me the desire to be a lifelong learner and instilled a drive to succeed.

If you've never done it before, pull out a journal and reflect on your early life experiences. What did you learn from your parents? What did your mother teach you? What behaviors did your father model? How did relationships with your siblings impact your growth? What did you learn about yourself in school? What subjects did you gravitate toward? What types of hobbies and interests did you have outside of your studies? Who were your friends? What did you learn from them? Answering these questions will give you a baseline to evaluate how you think about things today.

In my last book, *What Every Leader Needs: The Ten Universal and Indisputable Competencies of Leadership Effectiveness*, I talked a lot about calling and leadership legacy. It is imperative that we get a sense of what we are meant to do in life. When I talk about calling, I am referring to your life's mission and purpose. What do you want to contribute to the world? What type of impact do you want to have on others? The journey of self-exploration that leads to a deep understanding of calling can happen in many different ways. Early in our careers, mentors play an important role in helping us to define work values and beliefs. Get around people who are further in life than you are, not just one or two steps ahead in the journey. You want mentors who are eight or nine steps down the road. They can speak life into goals and dreams. A good mentor will have you focus on three areas:

a) What are you good at (i.e., what are your key strengths and capabilities)?

b) What are your hopes and ambitions (i.e., what do you want to accomplish in life)?

c) What's most important to who you are as a person (i.e., what are the things that guide your everyday living)?

If you want to go a level deeper into identifying who you are as a person, I highly recommend a therapist or a coach. Although some people have negative connotations associated with therapy, I've learned in my own life that therapy is whatever you want to make it. Early in my therapy journey, it was about understanding and accepting my bipolar disorder. I had to learn about the different forms of the disorder. I have Type II bipolar disorder, which is less severe than Type I bipolar, but there are still many things to be cognizant of if I want to live a healthy lifestyle. You may not have a mood disorder or mental health issues, but therapy is great for working on your relationships with others, for understanding how your past has shaped who you are today, and for making meaning out of what you experience on a consistent basis. If therapy is not for you, I'm a strong supporter of working with a life coach in your personal life or an executive coach related to professional endeavors. My firm works with clients from all walks of life. I regularly coach CEOs and C-suite executives on all aspects of their professional journeys. We set vision for their teams, understand how their strengths and blind spots impact their people and organizations, and consider how to influence direct reports through the power of relationships.

A great executive coach serves as a trusted advisor and thought partner. They get you to see things about yourself you didn't know before. Coaching usually has three components. There is the discovery phase, where you learn about your strengths, development areas, and work-related values. This is one of the most insightful parts of the process. From here, you get to build a personal development plan. This includes the three to four goals you want to work on to better yourself as a leader. The third and most exciting part is the actual coaching sessions. In many of my coaching sessions, I've focused on helping leaders navigate difficult personalities of colleagues and coworkers. I've helped them rebuild their brand when it has been tarnished or damaged. I've helped prepare people for roles of increased scale, scope, and responsibility.

If we want to build trust with others, we first have to fully understand ourselves. When we know and trust the person we are—all the good, bad, and ugly—it helps us to better interact with the world around us. I've seen trust destroyed between people when one person doesn't know how they are wired. They bring their struggles, challenges, and baggage into the relationship and can cause havoc for others. I've done this and have had it done to me. So get clear about who you are. It's the foundational step to building trust that will stand the test of time with others.

Live with a Deposit Mentality

There is power in intentional generosity. When we live with a deposit mentality, we seek to put people first. It doesn't have to be big, grand gestures. We can offer simple things like listening to a problem of a friend, helping out a colleague or coworker with a project, or making coffee in the morning for a spouse. Acts of kindness encourage people to trust us more. Recently, I worked with a senior executive in the financial services industry. Phillip was a generous and giving leader. He always looked for ways to add value to the lives of others. When I began working with Phillip, he had recently been promoted into a new role. As we mapped out his goals and personal development plan for the transition, we needed to make sure that he focused on his team, his peers, and his leadership across the enterprise. Our goals were centered on improving his ability to influence the actions and behaviors of others.

We first went to work on his relationships with his direct reports. I encouraged Phillip to make sure he took time for each of them. He went above and beyond with this. He invested in helping each of his people develop and grow. He frequently had conversations about their goals, hopes, and ambitions. He always made sure to do something for each of his people to help them pursue their objectives. He also had an open-door policy with all his employees. Employees two or three levels below his direct reports were encouraged to come to him if they needed anything. He went out of his way on a regular basis to support people. This created great trust and loyalty. Employees could count on him through thick and thin. Over a six-month period, I saw him build dynamic relationships. This resulted in increased productivity and organizational commitment to the vision he set for the team.

When it came to working with his peers, Phillip was highly collaborative. He volunteered for cross-functional projects to get exposure to the work of his colleagues. This gave people a glimpse into his working style and commitment to driving shared objectives. Phillip was generous with his time and never turned a coworker who needed help away. I got the chance to sit in on some of his leaders' team meetings, and Phillip was always actively engaged in conversations about the business. He offered insights and feedback about projects. He listened to the concerns and suggestions of others. He was humble and did not have to be the center of attention. People believed he had their best interests at heart. As I built my relationship with Phillip, I regularly asked him why he was so committed to supporting others. His answer was simple. If he was going to influence people, he first had to act as a servant leader. Phillip wasn't looking for reciprocity. He never kept score or looked for people to do him any favors. However, his approach garnered buy-in, alignment, and agreement with leaders across the enterprise. His intentional generosity had a positive impact on all those around him.

So how can you live with a deposit mindset? Start with those closest to you. Do it with your spouse, your kids, or your extended family members. From there, move out to your social circles. Be a resource and support system for your friends. Go out of your way to make others feel valued and appreciated. You'll be amazed at how this mindset and behavior will have an impact on your relationships. Intentional generosity is a lifestyle. It's not one-offs that take place occasionally. It's about how we engage and interact with the world around us at large. Be mindful, though, of those who may want to take advantage of your generosity. I always seek to give first, whether it's my time, insights, or ability to help others. If you start to notice that people are using you, however, simply disengage from the relationship. Transactional people are often hard to get along with. Don't take this as a reflection of your efforts. Continue to put people first, and you'll see it improve the quality of many of your relationships.

Never Manipulate and Use Others

It's pretty straightforward. Don't manipulate or use others. Most people do not have negative intentions when they step into relationships. Research shows that people usually give others the benefit of the doubt until proven otherwise. What I have found is that there are certain markers that will indicate when people are manipulative. These types of people are usually self-centered. They use the word *I* more than *we*. They like to be the center of attention and are often very charming or charismatic. We can all have the tendency at times to focus on ourselves and on our own interests and desires. People who are great at building relationships know how to prevent themselves from always getting what they want. They seek to bring value to the lives of others and do not operate with a win-lose mentality.

I've found that pride and arrogance are often tied to manipulation. When people are prideful, they tend to overlook others and put themselves first. Arrogance also prevents people from understanding how to add value to others. The sense of entitlement that comes with these areas limits our impact on others. That is why it is so important to be mindful of how you influence others. Are you seeking to help people or simply pursue your personal agenda? Are you looking to give in a relationship or to simply get something from another person? There is a natural give-and-take that takes place in relationships. Each person should want to be a positive influence on the other; however, when it comes to manipulation, this is often not the case.

In the corporate world, I've found that the most successful people do not focus solely on moving their agenda forward. Sure, they have personal goals and ambitions, and they have objectives that must be accomplished for their people and teams. However, they lead with a servant mentality. It's not about what they can get out of relationships but about how they can support others to maximize performance. In romantic relationships, manipulative people tend to take more than they give. They will use their influence to get the most out of others. As I've mentioned earlier in this chapter, this destroys relationships quickly. Once someone becomes manipulative, you cannot trust that they have your best interests at heart. If you see someone becoming manipulative, call them out on their behavior. Sometimes, people are unaware of what they are doing. Other times, they are behaving in a malicious fashion. When you are building relationships, make sure you do not become self-centered in your approach to dealing with others. Be intentional with your generosity. Give more than you seek to take. If you do these things, you will avoid going down the path of manipulation. Remember, relationships are about giving, not taking. The more we add value to others, the deeper the relationships will grow.

[1] A. H. Maslow, "A Theory of Human Motivation," *Psychological Review* 50, no. 4 (1943): 370–396.

[2] A. H. Maslow, *Religions, Values, and Peak Experiences* (New York: Penguin Publishing, 1970).

[3] E. H. Erikson, *Childhood and Society* (New York, New York: Norton Books, 1950).

[4] M. Deutsch, "Trust and Suspicion," *Journal of Conflict Resolution* 2 (1958): 265–279.

[5] J. B. Rotter, "A New Scale for the Measurement of Interpersonal Trust," *Journal of Personality* 35 (1967): 651–665.

[6] J. K. Rempel, J. G. Holmes, and M. P. Zanna, "Trust in Close Relationships," *Journal of Personality and Social Psychology* 49 (1985): 95–112.

[7] R. C. Mayer, J. H. Davis, and F. D. Schoorman, "An Integrative Model of Organizational Trust," *Academy of Management Review* 20 (1995): 709–734.

[8] P. Dasgupta, "Trust as a Commodity," in *Trust: Making and Breaking Cooperative Relations*, ed. D. Gambetta (Oxford, United Kingdom: Blackwell, 1988), 49–72.

[9] M. Dodgson, "Learning, Trust, and Technological Collaboration," *Human Relations* 46 (1993): 77–95.

CULTIVATING INFLUENCE

You don't have to be a "person of influence" to be influential.
In fact, the most influential people in my life are probably
not even aware of the things they've taught me.
—Scott Adams

When trust is developed, it opens the door to influence. Cultivating influence is about having a positive and meaningful impact on others. At their core, relationships are meant to enhance the quality of our lives. When we build relationships deeply enough, we can help others develop and grow. The most important relationships in my life have been with people who inspire and challenge me to be the best version of myself. They have had my best interests at heart; and as a result, I've trusted their guidance, counsel, and input. Influence plays out in personal and professional relationships. Dynamic, long-term, and sustainable partnerships with others change how we view the world and who we are as people.

In our personal relationships with loved ones and friends, influence starts to form over time. We first have to move through the stages of rapport building, understanding others, embracing individual differences, and developing trust. My relationships with some of my closest friends has been a great example of this process in action. They have encouraged, supported, and pushed me to look at myself differently. One of my best friends for over the last twenty years was one of the first people who taught me about the power of authenticity and accepting how events in my life helped shape my calling, purpose, and destiny. I had the same influence on him. I helped strengthen the spiritual part of his life and encouraged him to seek wisdom and knowledge outside of his past experiences. The funny thing, though, was that we never set out to change each other. Our relationship evolved so strongly over time that we both eventually came to value input and guidance from each other. Our ability to influence each other happened subtly over the course of our relationship.

In the professional world, influence is directly connected to leadership. The heart and soul of leadership is about the influence and impact we have on others. For leaders to effectively influence people, a number of factors must come into play. Vision setting and communicating expectations serve as foundational components of influence. Team effectiveness and collaboration play a critical role in how leaders impact others. Driving alignment and execution lead to the accomplishment of goals and objectives. Inspiration and innovation motivate and encourage people to think creatively. Despite these critical areas, I've found that relationship building and commitment to the development of others is the most important factor in the influence leaders have on their people. When leaders make personal investments in getting to know their people and helping them grow, it demonstrates their desire to see people reach their full potential. The best leaders with whom I have worked put people and relationships first. When they do this, it is easy for them to influence the actions and behaviors of others. This is not coercion or manipulation. It's about getting people to see how their efforts can make the business and organization better. It also makes employees' lives more meaningful and fulfilling. Influence takes place when people feel you have their best interests at heart.

Influence and leadership have been studied in the field of organizational psychology for decades. In the last ten to fifteen years, however, the specific field of leadership has attracted the interest of talented scholars and practitioners from around the world. The number of new leadership theories has grown substantially, and the field has advanced from theories that focus on understanding general leadership principles and processes to seeing leadership as a phenomenon that occurs through the relationships leaders have with their followers. Theories have been developed to understand both individual processes, such as perceptions, personalities, emotions, and cognitions, and group-level processes, such as the social and relational contexts through which leaders operate. There are over sixty different theoretical frameworks and a wide variety of methodological approaches that scholars have developed to study leadership.[1] Although we will not cover all of them in this book, there are several frameworks that are intimately linked to cultivating influence.

Neo-charismatic theories (e.g., transformational and charismatic leadership) deal with the process of change and the consequent transformation of followers. The process of change highlights charismatic and visionary factors, which are demonstrated in the characteristics and subsequent behavioral patterns of someone in a leadership role. The skill of cultivating influence is related to these types of leadership models because it is the daily actions of a leader that inspire followership from others. The information-processing theories of leadership focus on cognitive approaches to information processing and decision-making processes in leaders. Some of these areas include attribution theory, leader and follower cognitions (e.g., perceptions), and implicit leadership theories. The cognitive perceptions people form of their leaders determine how they will interact with them and whether they will follow their lead.

Social exchange theories focus on the relationships between leaders and their followers. Some of the most well-known work here focuses on the leader-member exchange (LMX) theory and the vertical dyad linkage. Much of my consulting work around cultivating influence stems from research in this space. Relationally intelligent leaders leverage their partnerships with others to accomplish goals and drive organizational performance. The dispositional and trait theories of leadership focus on the personality factors that impact leaders. Researchers in these areas investigate specific traits, abilities, or competencies that contribute to leadership effectiveness. Although research has found that there are certain traits and personality characteristics that enable leaders to influence others, all leaders can influence people by practicing certain habits. Behavioral leadership theory argues that the success of a leader is based on their behavior rather than their natural abilities. These theories involve observing and evaluating a leader's actions and behaviors when they are responding to a specific situation. Cultivating influence has a lot to do with the behaviors that leaders model for their people and how others look to emulate their actions.

The contingency theory of leadership argues that a leader's effectiveness is contingent on whether their leadership style suits a particular situation. According to this framework, a person can be an effective leader in one circumstance but ineffective in another. Relationally intelligent leaders who are skilled at cultivating influence understand how to flex their style to fit the needs of different situations and circumstances. Lastly, contextual leadership implies both a capability to discern trends in the face of complexity and uncertainty as well as adaptability while still trying to shape events. It allows leaders to adjust their style to the situation and to their followers' needs. Cultivating influence is also linked to the context through which people operate. You have to know the situation into which you're stepping in to, and the cast of characters with whom you're dealing with, if you are going to impact the lives of others.

WHY MACHIAVELLI WAS WRONG: MEANS TO AN END DOESN'T WORK IN THE END

As I started to explore the idea of relational intelligence for my doctoral dissertation in graduate school, I became fascinated with leadership and influence. I started to think about the various aspects of influence as I continued to conduct my research. I knew that people who built strong relationships could get things done through others. They could galvanize and inspire others to become the best versions of themselves. I also realized that there was a dark side to influence. Just as people could use influence to impact others, some could use it to serve their own ends. They could manipulate others to get to personal desired outcomes. They could operate with hidden agendas and ulterior motives. This led me to start exploring Machiavellianism.

In 1513, Niccolò Machiavelli completed a compelling narrative entitled *The Prince*, which offered advice on how to acquire and maintain power over others during times of change and uncertainty.

In his book, Machiavelli outlined a pragmatic and rational approach to keeping power that was based on expediency and devoid of the traditional virtues of trust, honor, and decency.[2] A primary theme throughout his book is the degree to which people can be manipulated. Specifically, he identifies tactics differentiating those who wield influence from those who are influenced. Behavioral researchers have been interested in Machiavellianism for the past fifty years. Beginning in the early 1970s, researchers began to examine whether the principles associated with two of Machiavelli's greatest works, *The Prince* and the *Discourses on Livy*, were practiced by individuals in today's society. They defined the Machiavellian personality type as someone who sought to manipulate others to achieve their own ends.

One of the most famous theoretical frameworks for studying the concept contains four components describing the characteristics associated with effective manipulation and control of others.[3] First, people with high Machiavellian tendencies (high Machs, as they are sometimes called) have a relative lack of affect and empathy in interpersonal relationships. They view people entirely as objects or means to personal ends. Second, high Machs show a lack of concern with conventional morality. People who manipulate others have a utilitarian rather than a moral view of their interactions with people. Third, high Machs lack psychopathological tendencies. People who manipulate others are not sociopaths or acting with malicious intent to hurt others. Lastly, high Machs have a low ideological commitment to others. Manipulators are focused on accomplishing their objectives in the present and give little regard to the long-term ramifications of their behaviors and actions. The basic premise of Machiavellianism is that high Machs are guided by expediency, as opposed to principle and genuine relationship building, in order to achieve certain end goals.

As I continued to study the concept, I partnered with several colleagues in my graduate program to conduct research on Machiavellianism in organizational settings. The basic premise for our research was that Machiavellianism was a multifaceted construct when it came to how leaders influenced their people. We defined organizational Machiavellianism as the belief in the use of manipulation, as necessary, to achieve one's desired ends in the context of the work environment. A key aspect of the organizational Machiavellian is that they will only use manipulation and deceitful strategies when it is advantageous to do so. These types of employees are not necessarily heartless, nasty, or vindictive; and they can be genuinely accommodating and respectful when it is in their best interest to be.

Our conceptual model had three components: maintaining power, management practices, and manipulativeness. We created an assessment tool to measure our model and were interested in finding out what other influence skills organizational Machiavellianism was related to. We explored its connections to social skills, emotional intelligence, extraversion/introversion, interpersonal influence, apparent sincerity, and other related constructs. Our results were compelling. We found that the manipulative dimension of organizational Machiavellianism was not related to EQ.[4] This was most likely because leaders with strong EQ could put themselves in other people's shoes. They did not operate with a win-loss mentality where people were means to an end. However, we did find a connection between manipulation and social skills. Specifically, high Machs were more likely to engage in negative behaviors at work, like emotional manipulation, lying and deceitfulness, and counterproductive work behaviors (e.g., abuse toward others, sabotage, theft, or withdrawal). Despite our findings, I still had questions about the difference between genuine influence and self-serving manipulation. How could a person tell the difference between the two? One could argue that the tactics were the same: you took the time to get to know people and then influenced them to do what you wanted them to do. I stored this information in the back of my mind and started looking for real-life situations and examples where people had the opportunity to influence others.

It wasn't until early in my consulting career that I started to see dramatic differences in the ways influential leaders reached others compared to how manipulative ones did. I started to see that leaders fell into one of two categories. The first type of leader puts the needs and interests of others before their own. They operate with a servant leadership mentality. They use their EQ and relational intelligence to support the actions and activities of their people. Research in the academic community supports this claim. High EQ is generally described as beneficial to those who lead people. Research has found that it is one's ability to effectively manage the emotions of others that lead to positive outcomes for managers and their direct reports.[5] This perspective places skills like understanding others, developing trust, and cultivating influence under the umbrella of positive psychology. People with strong relational skills have also been found to have higher levels of joy and happiness, life satisfaction, psychological health, and social network quality and size.

Many years ago, I worked with a marketing leader in the pharmaceutical industry who made a habit of putting others before herself. Alicia had great relational intelligence. She made people feel comfortable and took time to get to know those with whom she worked. When she first met new colleagues, she was curious and asked questions to learn about their backgrounds and experiences. She possessed strong EQ and displayed empathy on a regular basis. She developed trust by being honest, genuine, and authentic in all she did. Over time, this helped her cultivate influence and have a positive impact on the lives of others. I saw people put in tireless hours of work and effort because she did the same for them. Her direct reports trusted that she had their best interests at heart. They followed her lead and were able to accomplish the goals and objectives she set for her team.

The second type of leaders with whom I started to interact with were more concerned with their personal goals and priorities. They got along well with others, but things always had to be linked back to their agenda. They appeared to be skilled at building relationships but viewed people as means to an end rather than partners with whom they could learn and grow. I started to look at their behaviors to see how they got people to do things. Did they have strong EQ and know how to use it? Did they appear to be interested in the wants and needs of others? What did they do to influence people? My initial thoughts were that they could use their social skills to influence people while driving their own personal agendas. An obvious example would be a leader making use of high-level EQ capabilities to read and manage the emotions of others in order to manipulate others' behavior to suit their own interests. Yet in many instances, I found this wasn't the case. Most self-seeking leaders did not possess good EQ skills. They were more results-oriented than people-oriented. Some of these leaders led their teams with an iron fist. They used fear and intimidation to influence others.

The biggest thing I noticed with self-serving leaders was that they were great at getting people to accomplish short-term goals. Their manipulation tactics got people to perform for a few months, but breakdowns in trust and commitment would slowly occur. I found that research by organizational psychologists supported what I witnessed in these types of leaders. High Machs have been found to be emotionally detached in interactions with others. Their interpersonal orientation is often described as cognitive as opposed to emotional with little tendency to focus on the needs of others. In addition, correlations between Machiavellianism and empathy have been found to be negative.[6] Because high Machs have difficulty reading the emotions of others, their manipulation tactics do not work in the long term.

I remember working with a leader in the media and entertainment industry who used manipulation on a regular basis to get his desired outcomes. Greg was charming and charismatic when you first met him. He brought great passion and energy to his work. This initially excited others. You couldn't be around him and not pick up on his fire and intensity. We started working together when he was promoted into a senior vice president role overseeing content development. He had a new team of eight leaders with whom he had to build relationships to get folks aligned on his vision for the team. I quickly noticed that he did small things to get to know his people. He learned about what was important to each of his direct reports. He communicated his goals and priorities for the team. However, there were never discussions to get buy-in and support for his initiatives. He talked at his people rather than with them. I also started to see him use what he knew about others to manipulate them in pursuit of his personal agenda.

The first several months of his tenure in the role were highly productive. He got the team to move forward with his goals and objectives. He ingratiated himself to leaders higher up in the organization so they had a positive impression of his work. Over time, however, I started to see cracks in his system. He never gave credit to his people for their work. He always had to be the center of attention. He broke commitments and promises, which damaged the trust his team had in his leadership. People started to see that he used others. He wasn't concerned with the growth and development of his direct reports. He never had one-on-one meetings where he focused on their desires or interests. It was always about the business and pursuing his objectives. The lack of empathy for his people was concerning.

I tried to get him to see that his behaviors and actions were having a negative impact on his team, but my counsel and advice did not get him to change. He even started to tell me certain things in our coaching sessions, though I heard the opposite from his people. His employees didn't like working for him. They didn't trust him, and it slowly began to have a negative effect on his leadership. People started to see through his influence tactics. They compiled and conformed to what he said but did not respect him as a leader. The team's performance declined quickly, and some of Greg's direct reports started reporting things that were happening to HR. After several incidents, an investigation was launched, and Greg was let go a few months later because of the way he treated people. It was a valuable lesson to me about manipulation.

Machiavellian leaders may get things done in the short term, but their leadership style has detrimental effects in the long term. Although they appear to cultivate influence, they don't do it through relationship building. People follow their lead out of compliance rather than buy-in and commitment. Machiavellians may get to their desired outcomes, but they damage relationships in the process. You cannot have strong relational intelligence and operate with a self-serving mentality. Viewing people as means to an end never works in the long term. If you want to cultivate influence on others, it must come from a good place.

THE PROBLEM WITH NARCISSISTS

Early in my career, I was also exposed to different types of leaders when I worked on a large-scale talent development program. I got to work with people who built strong relationships with others. I was exposed to those who knew how to set a vision and get others to buy into their core mission. I interacted with passionate and fiery leaders who motivated and galvanized others to perform. I coached innovative leaders who knew how to unleash the creative talents and capabilities of their people and teams. I also got an up-close view into negative behaviors exhibited by certain leaders. I saw those who lied and manipulated people. I worked with those who used fear and intimidation to coerce others to get their goals accomplished. I saw those who lied and cheated to get ahead.

Some of the most alarming types of leaders whom I worked with were those who had a superiority complex. They were typically Machiavellian and knew how to effectively manipulate people. They were also entitled, self-absorbed, and hostile toward their people. They used power and authority to get people to comply with their demands. They were arrogant, egocentric, and vain. They always had to take credit for successes and loved to be the center of attention. These narcissistic leaders were often the most difficult with whom to work. They always had to be right and were hard to advise and coach. I remember working with a senior executive in the financial services industry who was being groomed for a CFO role. Stephen was a harsh and demanding leader. He had worked his way up through the finance organization by driving results and holding people accountable to stringent rules of engagement. I was asked to come in and work with him after reports were made that he had been leading with an iron fist.

When I first met with Stephen, I found him to be highly arrogant and conceited. For over two hours, he bragged about his personal accomplishments and what he had done to get to the current point in his career. There was never a mention of his team's contributions to his success. Every sentence out of his mouth started with an *I* rather than a *we*. I needed to figure out quickly how to get him to see that his leadership style was not going work in the long run. To do this, I started to discuss his desires and interests for the future. He wanted to be the company's next CFO. This goal consumed his behaviors and actions. He viewed his peers in the organization as competitive threats to his ascendance. We conducted a 360-degree assessment to get a better understanding of how he had been influencing others. The findings were scary. His direct reports feared him, and his peers hated working with him. However, he was skilled at ingratiating himself to his manager and senior leadership. He knew how to manipulate those above him and never gave them the opportunity to see the dark side of his leadership.

When I met with Stephen to give him the feedback, he was quick to get angry and defensive. He felt betrayed by his people and attacked by his peers and cross-functional colleagues. I knew it was going to be very difficult to get him to drive the behavioral changes needed to succeed. When we finally got through the feedback and began outlining his personal development plan, I witnessed his grandiosity, lack of empathy, and hypersensitivity. The sad part was his fragile self-esteem. At his core, he often felt inferior to others, which motivated him to act in harsh and demanding ways. We set some goals around building his relationships with his peers and repairing his brand, but it was difficult for him to implement the behavioral change needed to succeed. He continued to damage relationships as he pursued his agenda and quest for the CFO role. As his manager started to get more involved in the coaching process, it became evident that he was alarmed by the behaviors Stephen was demonstrating on a regular basis. After several months of trying to work with him, I realized he was not going to be able to change the way that he led others. His lying, deceiving, and manipulation had destroyed too many relationships across the enterprise. The narcissistic tendencies he had developed over time were hard to break. Our coaching engagement did not end well. Stephen was demoted several months later and ended up leaving the company. He felt people had betrayed him and never truly saw how his actions and behaviors had caused so much damage.

Dictators such as Adolf Hitler and Joseph Stalin and serial killers such as Ted Bundy, Richard Ramirez, and Jeffrey Dahmer are notorious examples of the malevolent potential of humans. The extreme cruelty of these individuals is exceptional. Still, in daily life, a substantial proportion of people violate social norms and moral values by engaging in transgressive behaviors, such as lying, deceiving, cheating, stealing, and bullying.[7] Over the last twenty years, a steadily increasing number of psychological studies have explored three specific personality traits associated with transgressive and norm-violating behaviors: narcissism, Machiavellianism, and psychopathy. Because these features are thought to play a key role in many norm-violating acts, several behavioral scientists have coined the term dark triad of personality.[8]

Narcissism originated from the Greek mythological figure Narcissus, a young male hunter who was so consumed by his own beauty and greatness that he arrogantly despised the attention and love of others. This myth covers the core features of narcissism as the concept is used today—namely, a blend of vanity and egocentric admiration of one's own qualities, which negatively impacts relationships with other people.[9] Some of the transgressive traits associated with narcissism include authority, self-sufficiency, superiority, exhibitionism, exploitativeness, vanity, and entitlement. Research has found that these behaviors are typically more prevalent among men than women. At a young age, boys more often exhibit conduct problems, delinquency, and violence than girls; and this gender difference continues into adulthood.[10]

Narcissism and its associated traits (e.g., grandiosity, arrogance, self-absorption, entitlement, fragile self-esteem, and hostility) are attributes of many powerful leaders and influencers. Narcissistic leaders have grandiose belief systems and leadership styles and are generally motivated by their needs for power and admiration rather than empathic concern for the people and organizations they lead. Interestingly, narcissists also possess the charisma and grand vision vital to effective leadership. In its healthy form, mature narcissism produces behaviors such as humor and creativity. However, pathological narcissism occurs when one is unable to integrate their own

131

idealized beliefs with the realities of their inadequacies. Pathological narcissists spend the balance of their lives seeking recognition from idealized parental substitutes as an emotional salve against their own shortcomings.

To date, literature on leadership and narcissism has been largely devoted to answering one overarching question: Is it good or bad for a leader to be a narcissist? As may be expected from a term laden with negative connotations, there is a significant focus in the research literature on the downside of narcissistic leaders. For example, because of their need for recognition, narcissists are more likely than others to self-promote and self-nominate and to employ their skills in deception, manipulation, and intimidation to secure leadership positions.[11] Although the quest for personal glory can sometimes motivate a narcissistic leader in the direction of positive, bold, and transformative innovation, even at their best, narcissistic leaders are bound to leave damaged systems and relationships in their wake. Narcissists are notoriously poor, overinvolved, and abusive managers.[12] Narcissistic leaders resist advisors' suggestions, take more credit for successes than they are due, and blame others for their own failures and shortcomings. They are also highly prone to lapses in professional judgment and personal conduct. However, because of their drive and grandiosity, narcissistic leaders make poor judgments and decisions with greater certainty and confidence and, thus, with greater influence than other types of leaders do.

To fully understand the negative consequences of narcissism in leaders, it is useful to consider the psychological components that underlie narcissists' behavior. Researchers have found a list of highly interrelated psychological underpinnings of narcissistic leaders. Some of these include arrogance, feelings of inferiority, an insatiable need for recognition and superiority, hypersensitivity and anger, lack of empathy, amorality, irrationality and inflexibility, and paranoia. Whether narcissists succeed or fail as leaders depends not only on their personalities but also on the circumstances in which they lead.[13] I have found that narcissists typically succeed for a short period when charisma and extraversion are important (e.g., sales roles) rather than in positions that require sustained relationships and trust. This is why most narcissistic leaders have trouble succeeding in the long term. They do so much damage to relationships that they leave a trail of destruction in their wake. You cannot have relational intelligence and succeed as a narcissistic leader.

I've also found that narcissistic leaders do better in situations in which their personal goals converge with those of their followers than in situations in which their success is likely to come at the expense of those around them. Narcissists are apt to emerge and often flourish in times when there is a call for a new order to be established, but they are unable to maintain the necessary stability once that new order has been established. Because relationally intelligent leaders cultivate influence over time, they must engage in behaviors that grow relationships. Narcissists cannot do this. Their self-absorption, lack of empathy, and inflexibility push people away. Narcissists may succeed in getting people to do things in the short-term, but they fail miserably when it comes to developing the relationships needed to successfully influence large numbers of people over time.

NOT EVERYONE NEEDS CHARISMA TO INFLUENCE OTHERS

My firm does a lot of work with nonprofit organizations, most of which are churches and faith-based organizations. When I think about influential leaders in the church world, charismatic people like T. D. Jakes, Pastor Steven Furtick, and Pastor Mike Todd come to mind. These types of leaders can captivate an audience. They inspire and galvanize people. They get people to see different things about themselves and motivate them to drive behavior change in their own lives. However, I've found that some of the most influential people in my life haven't had to be charismatic.

When I was in graduate school, I met Lisa, who had moved to my community about a year after I came down to Tampa, Florida. Lisa was part of the lights program, a group of Christians who were passionate about sharing their faith with others. Lisa had relocated from northern Florida with three other women to introduce people to Christ. At the time, I didn't really pay attention to my faith. I had grown up in a Christian home, where faith was one of the most important parts of my mother's life. We attended an Episcopal church every Sunday, and I served as an altar boy and sang in the choir some weekends. But although church was in our lives, I didn't have a personal relationship with Christ. In college, I strayed from my faith— not for any negative reasons but just because I had other priorities that took up my time. In graduate school, however, I started to feel as if something was missing in my life. I was in a doctoral program and preparing to become a business psychologist. I was excited about the prospects of starting my career. Despite all this, there was a void I couldn't explain.

The first time I met Lisa was at the physical fitness center at our apartment complex. She was social and outgoing, but there was something else that drew me into a conversation with her. We had a good talk about the superficial things most people discussed when they first met someone. We talked about sports, where she was from, and the type of work she did. I shared that I was working on my graduate degree in business psychology and that I loved golf. At the end of our conversation, she invited me to her apartment to meet her friends and have dinner. I was curious to learn more about her and accepted the invite.

When I got to Lisa's apartment later that evening, I found her roommates friendly and engaging to be around. We talked and laughed over dinner. It was a nice evening. At the end of the night, they asked if I wanted to come back Sunday morning for their Bible study. I had never heard of a Bible study group. It sounded interesting, and I said sure. On Sunday, I headed over to their place and met a couple of other people they had invited. We didn't know what to expect. Lisa greeted us with a smile on her face and opened the door. Some worship music was playing, which I found calming and peaceful. They started the group with a prayer, then one of Lisa's roommates read a passage from Scripture. They discussed the passage with us and asked if anyone had prayer requests. I didn't know what that meant, so I asked her to explain further. She talked about the power of prayer and what they believed as Christians.

Over the next several months, I started spending more time with Lisa and her friends. I felt a joy and love for life when I was around them. They rarely complained about things like so many of my other friends in graduate school did regularly. Yet Lisa never forced anything about her faith on me. She wasn't a charismatic person. She didn't have a larger-than-life personality. She didn't try to influence me to do anything with which I wasn't comfortable. She just shared what Jesus had done in her life. As my curiosity started to peak, I began to ask more questions. She encouraged me to read the Bible for the first time. She taught me how to pray. She explained that my relationship with Christ was just like a close friendship with family or friends in my life. This was new to me. I had always thought of God as someone up in the clouds who would strike down people like King Triton from *The Little Mermaid* if they sinned. A few months later, I accepted Christ as my savior. My faith has now become the cornerstone of my life. It guides everything I do. Lisa had a great influence on my life. Her influence helped set me on a course to find my true calling and destiny. You don't need to have a charismatic personality to cultivate influence on others. It happens through relationships. When people build dynamic and sustainable relationships, influence becomes easy. It flows naturally out of your desire to see others prosper and grow.

Most scholars define leadership in terms of emergence—the person in a group who exerts the most influence—or in terms of the perceptions others have of a person in a position of authority. A large body of research on leadership focuses on the competencies, skills, and behaviors that leaders exhibit on a consistent basis. The competency movement began with the work of David McClelland. His approach to leadership was designed to identify competencies that were specific to a particular job in a particular organization with no intention of generalizing.[14] The modern enthusiasm for competencies started after the publication of a book by McClelland's colleague Richard Boyatzis in 1982.[15] The competency movement spread rapidly after Boyatzis's book. But despite the plethora of research that has been conducted, most of the leadership competency frameworks can be captured in a model that was proposed Robert Hogan and his colleagues.[16]

Hogan's model identifies four broad classes of leadership competencies: (a) intrapersonal skills (e.g., emotional stability, courage, integrity, and patience); (b) interpersonal skills (e.g., listening, approachability, political savvy, and relationship building); (c) business skills (e.g., priority setting, intellectual horsepower, business acumen, and organizational skills); and (d) leadership skills (e.g., vision setting, care about others' development, effective team building, and support of others). The model is developmental in that people move from one stage to the next as they develop and grow. Intrapersonal skills develop first, probably during adolescence and one's high school years. Interpersonal skills develop next, most likely during one's college years. Business skills follow when a person enters the workforce. Lastly, leadership skills develop as people move up through organizations. People who learn how to influence others do so by leveraging skills they have developed from the interpersonal and leadership domains.

The reputational elements of leadership play a critical role as people begin to influence others. Specifically, literature on implicit leadership theories suggests the characteristics people look for in their leaders. Credibility as a leader depends vitally on perceived integrity—keeping one's word, fulfilling one's promises, not playing favorites, and not taking advantage of situations. The most important question people ask their leaders is this: Can I trust you not to abuse the privilege of authority? Research shows highly reliable correlations between trust in one's manager and a range of positive leadership outcomes, including job performance, job satisfaction, and organizational commitment.[17] Although research supports the notion that charismatic or transformational leaders can galvanize and motivate others, these traits are not a prerequisite to effectively influencing people.

Influential leaders make good decisions in a timely way. In times of crisis and uncertainty, the most effective leaders make prompt decisions that take into account the well-being and psychological safety of others. I saw this in many of the CEOs with whom I worked with during the COVID-19 pandemic. The strongest leaders made smart, practical decisions that had a direct impact on their teams in a positive manner. They quickly shifted from in-person to virtual, work-from-home models. Employees were given the opportunity to voice their fears and concerns. I witnessed several of my clients take actions that benefited their entire organizations. People who cultivate influence are also competent in contributing to their companies. Expertise is needed for legitimacy and respect from the team, not necessarily charisma and charm. If people believe in the competence of their managers, they will follow their lead.

Finally, good leaders are able to project a vision. They explain to their people the purpose, meaning, and significance of key undertakings. Vision facilitates team performance by clarifying roles, goals, and the path forward. I've found that visionary leaders do not always have to be the step-up-in-front-of-a-crowd inspirational type. The best leaders build vision with their teams by looking for input, buy-in, and alignment with others. They invest in relationship building so everyone has a say in the direction a team or organization is moving. Charisma can be an asset to a leader, but it is not more important than how leaders make others feel. The best leaders serve their people. They put the needs of others before themselves. They make commitments to people and stick to them. They develop trust by following up their words with actions. Because cultivating influence happens over time, the best leaders do it through the long-term relationships they develop with others. You cannot influence people from afar. True influence has to come from the interpersonal dynamics between leaders and their followers.

How the Best Leaders Influence Others

As I reflect on my career to date, I can see that there have been a number of leaders who have had a positive influence on my life. Each individual leader I've coached has taught me a valuable lesson about influence. One of the most impactful leaders with whom I worked was Trevor, a CEO of a midsize pharmaceutical company in North America. Trevor and I started our relationship when he was the vice president of sales for a medical device's organization. He was the son of first-generation immigrants from Europe. He grew up in a poor environment. His parents had to work extremely hard to earn a living. His father owned a small tailoring business in New York City. The business struggled for many years; but Trevor learned about discipline, dedication to one's craft, and perseverance. Trevor was fascinated with people. He would go to work with his father on a regular basis and study their customers. He was a curious child and always asked questions to learn about people's backgrounds and experiences.

During his educational years, Trevor gravitated toward business. He was a hard worker and paid his way through college. He worked three jobs while balancing his academic responsibilities. Trevor started his career as a sales rep for a small biotech pharmaceutical company. It was during this time that he cultivated and sharpened his people skills. He found ways to connect with people from all walks of life. This affinity wasn't an act. He genuinely valued and cared for others. Trevor's focus on building relationships with customers helped establish his early success. Year after year, he was in the top 10 percent of the company's sales performance.

People trusted Trevor. This afforded him more opportunities to influence. He quickly became a regional manager and started overseeing others' activities. As a leader, he always put people first. He knew that business results meant nothing if he didn't have employees who felt valued and appreciated, so he took the time to invest in the development of his people. He was always looking for ways to help them learn. He took pride in getting his direct reports promoted and advancing their careers. This became part of his reputation. He was known for accelerating the growth of his employees and helping them exceed performance expectations.

Our work began when Trevor was brought into the medical devices company as a vice president. As part of his onboarding and integration into the organization, I served as his executive coach. We quickly formed a strong bond and partnership. He viewed me as a trusted advisor because I was always honest and direct with him. I was authentic in our work together and never pulled any punches. Trevor valued our candid conversations and was always eager to improve. As our partnership has now spanned over fifteen years, I've seen Trevor grow in many ways. He has also helped make me a better consultant and leader in my firm.

I have learned four valuable lessons while working with Trevor. First, servant leadership is the best way to influence your people. When people know you are in their corner and will go to bat for them, they want to do their best for you. Trevor put his people first. This garnered loyalty and commitment from his teams. People knew his top priority was their success and well-being. Second, relational intelligence is more important than one's technical talents and capabilities. Trevor was a smart individual. He was strategic, had good business acumen, and had a deep understanding of the business. However, it was his ability to build relationships with people from all walks of life that drove his success. He was warm and genuine when meeting new people. He was compassionate and found ways to empathize with others. I saw this firsthand with many of his people and their customers.

Third, Trevor made learning his lifelong pursuit. He was always looking for new ways to grow. He was humble and admitted when he didn't know certain things. He leveraged the guidance and insights of others. Throughout his career, he consistently looked for ways to sharpen his game. Whether it was learning a new product or technology or figuring out how to connect in different ways with his customers, he looked for ways to innovate and improve. He encouraged and rewarded his people for doing the same. Over the course of our relationship, I have seen many of his people come up with new ideas and grow their business. This has happened because of Trevor's willingness to encourage diversity of thought in his people. Your reputation as a leader and your ability to influence are built over time. When you put people first, focus more on relationships rather than results, and strive to learn and grow, you leave a lasting impression on others.

Lastly and most importantly, Trevor was an authentic leader. We've discussed the importance of this in the chapter on embracing individual differences, but it is important to reiterate its impact on cultivating influence here. Trevor was candid, honest, and transparent with others at all times. I saw this with his people, with his peers, and with external stakeholders. His authenticity built trust with others. People were more transparent with him because he modeled the right behaviors. I've come to find that the best leaders cultivate influence on others through their authenticity. Researchers describe authenticity as owning one's personal experiences, including one's thoughts, emotions, needs, desires, and beliefs.[18] Authenticity involves being self-aware and acting in accordance with one's true self by expressing what one genuinely thinks and believes.

Researchers have concluded that authenticity is comprised of a number of mental and behavioral processes. These processes explain how people discover and construct a core sense of self and how this core self is maintained across situations and over time. Four central themes have emerged around the study of authenticity. These include self-awareness (i.e., knowledge and trust in one's thoughts, feelings, motives, and values); unbiased processing (i.e., objectivity about and acceptance of one's positive and negative attributes); behavior (i.e., taking action based on one's true preferences, values, and needs rather than merely acting to please others, secure rewards, or avoid punishments); and relational orientation (i.e., achieving and valuing truthfulness and openness in one's close relationships).[19]

A variety of definitions of leader authenticity have been advanced over the years. The earliest philosophical conceptions of authenticity arose in the 1960s and reflected the assumption that an organization's authenticity was manifested through its leadership.[20] The first attempt to formally define and operationalize the concept of leader authenticity was made in 1983.[21] These scholars viewed leadership authenticity as encompassing three components: acceptance of personal and organizational responsibility for actions, outcomes, and mistakes; the nonmanipulation of people; and cultivating an understanding of self over job duties and responsibilities. Fourteen years later, authenticity research reemerged within the field of education. Some scholars defined authentic leadership as being composed of authenticity, intentionality, spirituality, and sensibility.[22] In 2001, Paul Begley introduced an alternative perspective that was both broad in scope and narrow in context, as it equated authenticity with effective and ethical leadership. He argued that authentic leadership implied a genuine kind of leadership—a hopeful, open-ended, visionary, and creative response to situations and circumstances.[23] He also recognized the importance of self-knowledge, a quality that was central to most conceptualizations of authenticity.

Popular conceptions of authenticity have included pursuing purpose with passion, practicing solid values, leading with heart, establishing enduring relationships, and demonstrating self-discipline. I've found that most of the influential leaders with whom I work possess some, if not all, of these skills. They also believe in the greatness of others. They bring to relationships a desire for self-exploration and self-discovery and a tendency to develop and grow. The best leaders are authentic. They cultivate influence by being true to themselves and to all those around them. Relationally intelligent leaders are authentic. Authenticity enables them to build strong, sustainable partnerships with others that stand the test of time. Because they want to see the best in others, they cultivate influence that helps guide and direct people to reach their full potential.

PUTTING IT INTO PRACTICE

Cultivating influence is the fifth and final skill of relational intelligence. People influence others after relationships have had time to develop and grow. When you are able to establish rapport, understand others, embrace individual differences, and develop trust, you set the stage for having a positive influence on the lives of others. Influence is a responsibility. It has to come from a genuine and authentic place. You cannot use or manipulate people to get to desired outcomes. If you do these things, you will lose credibility and trust quickly. You also have to think about more than yourself. Self-centered, egotistical people don't have a positive impact on others. They are driven by personal motivations and do not have the capacity to care deeply for people. Cultivating influence does not have to be grand and dramatic. Some of the most influential people in our lives tend to be those with quiet strength. They may inspire us more by the type of people they are rather than any showy way they engage with others. If you want to influence those around you, find ways to be true to yourself. Put other people first. Commit to a lifelong journey of growth and development. In addition, focus on these three areas and you'll start to have a positive influence on those around you.

Look for Mentors and Role Models

If we want to grow in any area of our lives, we have to find people who give us the insights and wisdom needed to succeed. When it comes to cultivating influence, surround yourself with people who have a positive impact on others. Look for people in key leadership roles—those who steward activities and responsibilities for their teams or those who garner buy-in and support from their people. You can spot a great leader quickly. They are usually delegating and empowering others to become the best versions of themselves. I regularly advise my clients that mentoring is a great way to grow the capabilities of their employees. Mentors help accelerate the journey to personal and professional development.

When I work with companies to help develop mentoring programs, there are several factors that need to be put into place. First, mentees need to realize that their mentors' time is valuable. A mentor takes time to support a mentee's growth, and that time should be respected. Mentors can help with this by setting clear time management expectations at the beginning of the relationship. Putting in place a consistent rhythm helps structure the time spent together. Second, the mentor and mentee need to be clear about what they want to get out of the relationship. Does the mentee want to increase their knowledge in a particular area? Do they want to learn how to better navigate the culture of the company? Do they want to sharpen their influence skills with leaders at higher levels in the organization? Does the mentor believe they can add value about how to have broader influence and impact on others? Can they translate what they do into simple steps that the mentee can follow? Before seeking a mentor, the mentee should get clear on their goals. If you want to be around people who exert great influence, make that known to your mentor. Tell them that you want to grow as a leader and that you have a desire to make an impact on the people around you. At the same time, mentors need to manage expectations by being clear about what they can offer. When a mentee is vague about their goals, a good mentor will challenge them to be specific about their desired outcomes.

Third, mentorship should be energizing for both parties. The mentor should get excited about sharing what they know, and the mentee should be committed to learning and growth. This is where chemistry between the two comes into play. Do they have similar personality styles? How do they relate to each other? What do they have in common? If there are some similarities between the two, the mentee is more likely to tap into what the mentor knows. Lastly, the two have to acknowledge the work that goes into the partnership. For the mentees, this means having a curious and inquisitive mindset. Mentees should ask questions and thank their mentors for the guidance and stewardship. Mentors should go the extra mile to help bring out the best in their mentees.

If you want to find a great mentor, be proactive and take initiative. Figure out how you want to grow, and find the right people to help you do so. I started doing this when I was in college. I knew there was so much I had to learn about my field, so I went out and found people who would help me develop the skills I needed to succeed. I found professors who were experts in studying leadership. I found older students who were thriving in our program and befriended them to learn the things they knew. I looked for internships where I would learn from people with different backgrounds and experiences. By finding mentors in different areas of my life, I started to get an exposure to different ways of thinking and interacting with the world around me. I encourage you to do the same. It doesn't matter how old you are or how advanced you are in your career. There are always things we can learn from others.

Work on Your Sphere of Influence

When I work with clients on developing their leadership skills, some of the questions I get asked are the following: How can I become a better leader? What can I do to improve how I make an impact on my people and my teams? How can I strengthen my relationships with my peers and senior leadership? The answer to almost all these questions starts with working with the people who are closest to you. If you want to be a better leader, work on strengthening relationships with your direct reports. Be intentional about getting to know them and the things that are most important to their success. Once you have this information, do what you can to provide support. Inspire, motivate, and encourage what they do. Be a resource to them. That's how you influence people. Give more of your time and they will follow your lead. The same applies to working with your peers. Spend more time with those you partner with most. Make work about collaboration and teamwork. Use your influence to support them and to broaden initiatives for the organization.

If you want to influence your boss or those above you, never bring problems without potential solutions to them. Trust is of paramount importance when influencing your boss or manager. They have to have confidence that you can get the job done and that you can do it successfully. When you have their trust, they will be open to more of your suggestions, input, and counsel. This works at the top of an organization all the way down to the frontline leaders. Cultivating influence comes from delivering exceptional work and making your manager look good. If you can take problems or challenges off their plate, this will make you even more impactful.

In your personal life, your sphere of influence can be as small as your core family. Do you have a positive impact on your parents? Are you available and a support system to your siblings? Do you go out of your way to make life easier for your spouse? Do you make time for your children? Whether we want to or not, we have the most influence on the people in our families. This can be good or bad depending on the circumstances. I will share about my family and how to use relational intelligence to strengthen your own in the next part of the book. For now, make sure you're intentional in the relationships that matter most in your life. You should be a positive ray of light to your loved ones. You'll be surprised how one word of encouragement at the right time can springboard someone into their destiny. I've had it happen in my life. I've tried to do it for others. Seek to do the same for those you care about most. Such intentionality will not only improve the quality of their lives, but it will also strengthen the connections you have with them.

Serve Others

I believe that influence is about serving others. If you want to lead people, put them first. The best leaders are often the most selfless ones. Yes, good leaders have goals and priorities they need to pursue. Their companies need to make money and grow. But influence cannot just be all about one's own goals. If you want to influence people, they have to know you have their best interests at heart. One of the best ways to do this is by considering the words you use. In my coaching work, I've seen leaders who use words to inspire and build people up, and I've seen leaders who are destructive in how they engage and interact with others. This is especially the case with written communication and email. One of the most damaging things failed leaders do is communicate down to their employees. I've seen leaders disrespect and put people down over email. I've seen them instill fear and apprehension in their people. They will argue that tough leadership is needed to drive results, but this is far from the truth. Our words are a witness to who we are as people. Influential leaders are careful to not speak rashly, impulsively, and out of anger. They take time to reflect on how they interact with their people and teams in good times and bad.

I encourage all my clients to speak with measured words. Words of encouragement and support can have a tremendously positive effect on the people around them. When employees feel valued and appreciated, it inspires commitment and loyalty to the organization. It promotes creative thinking and innovation. Support helps people maximize their potential and achieve desired outcomes. I've worked with many CEOs who understand the power of words.

Michael, a CEO in the telecommunications industry, was an expert at communication. I started working with his leadership team when they were looking to hire a new CIO. I found out right away how he used words to build people up. In our first meeting, he was quick to compliment me and the work of our firm. He was referred to us by a colleague that I had worked with many years ago. Michael didn't have to make the effort to establish that connection. I was trying to get him as a client! With time, though, I continued to see that such care was a staple aspect of his leadership. I saw it with his direct reports. I saw it with the candidates he had us assess. I saw it with the broader organization. He inspired people through his words and actions. He moved people emotionally when he was in front of an audience. He was always honest, transparent, and clear in his interactions with others.

Words are essential if you want to cultivate influence on others. Trust is earned by how you communicate with people. What you say and how you say it matters. In our professional lives, words can bring people together and get them aligned on the right priorities. Words can encourage and build people's self-confidence. You can unlock others' true potential by the things you say on a consistent basis. In our personal lives, our words strengthen the bonds we have with family and friends. The things we say to those closest to us can mean the world to them. At the same time, one wrong word used at an inappropriate time can be crushing to a loved one and damage a relationship for years. Choose what you say wisely. Our words have a tremendous influence on the people around us.

1   J. E. Dinh, R. G. Lord, W. L. Gardner, J. D. Meuser, R. C. Liden, and J. Hu, "Leadership Theory and Research in the New Millennium: Current Theoretical Trends and Changing Perspectives," *The Leadership Quarterly* 25 (2014): 36–62.

2   D. S. Wilson, D. Near, and R. R. Miller, "Machiavellianism: A Synthesis of the Evolutionary and Psychological Literatures," *Psychological Bulletin* 119 (1996): 285–299.

3   R. Christie and F. Geis, *Studies in Machiavellianism* (New York: Academic Press, 1970).

4   S. R. Kessler, A. C. Bandelli, P. E. Spector, and L. M. Penney, "Re-Examining Machiavelli: A Three-Dimensional Model of Machiavellianism in the Workplace," *Journal of Applied Social Psychology* 40, no. 8 (2010): 1,868–1,896.

5 P. Salovey, J. D. Mayer, and D. Caruso, "The Positive Psychology of Emotional Intelligence," in *Handbook of Positive Psychology*, eds. C. R. Snyder and S. J. Lopez (New York: Oxford University Press, 2002), 159–171.

6 C. Wastell and A. Booth, "Machiavellianism: An Alexithymic Perspective," *Journal of Social and Clinical Psychology* 22 (2003): 730–744.

7 D. Ariely, *The (Honest) Truth about Dishonesty* (New York, New York: HarperCollins, 2013).

8 D. L. Paulus and K. M. Williams, "The Dark Triad of Personality: Narcissism, Machiavellianism, and Psychopathy," *Journal of Research in Personality* 36 (2002): 556–563.

9 W. K. Campbell, J. D. Miller, and L. E. Buffardi, "The United States and the 'Culture of Narcissism': An Examination of Perceptions of National Character," *Social Psychological and Personality Science* 1 (2010): 222–229.

10 T. E. Motiff, A. Caspi, M. Rutter, and P. A. Silva, *Sex Differences in Antisocial Behavior: Conduct Disorder, Delinquency, and Violence in the Dunedin Longitudinal Study* (New York, New York: Cambridge University Press, 2001).

11 R. Hogan, R. Raskin, and D. Fazzini, "The Dark Side of Charisma," in *Measures of Leadership*, eds. K. E. Clark and M. B. Clark (West Orange, New Jersey: Leadership Library of America, 1990), 343–354.

12 R. Hogan, G. J. Curphy, and J. Hogan, "What We Know about Leadership: Effectiveness and Personality," *American Psychologist* 49 (1994): 493–504.

13 B. Glad and B. Whitmore, "Jimmy Carter and the Soviet Invasion of Afghanistan: A Psychological Perspective," in *Politics and Psychology: Contemporary Psychodynamic Perspectives*, ed. J. Offerman-Zuckerberg (New York, New York: Plenum Press, 1991), 117–142.

14 D. C. McClelland, "Testing for Competence rather than Intelligence," *American Psychologist* 28 (1973): 1–14.

15 R. E. Boyatzis, *The Competent Manager* (New York: Wiley Publishing, 1982).

16 R. Hogan and R. Warrenfeltz, "Educating the Modern Manager," *Academy of Management Learning and Education* 2 (2003): 74–84.

17 K. T. Dirks and D. L. Ferrin, "Trust in Leadership: Meta-Analytic Findings and Implications for Research and Practice," *Journal of Applied Psychology* 87 (2002): 611–628.

18 S. Harter, "Authenticity," in *Handbook of Positive Psychology*, eds. C. S. Snyder and S. J. Lopez (Oxford, United Kingdom: Elsevier Science, 2002), 382–394.

19 M. H. Kernis and B. M. Goldman, "From Thought and Experience to Behavior and Interpersonal Relationships: A Multicomponent Conceptualization of Authenticity," in *On Building, Defending, and Regulating the Self: A Psychological Perspective*, eds. A. Tesser, J. V. Wood, and D. A. Stapel (New York, New York: Psychology Press, 2005), 31–52.

20 M. M. Novicevic, M. G. Harvey, M. R. Buckley, J. A. Brown, and R. Evans, "Authentic Leadership: A Historical Perspective," *Journal of Leadership and Organizational Studies* 13 (2006): 64–76.

[21] J. E. Henderson and W. K. Hoy, "Leader Authenticity: The Development and Test of an Operational Measure," *Educational and Psychological Research* 3, no. 2 (1983): 63–75.

[22] N. Bhindi and P. Duignan, "Leadership for a New Century: Authenticity, Intentionality, Spirituality, and Sensibility," *Educational Management and Administration* 25, no. 2 (1997): 117–132.

[23] P. T. Begley, "In Pursuit of Authentic School Leadership Practices," *International Journal of Leadership in Education* 4 (2001): 353–365.

THE
APPLICATIONS
OF RELATIONAL
INTELLIGENCE

FAMILY RELATIONSHIPS

In truth a family is what you make of it. It is made strong, not by number of heads counted at the dinner table, but by the rituals you help family members create, by the memories you share, by the commitment of time, caring, and love you show to one another, and by the hopes for the future you have as individuals and as a unit.
—Marge Kennedy

Our families are the first place where we learn about relational intelligence. In them, we learn how to build rapport with others. We learn how to understand what makes the people closest to us tick. We learn how to embrace individual differences. We are exposed to the way trust is developed and influence is cultivated. Such knowledge often starts with the way parents interact with their children. Mothers and fathers play a critical role in shaping how their kids see the world around them. This can be good or bad depending on the household in which they are raised. I've worked with clients who had great upbringings. They learned important values and beliefs that have helped shape who they are today and the types of leaders they can become. They learned about hard work and discipline. They learned how to treat others with respect and to live with integrity. They learned how to develop empathy and show compassion toward others.

I've also worked with leaders who grew up in hostile environments. I've heard horror stories from people who were physically and sexually abused. Leaders have told me about parents who struggled with drugs, alcohol, and addiction. Some people had to deal with parents who had mental, emotional, and psychological disorders. These types of situations and circumstances do one of two things to people. Children of dysfunctional households either develop the same problems with which their parents had to cope, or they learn what not to do as adults. It can be scary when people adopt the same negative habits, patterns, and beliefs as their parents. These types of leaders often struggle with building relationships with their people, teams, and organizations. I've learned that although we don't get to choose who our families are, we do get to choose how we want to interact with them.

For years, psychologists have studied the relationships between parents and their children. Research on attachment theory has found that there are two functional roles parents have for the early behavioral development of children.[1] The protective function serves to keep a child close enough to their mother or father in times of potential danger so they can be protected. When there is no danger, parents become a secure base from which a child can explore their environment.[2] Child attachment relationships can be broadly classified as secure or insecure, and the quality of care a child experiences can determine the quality of their attachment relationships as they develop and mature.

In the late 1970s, researchers experimentally defined three sub-groupings of attachment relationships: secure, anxious-avoidant, and anxious-resistant (or ambivalent) attachment styles.[3] A secure attachment is characterized by intense feelings of intimacy, emotional security, and physical safety. Research has found that individuals in securely attached groups of children are more positive in their interactions with primary caretakers, showing little anxiety when separated from their mothers.[4] Secure attachment promotes an overall sense of self-worth and belongingness in children and serves to advance a child's emotional and social development. This lays the groundwork for children to develop strong relational intelligence later in life.

When children experience an insecure attachment relationship (as the result of trauma or neglect), significant deficits in their development of self occur. Their ability to relate to others suffers as well. These effects can have long-term negative psychological and relational consequences for a person. The anxious-avoidant group of children is characterized by their low need to accept physical contact from their parents when united after separation. Studies on mate selection and attachment style have found that as anxious-avoidant children grow up to adulthood, their intimate relationships are often characterized by such complications as withdrawal and emotional distance.[5]

Anxious-ambivalent children are characterized by intense distress when their parents depart and an inability to be soothed upon their return. Children with this type of attachment style show an unusual amount of internal conflict regarding the perceived physical and emotional availability of their attachment figure. Research on the consequences of this attachment style indicates that anxious-ambivalent children experience developmental delays compared to securely attached children. Specifically, children with an anxious-ambivalent attachment style show inhibitive exploration tendencies, precociousness, and self-protection while showing increased recklessness and accident proneness.[6] These studies show that it is no wonder that the way we are raised by our parents can have a positive or detrimental effect on how we build relationships with others throughout our lives.

SINS OF THE FATHER

I've had a complicated relationship with my father for many years. When my parents divorced over religion, I was five years old. I don't remember much of what took place around that time. However, I do remember a few flashbacks of specific events. On one occasion, I remember my mother coming home from work and wanting to take me and my younger brother to a local carnival that was on church grounds. My father snapped at her and told her that his kids weren't going anywhere near a church. On a separate occasion, I remember my father telling us stories from the Quran. I vividly remember the story of Joseph and his imprisonment in Egypt. My father talked about how Joseph was sold into slavery, but because he had the favor of God, anything he touched was blessed. That appealed to me. It seemed that I could have favor with God by living an honorable life.

My most memorable experience from that time was not a good one. My mother had my father served divorce papers after we returned from summer vacation. They had been having problems for months, and my mother felt she had no other alternative. She felt she had to choose between her faith and her husband. She chose her faith. We were with our grandparents when he received the news. We stayed with Grandma and Grandpa the entire weekend. My mother did as well. When we came home late on Sunday night, our home was empty—no furniture, no beds, and no TVs. My father had several friends come over the day before to empty out the house. Anything he bought or felt was his, he took. I remember crying with my brother on the living room floor because we had no beds to sleep in that night. The next several months were extremely difficult. My mother's parents had come into some money from the passing of a relative, so they bought my father out of the house my parents had bought together. That made my father furious. He felt that my mother got to keep the house and her children while he was kicked out on the streets.

Over the next several years, my father was in and out of our lives. He went back to Egypt and remarried. He returned with his new wife and would see us on weekends once in a while. On some weekends, he would pull up in his car, and we would cry in the driveway because we didn't want to leave home. On other weekends, we would go with him and spend most of the time at his mosque, running around with other kids. My brother and I didn't like his new wife. She spoke very little English and had a ferocious temper. He would leave us with her often while he went out with his friends. We started seeing less and less of him as time progressed. As I look back on it now, the distance wasn't solely his fault. We didn't want to be with him. We didn't want to spend hours at his mosque or with his wife.

The family on my mother's side wasn't helpful. My grandmother constantly bad-mouthed our dad. When I acted up or misbehaved, she would scold me and say, "You're selfish just like your father." This would hurt me deeply. Everyone seemed to dislike my father, and she would say I was just like him. It made me want to spend less time with him. Eight to ten years went by before he came back into my life. When we did start to talk again, I was just finishing my junior year of high school. I was dating my high school sweetheart, whom my mother feared I was going to get pregnant. She reached out to my father to see if I could spend the summer with him in Virginia. When I first arrived on his farm, it was strange to see him after so many years. There was much relationship building we needed to do. My father did a lot that summer to try to learn about me and understand what was most important at that point in my life.

About a month after I got to Virginia, my father was talking to me one night and wanted to share about a self-help audio program that he had been listening to. He told me the program could help change my life. It would build my self-esteem and help me set goals for my future. He gave me the first cassette tape of Tony Robbins's *Personal Power*. I remember listening to it in his basement that night and becoming fascinated with discovering and unleashing my full potential. I spent the next thirty days going through Tony's program. I had always set goals for sports and athletics in high school, but Tony taught me how to set goals in all areas of my life. I left my father's farm at the end of that summer with a new sense of purpose. I look back on that time now as one of the most important contributions he made in helping me become the man that I am today.

But we had another falling out a few months after that, and I didn't talk to him for the ten following years. I don't even remember what the fight was about or who started it. I just remember feeling that this was how it was with my father. He was a stubborn, prideful man who never really took the time to see the perspectives of others. He did not have strong relational intelligence. A few years after the falling out, I changed my last name to Bandelli in honor of my grandfather, who served as the father figure when I was growing up. I wanted the legacy of his name to live on and be passed down to my own children. I'm sure this was hurtful and insulting to my father once he found out.

When I was in the second year of my doctoral program, I reached back out to him to try to reconnect and reconcile. My father was thrilled that I wanted to spend time with him and rebuild the relationship. After about a month of getting to know each other again, he started talking to me about getting into the real estate industry. This was a year or two before the 2008 economic collapse, which was caused mainly by the housing crisis. My father was trained as a civil engineer and had his own construction and real estate company. Given that we had two different last names, he wanted to sell me my first house and teach me how to flip it a few years later. It sounded like a great idea. I would learn about real estate, get to know my father more deeply, and learn from him. It seemed too good to be true for a twenty-four-year old.

Over the next three months, my father did a number of things to ensure I got the loan for the house. He moved thousands of dollars around into my bank accounts and told me to start spending money so it would look like there was a paper trail of cash flow. He asked me to request personal loans from several of my friends to help with the down payment for the home. I trusted him and his intentions, so I followed his lead. One of my most memorable experiences with him from that time was when we took a road trip down to the lake house I was going to purchase in North Carolina. The place looked amazing. It was supposed to be part of a three-hundred-home development set around a large lake. I fell in love with the house, and we quickly moved to draw up the mortgage documents. At the time, I was making about twenty-five thousand dollars a year as a poor graduate student. However, my credit was great, and I had spent the previous three months borrowing money and spending it recklessly. However, I hadn't had an inspection done on the house. I didn't know anything about that. I trusted that my father had my best intentions in mind.

The agreement to which he committed was that I would purchase the house since we had different last names. He would sell the house to me. He told me that he would pay the mortgage for two years until we flipped the house. I thought that was great. On the day of the closing, I remember sitting across the table from him and his wife as I signed many documents and papers. I didn't even know what I was signing. I just knew my father wanted a relationship with me and wanted to teach me about real estate. I signed for two home equity loans that day—one for $750,000 and a second for $150,000. He was selling me a $900,000 home that I found out later wasn't even worth $400,000. I finished signing the papers, and we went out to dinner to celebrate.

This also happened to me when I was having my first major manic episode. I didn't realize I was in the middle of an episode at that time, but my habits and actions were extremely reckless. I spent the thousands of dollars my father had put into my accounts. I slept two to three hours a night and worked sixteen-hour days. Three months later, I fell into a deep depression. I was in Cincinnati for my first doctoral internship, and my father came out to visit me one weekend. As the weekend drew to a close, I told him not to leave because I felt I would hurt myself or worse. He packed up my things with me, and we drove sixteen hours back to his home in Virginia to get me the help I needed. Although the house buying situation influenced by my father had exacerbated my mental health situation, he did come through for me during one of the darkest periods of my life. I look back on that time now and realize it was the second time he stepped into my life and helped shape the course of my destiny. I've never told him how grateful I was that he was there in my time of need.

For the next six months, I struggled with my bipolar diagnosis and spent most of my time in my mother's home as I recovered and recuperated. I forgot about the house I had purchased from my father. It was the furthest thing from my mind. I had to finish my doctoral program and start my career. One night, I went to Macy's to do some shopping for the holidays. When I stepped up to the cash register to pay for my items, my Macy's card was declined. I tried my American Express card. That was declined as well. I had never missed a credit card payment, so I was shocked that my cards weren't processing. I went home and called all my credit card companies. They said the cards had been closed because of a delinquent payment on my credit report. I was shocked and puzzled to hear that. I looked up my credit report. The mortgage that was taken out on the house was never paid. My father had never made a single payment over the previous twelve months. The house fell into foreclosure, and my credit was damaged for seven years.

When I confronted my father, he simply told me that the economy was collapsing and that he was losing so much money he couldn't pay for the mortgage. I didn't believe a word he said. He had manipulated me into purchasing a home I couldn't afford. I felt betrayed. He had taken advantage of me. The man to whom I looked up and whom I respected had lied to and cheated me. We didn't talk again for thirteen years. Over that time, I forgave him. That action was more for me than it was for him. But I never reached back out to start a relationship. He tried to communicate with me several times during that period, but I didn't want him in my life. It wasn't until a close friend talked to me about what had happened that I started to change my mind. Her father was murdered when she was a child, and she told me she would give anything to talk to him again. She told me that time was precious and that I should give my father a chance before it was too late to do so. I reached out to my father a few months later. It's been two years now that we have been talking to each other. Our relationship is growing slowly. Full trust will never be there, but I've come to take my father for what he is. His intentions are usually good, but he does have a selfish and manipulative side. I inherited some of that from him and have spent years removing those habits and traits from my life.

Relationships with our parents shape so much of our lives. Healthy relationships can help us grow and thrive. Problematic relationships can leave us damaged and carrying baggage for years. Relationally intelligent parents invest in the development of their children as people. They teach them how to be empathetic and learn about others. They expose children to different types of people from various backgrounds, cultures, and ethnicities. They teach us the importance of trust and commitment. Their influence can help shape the people we become in adulthood.

Researchers in the field of family psychology have studied healthy and problematic family functioning for years. According to the Circumplex Model of Marital and Family Systems, family functioning is best understood in three concepts. Cohesion is the emotional bond between family members. Flexibility is the quality of family leadership, organization, roles, rules, and negotiations. Communication consists of the positive communication skills used in the family.[7] With respect to cohesion, unbalanced family functioning can result from either disengagement or enmeshment.

Disengaged families are characterized by too much independence, underinvolvement in family business, and few feelings of togetherness. Children from disengaged families are more depressed, present more externalizing symptoms, and are less empathetic.[8] Healthy family functioning, with respect to cohesion, is characterized by a well-balanced closeness between family members, where the family is seen as a network of support.[9]

Unbalanced family functioning in the category of flexibility can result from either too much or too little family change in the face of development challenges. Chaotic families are characterized by a lack of leadership from the father figure, dramatic role shifts, and erratic discipline. Children from chaotic families show more suicidal ideation and lack of insight and are more likely to have conduct disorders and commit homicide.[10] Rigid families that cannot change even if it's crucial are characterized by authoritarian leadership, strict discipline, and hard-to-change roles. Rigidity is connected with inadequate problem-solving skills and suicidal ideation in adolescents. Children from such families report high levels of loneliness and low sense levels of coherence. Healthy families are characterized by solid but ready-to-change rules, roles, and behavioral patterns, leading to optimal adaptation to environmental challenges.

The third major characteristic of family functioning is communication between family members. This is the most critical area, as it pertains to developing relational intelligence. Many researchers have highlighted the importance of open, congruent, and overall positive communication as a source of development and well-being in a family.[11] Fathers play a critical role in this for the entire family. The behaviors fathers display to their children stick with them for years to come. Healthy behaviors lead to productive lifestyles for their children. Unhealthy behaviors can leave scars that will take years of therapy to be healed and removed.

Strong relational intelligence is a crucial factor in the growth and development of children. The roles parents play in helping to shape how their children start to form connections and build relationships with others are critical. When parents create loving, caring, and supportive environments for their children to explore their interests and curiosities, children start to learn the necessary skills for socializing and building strong interpersonal relationships. When there is a lack of supportive environment, negative patterns and poor relational habits are formed. Issues like low self-esteem, pride and arrogance, or self-entitlement can develop and leave a lasting, destructive impact on children's lives. What we teach our children matters. Often, it is not only what we say to them that is important. It's what they see us do that leaves a lasting impression.

SIBLING RIVALRIES

For most of my life, I've had a really strong relationship with my younger brother. We are two and a half years apart and spent most of our childhood doing things together. Our extended family members often referred to him as "me too" because he tried to imitate everything his older brother did. The divorce of our parents hit me harder than it did him. He was two and a half at the time. I was five. Growing up in a single-family household had its good and bad moments. The absence of our father created a tight bond between the two of us. Our grandfather served as the male figure and role model when we were kids. He would visit two to three times a week and take us to the baseball fields. We would cook barbecue and shish kebabs in the backyard during summers. He took us to the local flea market to buy baseball and basketball cards. I always enjoyed the time we got to spend with him. It brought happiness and joy to our lives at a time when there was a lot of instability with our father.

We deeply valued the relationship we had with our grandfather, and both of us looked up to him as a role model and father figure. Over the next several years, he helped with our growth and development. When I was thirteen years old, my grandfather came down with lung cancer. It was devastating to our family. Within eight months, he lost over one hundred pounds due to chemotherapy and the spread of the disease. A few months later, he passed away. I saw him a few days before he passed. He was in and out of consciousness at that point, so visits to see him were very painful. As I sat beside his bed that night, he turned to me and squeezed my hand. He looked me straight in the eyes and said, "It's your responsibility now to take care of your mother and your brother. I know you will be a strong role model for Joe. Make sure that the two of you remain close." I told him I would. I kissed him on the forehead and told him I loved him. At the time, I didn't know that would be the last time we would ever have a conversation.

My world came shattering down a few days later when I found out he had passed away. It was the first time my brother and I had been exposed to a death of a family member. I remember the day we drove to the funeral. There was a sadness neither of us could shake. Over the next several years, I made it my priority to have a positive impact on my brother's life. I encouraged him to play sports with me, and we played basketball together all the time. I made sure he focused on his studies and did the best he could in school. There was never sibling rivalry between the two of us because we were three grades apart in school. Some of the most memorable experiences we had together were when I was a senior in high school and he was a freshman. I drove him to school every day, and we would laugh and joke about life. It was an extremely important time in our bonding and the development of our relationship.

When I went off to college, our relationship started to change, though not in a bad way. I was figuring out what I wanted to do with my life, and he was figuring out how to stand up as his own person. Although we share many similar traits, values, and beliefs that were instilled by our mother, we are two totally different people. I am the stereotypical businessman—polished, put-together, and always wearing a three-piece suit. My brother is the complete opposite. He's covered in tattoos, grows his hair out regularly, and lives a much more laid-back lifestyle. I live in New York City. He lives in Los Angeles. I'm into business and psychology. He is into films and the arts. He has a successful career making horror movies and has done so for many years. When I started my career, we lived together for a few years while he was in film school. It was a turbulent time in my life. I was not on meds for my bipolar disorder, and he witnessed firsthand my many reckless habits and behaviors. He saw me manipulate and use women. He saw my horrific drinking. The worst part was that he had a front-row seat to the start of my cocaine addiction.

In the beginning, we both thought it was fun. He would participant in some of the party activities when they took place. I planned a trip for his thirtieth birthday to Las Vegas for him and a few friends. It was about a year and a half into my addiction. I spent the whole weekend in the hotel room doing cocaine while they went out and celebrated his birthday. The day before we left, I had been doing cocaine since we woke up in the morning. He was angry and frustrated that I chose to spend all our time there doing drugs rather than enjoying the time with him. He came up to me at one point during the day and said, "Adam, you have a serious problem. All you do is cocaine. It's going to destroy your life. That career you care so much about is going to go down the drain. You need to tell your fiancée and Mom. You need to get help!" I told him to fuck off and that he didn't know what he was talking about. That started the split in our relationship. I damaged the trust we had and have spent a long time trying to rebuild it.

As my addiction got worse over the next year, we started spending less and less time together. He never wanted to be around me. But out of respect and loyalty, he said nothing to my wife or our family. He had to deal with the burden of being the only one who knew about my issues. If I had an overdose and had died, he would have had to live with that for the rest of his life. It was unfair that I did this to him, and he had rage and hostility toward me. I deserved it for what I put him through. After rehab, I tried to make amends. I told him how sorry I was for putting such a heavy burden on him. I also felt like a failure for letting my grandfather down. I had not remained Joe's role model. If anything, my life had become a story of what not to do. We are in a better place today than we were back then, but the damage that was done will take years to heal. I took a relationship that was strong and positive and destroyed the trust we had shared.

The sibling relationship is unique. It is characterized by both love and warmth as well as conflict and rivalry. However, it is also one of the most neglected relationships in psychological research and practice. This is puzzling because there are a number of reasons why sibling relationships are important for individual development. First of all, statistics indicate that around 90 percent of the population has a sibling,[12] so it is a very commonplace relationship. Second, the sibling relationship is one of the most enduring relationships in a person's life span, starting at birth and continuing to death. Third, research has found that brothers and sisters spend a lot of time together, more than anyone else, including their parents.[13] Fourth, sibling relationships affect other relationships within the family, as indicated by family systems theory, which assumes that all individuals and dyads within the family influence one another. Lastly, sibling relationships strongly affect psychosocial and relational functioning. Due to the frequency and amount of interactions, the durability of the relationship, the existence of ascribed roles, accessibility, and the degree in common experiences, these relationships form a unique and important context in which people develop social and emotional skills.[14]

Positive parent-child relationships contribute to the development of closeness and positivity among siblings. Psychologists who study attachment theory have found that children form internal representations of relationships from interactions with their primary caregivers, which they subsequently use in developing and maintaining other relationships. Social learning theorists have demonstrated that the behavior patterns children enact with their parents are generalized to siblings and peer relationships.[15] Behavioral scientists from both theoretical areas have found that positivity in the parent-child relationship is linked with levels of positive affectivity in other relationships. Conversely, negativity in the parent-child relationships is linked to suspicion concerning relationships and to aggressive, self-protective behaviors. Such negative expectations and behaviors undermine the quality of sibling relationships.

Researchers have found that differences in relationship quality between each sibling and their parents contribute to variations in the affective quality of sibling relationships.[16] When siblings are treated differently by a parental figure, feelings of inequity among the children engender rivalry and anger, which in turn create negativity in the sibling relationship. Central to this framework is the assumption that siblings in middle childhood engage in social comparison processes, through which they compare the quality of their own relational experiences with their parents and those of their siblings. The quality of parent-child relationships also depends in part on the relationship between the parents. Open hostility and negativity between spouses have consistently been shown to be associated with low levels of positive emotional experiences in parent-child relationships. This, in turn, creates less positivity and more negativity in sibling relationships.[17] Parental conflict also creates emotional demands on parents that compromise their ability to foster positive relationships with each of their children. Because children model what they see, such parental conflict also creates tension in sibling relationships.

A prime time for change in sibling relationships occurs in late adolescence into early adulthood. Consistent with identity development research, behavior scientists have found that the period from eighteen to twenty-five years of age is a time for self-exploration, as people face three primary tasks that define adulthood: taking responsibility for oneself, making independent decisions, and establishing financial independence. These tasks largely take place in the context of romantic relationships and workforce entrance. Two role transitions that often accompany leaving home and workforce participation are marriage and childbearing, both of which have the potential to enhance closeness in sibling relationships or exacerbate previous difficulties. When siblings create their own family units through marriage and cohabitation, the social fabric of the original family changes to accommodate new relationships. Different role transitions are usually experienced simultaneously across multiple family members, increasing the complexity of sibling relationships. For example, younger siblings may transition into higher education or the workforce just as older siblings are transitioning into marriage or parenthood. Thus, the siblings may be simultaneously focusing more on individual goals and interests during these transitions, and this self-focus may present barriers to communication and support within the relationships.

Relational intelligence plays a critical role during all these transitions. For siblings to continue to maintain strong connections, there needs to be an intentional focus on sowing into the relationships. Skills like further developing the trust that exists or having a positive influence on one another's lives become critical. If siblings stop pouring time and energy into their relationships with one another, they can suffer and fall apart. Relationally intelligent people understand this. They make it a priority to strengthen relationships over time. Our siblings are some of the most important people in our lives, and like in any other relationship, if we don't invest in growing them, we miss out on opportunities to have a positive impact on the people who should matter the most.

GOLDEN CHILDREN AND BLACK SHEEP: EVERY FAMILY HAS THEM

A large part of the work my firm does is in the area of senior executive selection. When clients hire us, we come in to help them identify and select the best talent for their organizations. Our executive assessment process is comprised of several different areas that enable us to make accurate predictions about a candidate's success in a given role. When we work with a company, we always begin our process by selecting key stakeholders to build a scorecard. The scorecard holds key role imperatives and critical leadership behaviors a person must demonstrate to drive success for the organization. Scorecards are specific to different roles, levels, and functions in an organization. A strong scorecard will capture key performance indicators (KPIs) for the role, leadership skills and behaviors that are important to the company, and organizational culture factors candidates must possess to be a strong fit.

Once we have the scorecard in place, we put candidates through a psychological battery of personality tests. These tests explore a person's strengths, their risk factors and derailers, and their values and beliefs. The personality test results give us an initial glimpse into how a person is wired and what makes them tick. They are our way to "get under the hood" before we sit down and meet with the candidate. The most important part of the process is our three-hour behavioral interview. This experience is not your typical job interview. As business psychologists, we focus on the mix of psychological leadership traits and business skills that impact performance. Our ability to provide senior executives with highly nuanced behavioral insights enables us to more accurately assess a person's strengths and weaknesses. This, in turn, enables us to predict (with relatively high accuracy) if someone will be a good fit for the role and the company's culture.

To get the data and information we need to know about someone, we have people share their leadership journey. When I sit down with a candidate, I have one simple request: for them to tell me their life story. I want to learn about all the events that have helped shape who they are as a person and the type of leader they are when we meet. We'll talk about a person's family and childhood. We'll talk about their friendships and the types of activities and hobbies they were involved in growing up. We'll talk about their high school sweetheart and where they went to college. We'll talk about successes that gave them confidence in themselves and setbacks or failures that taught them valuable life lessons. We'll talk about their career history and the companies where they have worked. We'll talk about their spouse and their children. We'll cover all aspects of their life so we can get a clear picture of who they are as a leader.

Some of the most important parts of the conversations are when people talk about their family and upbringing. I'm fascinated by the power of parent-child relationships. The values and beliefs parents instill in their children shape how they see the world around them. When parents are strong role models for their children, they inspire their kids to strive for all that they can be. When the family is dysfunctional, it can damage a person for years. I've found that positive or negative early life experiences can serve as motivational forces to drive change in a person's life. Contextual factors do matter, and nurture usually plays a more dominant role than nature. However, people often tell themselves narratives that become part of their identity as they mature and transition into adulthood. These narratives impact the quality of their relationships across all areas of their lives.

Some of the funniest and entertaining stories also come from childhood. We all have family members who require a little special attention. There's the old, eccentric uncle who's always telling stories from forty years ago. There's that aunt you cringe seeing every holiday because you know she's going in for a kiss on the lips with every greeting. There's that one grandparent who smells like dirty mothballs. There are cousins on your mother's side of the family who are just strange. There are cousins on your father's side of the family who are self-centered egomaniacs. And every family has a golden child. They're the person with a larger-than-life personality. They can do no wrong in their parents' eyes. They typically like to be the center of attention. Every family also has a black sheep. They're the wallflower who keeps to themselves. They're the ones you usually don't see at Grandma's annual holiday party. They often get forgotten about or overlooked in most situations.

A few years back, I helped a client select a candidate for a senior vice president role in the sports and entertainment industry. During our assessment interview, Mark discussed some of the people who had an impact on him while he was growing up. He talked about the role his father played in developing his self-confidence, discipline, and work ethic. He touched on the things he learned from his mother, like empathy, compassion, and concern for the well-being of others. He also talked about some of his extended family members who taught him what not to do as a person. He mentioned one of his cousins who was a high-maintenance egomaniac. I remember laughing as he told me the story about this cousin on his mother's side of the family. Dan the Man, as the family playfully referred to him, was a cocky and highly conceited individual. He always had to be the center of attention at holiday parties and family gatherings. He made sure he had the last word in any conversation. He was always giving out unsolicited advice on topics he didn't know anything about. He also got a kick out of poking fun and making jokes about others.

Dan the Man had little awareness of the impact he had on others. He had poor EQ and couldn't pick up on the subtle verbal and nonverbal behaviors of family members who were turned off by his brash and arrogant ways. This got me thinking about how relationally intelligent people learn how to interact with the divas in their families. One of the most critical skills that come into play is our ability to understand others. Most of the golden children in a family have some sort of self-esteem issues or have been coddled by their parents more than they should be. In Dan the Man's case, he had pride issues that made him stick out his chest and try to prove his value to others. Over time, Mark had to learn how to engage his cousin in conversation. It wasn't about pushing back and trying to confront Dan the Man. This would only end up in a pissing contest about who had the larger voice or could dominate the airtime in a discussion. Relationally intelligent people know how to adjust their style to meet the demands of different situations. They know that skills like ingratiating themselves to others and tailoring messages to lower people's defense mechanisms are important. We can usually do this with colleagues or coworkers, but it can be extremely frustrating to have to do it with our own family. It's also the family members who usually push our buttons the most that challenges us to practice our relational intelligence skills.

Many relational intelligence skills start to take shape at an early age because we are forced to adapt to interactions with our families. We have to learn how to establish rapport with those who have very different ways of thinking than we do. We need to be curious and seek to understand what makes others tick. We have to develop an appreciation for the things that make our family members different from one another. We have to find ways to develop trust even though we may not trust some of the intentions or actions of others. Sometimes, we can only cultivate influence by first seeking out insights and input from others. I've found in my life that we learn valuable lessons of what not to do and how we shouldn't treat people based on some of the dysfunction we see from those closest to us. We take these hard-learned lessons and apply them to how we develop relationships later in life. We don't get to choose our families, but we do get to choose what we want to learn from them. Relationally intelligent people are naturally curious about others. They are typically great people watchers who can assimilate new and different information from all those around them. Our first exposure to these opportunities is often through our families. Good or bad, we learn powerful lessons about people and relationships from our loved ones.

1   J. Bowlby, *Attachment and Loss: Attachment*, vol. 1 (London: Hogarth Press, 1969).

2   J. Bowlby, *A Secure Base* (New York, New York: Basic Books, 1988).

3   M. D. S. Ainsworth, M. C. Blehar, E. Waters, and S. Wall, *Patterns of Attachment: A Psychological Study of the Strange Situation* (Hillsdale, New Jersey: Erlbaum Publishing, 1978).

4   A. F. Lieberman and J. H. Pawl, "Clinical Applications of Attachment Theory," in *Clinical Implications of Attachment*, eds. J. Belsky and T. Nezworski (Hillsdale, New Jersey: Erlbaum Publishing, 1988), 327–351.

5   D. Benoit and K. C. H. Parker, "Stability and Transmission of Attachment across Three Generation," *Child Development* 65 (1994): 1,444–1,456.

6   L. A. Sroufe, "The Role of Infant-Caregiver Attachment in Development," in *Clinical Implications of Attachment*, eds. J. Belsky and T. Nezworski (Hillsdale, New Jersey: Erlbaum Publishing, 1988), 18–38.

7   D. Olson, "FACES IV and the Circumplex Model: Validation Study," *Journal of Marital and Family Therapy* 37, no. 1 (2011): 64–80.

8   M. Kaufman, "How Families Facilitate the Development of Empathy in Children: A Family Systems Theory Perspective," *Developmental Psychology* 31, no. 6 (2011): 923–933.

9   C. D. Sherbourne and A. L. Stewart, "The MOS Social Support Survey," *Social Science and Medicine* 32, no. 6 (1991):705–714.

10 P. J. Darby, W. D. Allan, J. H. Kashani, K. L. Hartke, and J. C. Reid, "Analysis of 112 Juveniles Who Committed Homicide: Characteristics and a Closer Look at Family Abuse," *Journal of Family Violence* 13, no. 4 (1998): 365–375.

11 V. Satir, *Peoplemaking* (Palo Alto, California: Science and Behavior Books, 1972).

12 A. Milevsky, *Sibling Relationships in Childhood and Adolescence: Predictors and Outcomes* (New York, New York: Columbia University Press, 2011).

13 R. Sanders, *Sibling Relationships: Theory and Issues for Practice* (Basingstoke: Palgrave Macmillan Press, 2004).

14 V. G. Cicirelli, "Sibling Influence throughout the Life Span," in *Sibling Relationships: Their Nature and Significance across the Life Span*, eds. M. E. Lamb and B. Sutton-Smith (1982), 267–284.

15 G. R. Patterson, "A Microsocial Process: A View from the Boundary," in *Boundary Areas in Psychology: Social and Developmental Psychology*, eds. J. C. Masters and K. L. Yarkin (New York: Academic Press, 1984), 43–66.

16 G. H. Brody, Z. Stoneman, and J. K. McCoy, "Associations of Maternal and Paternal Direct and Differential Behavior with Sibling Relationships: Contemporaneous and Longitudinal Analyses," *Child Development* 63 (1992): 82–92.

17 E. M. Cummings, "Coping with Background Anger in Early Childhood," *Child Development* 58 (1987): 976–984.

FRIENDSHIPS

A true friend knows the song in my heart and
sings it to me when my memory fails.

—Donna Roberts

Some of the most enduring relationships in our lives are with our closest friends. Close friends are the people who stick by our side through thick and thin. They can be counted on in times of challenge and adversity. They know us inside and out. They have our best interests at heart and know how to encourage and support us when we're down. Our closest friends are usually great listeners. They don't try to give us advice all the time. They want to give more to you than they want to take from the relationship. They are there when we need a shoulder to cry on. They share some of the most precious and important moments in our lives. They are empathetic and compassionate. They are willing to walk a mile in our shoes and will go a step further and carry us when our strength fails. They accept our flaws and blemishes but challenge us to develop and grow. They tell us the things we need to hear at the right moments rather than just tell us what we want them to say. They inspire us by being positive role models in our lives. They influence us to become better versions of ourselves.

Some of our closest friendships start at an early age. We can all remember someone we met in elementary school whom we connected with instantly. We may have had similar hobbies and interests and enjoyed spending time together. In high school, our relationships change. Many of us made friends through sports and extracurricular activities. Our friendships evolve as we grow and mature. The skills of understanding others and embracing individual differences become of utmost importance. We often get greater exposure to people with different backgrounds, cultures, and beliefs during young adulthood. If we develop relational intelligence skills in the right way, we have a greater appreciation for people from all walks of life. If we don't, we stunt our growth. We can get locked into closed mindsets that affect us for years to come.

In the college years, many of us move away from home for the first time. We get thrown into a whole new environment. We may meet friends in classes or through fraternities and sororities we join. Such bonds are unique relationships, as most people who join groups go through some form of initiation or pledging that bonds people together. I have vivid memories of the friends I made in my pledge class. We got to go on scavenger hunts together in New York City. We had to deal with the grueling humiliation and abuse we were put through by our older brothers in the fraternity. We learned how to rely on one another and develop trust. Elected as pledge leader for my class, the burden I had to carry was to provide guidance, encouragement, and support to my brothers as we worked our way through the pledging season. I spent long nights with my brothers; and I learned about their goals, hopes, and dreams for the future. We handled adversity and struggles together. We had fun and made some great memories.

My fraternity held an annual lip sync contest in which all Greek life groups participated. It was customary for all the pledge classes to get up on stage and make fools out of themselves there. I told my brothers we weren't going to do that. We were going to win the contest! I had to convince eight White guys with no rhythm to practice dance moves for the six weeks leading up to the competition. This was in the late '90s, when Sisqo's "Thong Song" came out. I recorded the music video from MTV and watched it probably three hundred times to get down every dance move. I taught myself how to do the dance, then set up practice three nights a week to teach my brothers. We would sneak into the gym at 2:00 a.m. and practice in front of mirrors so we could get aligned and in sync. The night of the lip sync contest, I dyed my hair silver and bought everyone outfits like in the music video. We won the contest easily. It was a blast, and it also taught me a valuable lesson about trust and relationships. There would have been no way I could have influenced all these guys had I not sown into each individual relationship. My brothers trusted me. They knew I had their best interests at heart and followed my lead. I'm still friends with many of the guys from my fraternity. Those bonding experiences helped solidify friendships that have lasted the test of time.

Birds of a Feather

I've known my best friend Justin for over twenty-five years. We met our junior year in high school. I had transferred that year from a private Catholic school that wasn't a good fit. He had moved from Long Island, where he spent most of his childhood, to Central Jersey. Justin sat behind me in history class. At the time, I was focused on my academics and getting good grades. It was important for me to do well in school so I could position myself to get into the best college possible. He was hoping to do the same with his academic pursuits. We were also both trying to make new friends, as we had just started in that high school. I remember him always having a good sense of humor. We joked around together and established a good connection.

Over the next several months, our friendship began to develop. We shared many of the same values, particularly physical fitness and important career and life aspirations. We would go to the gym together regularly, and he taught me how to weight-lift. We both loved sports. Basketball and football were two of the main activities we watched and played together. Justin struggled that year since he had left all his friends in Long Island. I understood that it was a rough transition for him; I was experiencing some of the same feelings having left my group of friends from Catholic school as well. Our bond strengthened over the next two years. We developed a strong understanding and appreciation for each other. There was never any type of competition between the two of us. We each had our swim lanes and supported each other in our academic and social endeavors.

In college, our relationship blossomed. Justin hit his intellectual stride. He began focusing on pursuing a career in English and African American studies. At the same time, I was developing my passion for industrial-organizational psychology. I was involved in all sorts of extracurricular activities at my university. From fraternity life to academic societies to pursuing leadership roles on campus, I was learning how to develop relationships with people from different backgrounds and cultures. Justin was doing the same at his university. We worked hard to push and support each other. When we got to spend time together, we had discussions about life goals, dreams, and our professional ambitions. I wanted to pursue my doctoral degree in organizational psychology, and he wanted to do the same in English literature. During those years, we shared many experiences. Through summer vacations at the beach, meeting women and dating, and listening to hip-hop music and jamming out together, we nurtured and cultivated a strong bond.

One of the most interesting things that developed over those years was how we created a shared vocabulary and way to communicate with each other. We came up with words and phrases only the two of us understood. This started in high school when we watched Eddie Murphy's stand-up specials together. We took phrases and things he said in his shows and made them part of our regular communications with each other. These shared sayings and ways in which we talked to each other strengthened our relationship. We could be in the middle of a party or social event, and Justin would say one word and I would know what he was thinking and feeling. This taught me a powerful lesson about the use of language and how it could tighten the bond between people. Over the years, I've found that other close friends have understood the same. My brother has a similar way of communicating with his closest friends. Shared experiences with others create methods of communication and understanding.

In our late twenties, my friendship with Justin began to evolve and grow deeper. We developed a trust that was unbreakable. During those years, we supported each other a great deal. Justin moved around a lot during this period. He spent time in New Mexico, Pennsylvania, and Upstate New York. I moved to Florida and spent four years there working on my graduate degree. I was there for him during a major breakup with a woman to whom he was engaged for several years. He was there for me during my first major manic and depressive episodes. These life events and challenges forced us to mature our relationship. When we spent time together, our friendship became more of a therapeutic one, as each of us served as a counselor, life coach, and shoulder to cry on. This was also a time when we provided emotional and intellectual support for each other as we prepared for our careers.

In our thirties, life hit both of us in different ways. I struggled with accepting my bipolar disorder and almost lost my life to addiction. Justin got married and started having children through periods when he struggled with completing the dissertation for his doctoral degree. Although we faced different things during those years, the bedrock of our history and shared past experiences helped steady and sustain our relationship. Like a water well, we knew there would always be something meaningful to draw from each other regardless of our own personal challenges. We encouraged, supported, and pushed each other to get through some of life's most difficult periods.

As I look back on it now, there have been many things that have defined our relationship over the years. We have served as nurturing support systems for each other during times of great need. We've challenged each other to face our demons and grow as men. I've always been able to bring a problem to Justin, and he's helped me think through it logically and with a solution-focused perspective. There has also been a dimension of vulnerability to our relationship. Both of us have had times when we came to each other and needed to admit flaws and weaknesses. Such vulnerability takes trust and the belief that the other person has your best interest at heart. This has always been easier for Justin to do than for me. I have often been emotionally stubborn, closed off, and hardheaded when it comes to accepting my deficiencies. Justin has taught me to be more authentic and to own who I am as a person.

The way we both describe our relationship is as one of love and respect. We have never had a major falling out because we honor and value each other. We've always focused on loving, supporting, and accepting who the other is as an individual. We both have had our crazy moments, but we've come to appreciate the humanity in who we are as people. There's also been the importance of humor throughout our relationship. We've had many laughs and good times together, which have made our relationship enjoyable. The mix of mutual support, joy, respect, encouragement, love, and trust that we started developing as kids have created a friendship that has stood the test of time.

People commonly possess implicit theories of relationships characterized by two distinct belief sets: growth beliefs and destiny beliefs.[1] Growth beliefs reflect the notion that relationships are malleable, develop gradually over time, and require regular maintenance. Destiny beliefs capture the notion that relationships are relatively fixed, that they are either successful or unsuccessful from their start, and that friends are either inherently compatible or incompatible. An important distinction between growth and destiny beliefs concerns the functional role these beliefs serve in orienting people toward different relational goals. Growth beliefs orient people toward relationship cultivation. They help people determine the types of people they want in their lives and how they can learn and grow from others. Destiny beliefs, on the other hand, provide an evaluative framework by which friends can assess whether a relationship is worth pursuing. Relational intelligence plays a vital role in growth beliefs theory because it relates to how we develop a deeper understanding of our friends, embrace individual differences, and invest in trust for the relationship to flourish and grow.

For years, social psychologists have treated friendship as an affinity-based peer relationship that may vary quantitatively in some dimensions (e.g., intimacy, agreeableness, and satisfaction). There are many different types of friendship categories that have been researched over the last three decades. Utility friendships are best understood as having the primary purpose of making it possible for people to obtain valued outcomes from themselves through exchanges with others. The primary value of utility friendships is the degree to which relationships serve as a means to each friend's desired outcomes. For example, a friend may have particularly helpful skills or relatively greater popularity or physical strength. Because the relationship is based on a history of conferring benefits with one another, if that utility falters, so does the relationship. Friendships based on utility mirror the common idea that the point of a friendship is to provide benefits for the friends, a view that has been found in social exchange and interdependence theories of relationships.[2]

Pleasure friendships have the primary purpose of providing enjoyment to two people. As long as two people continue to obtain pleasure from the friendship, they will remain friends. This form of friendship mirrors the contemporary focus in psychological research on how friendship contributes to satisfaction and positive emotions. For example, one study shows that for older adults, friends are important because they are associated with short-term pleasurable feelings resulting from spending time together playing sports, engaging in hobbies, or attending cultural events.[3]

A third category, virtue friendships, has been described as the best type of friendship because it includes three distinct features. First, two people are friends because they admire each other's good qualities. The good qualities (e.g., honesty, sympathy, generosity, fairness, and courage) are what attract and bind the friends together. Because good qualities can be assumed to be a stable pattern of acting and being, these friendships are expected to last longer. Second, virtue friends see the friendship and their shared activities and goals as valuable to themselves. These are distinct from utility and pleasure friendships, where the primary goal of interactions is to obtain personal outcomes. Lastly, virtue friends want the best for one another. This means that obtaining benefits and experiencing pleasure for oneself are secondary to the value of one's friend and of the friendship itself. Virtue friends benefit one another, but they do so spontaneously to enhance each friend's welfare without keeping track of or equalizing benefits.[4] Relationally intelligent people usually have many virtue friendships because of the desire to give rather than the need to receive. Trust developed enables them to have a positive influence on the lives of others. Dynamic relationships are formed because there is a mutual desire for deep connection and for strengthening the emotional bond between two people.

Turning points and contextual shifts are impactful moments in any relationship. These are when friends reevaluate the relationship, its importance and meaning, and the reasons for future investment.[5] Such transitions reformulate the relationship, encouraging a new perspective from both individuals. Turning points can be obvious and dramatic, like one friend having a child or another getting married, but they can also be subtle, such as beginning to use inside jokes or creating shared routines. Turning points occur throughout the duration of a friendship. Because relationships go through moments of change both toward and away from one another, turning points have been found to be associated with changes in relational closeness.[6] Throughout the duration of a friendship, turning points mark changes in commitment and are inflection points of progress. Relationally intelligent people use turning points to strengthen their bonds with their friends. They show empathy and compassion to the changing needs of others. They provide guidance, counsel, and support to friends during seasons of change and uncertainty. This sustains the relationship over time and helps it evolve as both people continue to develop and grow.

LINE LEADERS AND THE HEAD OF THE PACK

I've always been amazed by the stories my clients share when asked to recall early life friendships that have contributed to lessons they have learned about themselves and their relationships. Some people will talk about friendships on sports teams or with academic extracurricular activities. Others will go into the history of their relationships with their siblings. About seven or eight years ago, I worked with a CEO from a pharmaceutical company. Nick was a passionate and inspirational leader. He was the type of person who instantly had a positive influence on those around him. People bought into his vision, and he had the unique ability to galvanize people around a collection of mission and purpose.

When we met for his assessment interview, we talked through his early life experiences and the close friendships he developed with others. Nick took me all the way back to when he was seven or eight years old. In elementary school, his teachers started to observe him exercising social influence on his classmates. He laughed about how he would regularly volunteer to be the line leader when the class got ready to go to the cafeteria or outside for recess. He also talked about how he began using prosocial strategies, like cooperation, unsolicited help, and positive alliance formation, with his classmates. If he and his friends were building forts or engaging in team-related activities, he was usually helping others. He didn't remember why he started engaging in these behaviors. He just naturally became the head of the pack in his interactions with others.

As he moved into middle school, Nick began playing a variety of sports. In baseball, soccer, and football, he began cultivating deeper friendships. He acquired skills like teamwork, influence, and partnering with others to accomplish a goal. He was also being exposed to different types of interpersonal styles in many of the coaches he worked with. Although these experiences helped shape his early ideas of friendships and relationships, it was the game of basketball that had a lasting impact on him during the early part of his life. The friendships he built with his teammates still last to this day. These relationships taught Nick the power of building strong connections with others. They have also taught him the power of words and storytelling. Nick excelled at basketball during high school. He was nominated as captain of his varsity team as a sophomore and took the responsibility seriously. The influence he had on others also played into the strong relationships he had with his friends. He was never overly assertive and aggressive with people. He naturally took on a leadership role in planning activities and bringing people together.

Nick started his career as a sales rep for a medical devices company. Early in his tenure, he put the same skills he had developed with his close friends into practice. He knew how to influence the thoughts and actions of others. He used the power of words to cultivate trust in his most important relationships. He practiced the skill of reciprocity. Within eighteen months, he was promoted to district manager with responsibility for nine sales reps. This was his first management experience as a professional. In getting to know his team, he did four important things. First, he took time to connect with each person on the team. He took rides with them to visit their customers and invested in building personal and professional relationships. He knew how to use relational intelligence to form lasting bonds with his people. Second, he brought the team together on a regular basis to establish and reinforce his vision. This gave the team a collective goal and a unified purpose. Third, he modeled the right behaviors. He never asked his sales reps to do something he would not have done. This garnered loyalty and commitment from the team. Lastly, he was always supportive and encouraging. He celebrated successes in public and provided development feedback in private conversations. These leadership behaviors served as a foundation for inspiring his team.

As Nick moved up in the organization from district manager to regional manager, then to vice president of sales, he continued to focus on the skills and behaviors he had implemented at an early age with his close friends. After twelve years with the same organization, he was approached by a headhunter to join a pharmaceuticals biotech start-up. Nick joined his current employer as vice president of sales and marketing. New responsibilities for marketing gave him the opportunity to learn a new part of the business and to expand his influence on a larger team. Within three years, the company doubled its revenues, and Nick was promoted to president and general manager for an entire division of the company. Although he had immense responsibility as a GM, he continued to take time for people and to invest in relationships. This was a hallmark of his leadership. He became known for inspirational speeches delivered every year at the company's national sales meeting. He was great at rallying the troops and giving people purpose and mission. He attributed all these behaviors from the things he learned when he built relationships early in life. It was some of his closest friends who taught him how to connect with others and build long-term, sustainable relationships.

Over the next two years, Nick's leadership continued to shine. He cultivated strong relationships with investors and the board. The company was successful in expanding across Europe and into Asia. Given these accomplishments and the financial success the company had during that time, he was promoted to CEO. We continued to work together as the board and former CEO outlined the transition.

What inspired me the most was how he handled the relationship with his predecessor. He ensured the current CEO that he understood his vision for the future. Nick committed to keeping lines of communication open after the transition. People gravitated to him throughout his entire career. His commitment to others, the investments he made in relationships, and his passion for the business had a positive impact on all the people with whom he interacted. He attributes most of his success to the things he learned about building relationships at an early age. Cultivating the skills that he developed in childhood with friends and teammates helped prepare him for leadership later in life. It was his ability to build relationships and influence others that made him such a great success.

Many studies on friendships and childhood leadership focus on children who emerge as leaders once they are placed in peer groups to participate in a collaborative task. In contrast to adult leadership, which is typically defined with reference to internal characteristics, such as personality traits (e.g., extraversion, agreeableness, and conscientiousness) or intelligence, children's leadership is often described in observable actions or behaviors. Specifically, child leaders exercise social influence through two primary behavioral means: prosocial behaviors and coercive dominance. Children who use prosocial strategies engage in behaviors like cooperation, unsolicited help, and positive alliance formation. These behaviors can be used strategically for goal attainment and are particularly used by younger children in early elementary school.[7] Coercive dominance in the broadest sense refers to force submission sequences in which force can be verbal, physical, or personality based (e.g., hitting, pushing, intimidating by physical stance, or using threats of violence to achieve a personal goal). Research has shown that children who emerge as leaders over time care about others and manifest good interpersonal skills.[8] They are sensitive to the needs and concerns of their fellow classmates or friends.

Friendships foster the acquisition of skills and competencies essential to a child's behavioral and social adjustment. It is through early-age friendships that children begin learning how to influence others. Findings from genetically-formed research, such as twin studies, indicate that leadership behaviors in adults and children are partly explained by genetic factors with estimates of genetic effects varying from 20 to 50 percent.[9] Individuals' genotypes can also influence their environmental experiences with peers, including their friendship choices. This is a phenomenon called gene-environment correlation. Accordingly, children with a greater genetic likelihood for leadership may be more likely to choose friends who will follow their lead. I've found that many of the leaders with whom I work today can recall situations growing up when they naturally assumed leadership roles with their friends. This contributes to how they evolve as leaders and the impact they have on the lives of others.

Researchers have found that leadership is an important dimension of friendships and peer relationships. Preschool leaders are frequently sought out by their friends for companionship, ideas, and decisions; and they readily adapt to new situations and interact easily with others. Not surprisingly, children with leadership skills also attract friends easily. Several of the personal characteristics that foster leadership, such as understanding others, showing empathy, sharing, developing trust, and helping behaviors, have been found to predict the number of close friends a child has.[10] Because friendships are voluntary and more egalitarian, group-based relationships, they provide a unique context for children to develop interpersonal morality and mutual concern. Social psychologists have found that friends tend to engage in more frequent and positive interactions (e.g., social contact and conflict management) that enable them to develop stronger relationships later in adulthood.[11]

Relational intelligence plays a critical role in how both children and adults build friendships. There is no standard that may be used as a point of reference in determining whether a relationship may be categorized as a friendship. Friendship is multidimensional in nature and can be established in a number of different ways. Social scientists who study friendship have looked at the construct from three different areas. First, friendships are based on interdependence in that the behavior of each person in the relationship is influenced by the behavior of the other. Second, friendships grow based on the continuity of interaction over an extended period of time. Third and most importantly, there is a social and emotional component (e.g., companionship, emotional support, stimulation, and belongingness) rather than simply means to personal goals and objectives.

Relationally intelligent people build friendships easily because they know how to connect with others. They are skilled at establishing rapport in the early stages of relationships. They ask questions, are curious and inquisitive, and genuinely want to learn about others. They acknowledge and embrace the differences between people. I'm always amazed at the leaders with whom I work who have broad social networks and friendships with a variety of people from different backgrounds and cultural ethnicities. This helps them appreciate the intrinsic value people bring to relationships. Relationally intelligent people are also great at building trust over time. Some of the strongest friendships in my own life have been developed through trust and mutual support. Such people have influenced me in ways I never would have thought possible. Influence began to take place because they invested in getting to know me as a person. With such friendship, there aren't habits of judgment or harsh criticism. Don't get me wrong, some of my closest friends have challenged me to develop and grow. However, they do it from a place of love and support. You might not have been a line leader when you were growing up, but the time you invested in getting to know people and build friendships was what might have enabled you to have a positive influence on the lives of others.

DEALING WITH HIGH-MAINTENANCE FRIENDS

We all have that one friend in our social circle, the one who requires a little extra attention. They often have urgent needs that cause everyone to drop what they are doing to help support them. They are typically the most arrogant and self-centered members of a circle of friends. They like to cling to stories of personal wrongs from the past. They are offended easily and can cause problems for others. They talk a lot, more so than anyone else in your group. The discussion always seems to revolve around their life, their issues, and what's most important to them. They are seldom satisfied with service at a restaurant. They make comments and gossip about others. They're draining and live in a state of perpetual drama.

Jennifer, a colleague of mine today, had a large circle of friends from her time in the restaurant industry. She spent many years working at one of the most renowned restaurants in New York City. I remember Jennifer telling me stories about her friend Marissa, who stood out from the pack. Marissa was the high-strung friend who always had to be the center of attention. The world revolved around her, and if you interfered with this, she would let you know. She was a nice person at heart and was always fun to be around for a night out. She was playful, funny, and often the life of the party. Her friends gravitated toward her because of her high energy and enthusiasm. However, being around her for long periods was draining. Everything had to be about what was going on in her life. When she reached out to my colleague, Jennifer had to drop everything and make sure to attend to her needs.

I remember one story Jennifer shared with me about celebrating Marissa's thirtieth birthday. For years, Marissa was used to having big birthday bashes. Her family always made a big deal for birthdays when she was growing up. As she got older, her family stopped celebrating in a big, elaborate way, so Marissa expected her friends to take the reins. For several years, Jennifer and the rest of Marissa's friends threw massive parties for her. One year, they convinced her that they needed to borrow her car for the day. Marissa begrudgingly agreed. Jennifer took the car to a body shop and had a new stereo surround sound system installed. After the car was ready for pickup, Jennifer and her other friends drove it to her work to pick Marissa up. They had balloons and party favors when they arrived. They took her to Hot 97's Summer Jam festival that night, where they all celebrated in style.

The next year, the girls didn't throw a major bash for Marissa. Some of the girls had hit hard times financially, so there wasn't much money to plan a big party. Instead, they took Marissa out to dinner in New York City. It was a nice evening, but Marissa was so upset and frustrated that they didn't throw a big event that she didn't talk to the entire group for a month. When she did come around and started speaking to them again, she told them how hurt she was that they didn't go all out like she had expected them to do. Jennifer and her other friends were astonished. Marissa's expectations were unreasonable and unfair. It didn't matter, though. Marissa always had to come first even though she never made a big deal for other people's birthdays.

The following year, Marissa was turning thirty. Her friends didn't want to hear all the complaining again, so Jennifer took on the responsibility of planning a major surprise party at a famous nightclub. For months leading up to the party, Marissa's friends planned the event. They reached out to people from her high school and college to invite them to the festivities. They each saved money to cover the fees for the nightclub and purchase a VIP section with bottle service. Because her friends knew they wouldn't hear the end of it if they didn't go big, they had to plan a grand gesture. I asked Jennifer why they did all this when Marissa never reciprocated. She didn't have a compelling answer. They all liked Marissa. She was fun to be around. But it all boiled down to her friends not wanting to deal with her complaining and bitterness if they did not plan something big.

The night of the party, they told Marissa they were going to the city again for a low-key dinner. That was early in the afternoon so she could get ready for a night out. Her friends chipped in for a limo that picked Marissa up at her house that evening. Forty people showed up at the nightclub for the VIP party. It was an expensive night. I think Jennifer told me it cost something like four thousand dollars for the entire event. Marissa had to be the center of attention. She had to be the best dressed of all her girlfriends. She insisted on wearing a tiara all night. Two women who showed up to the party were dressed a little nicer than her. Marissa proceeded to spend most of the evening bashing and bad-mouthing these women. "How could they do that?" "This is my evening!" "It should be all about me!" she said. Marissa was like that most of the time with her friends. She was direct, blunt, and overbearing on most occasions. Her friends could never say anything to confront or challenge her. It would just make things worse. That was the strange thing about her relationships with her friends. Everyone knew what they were going to get from Marissa, but no one ever said anything. She was never manipulative or conniving, but you just had to accept Marissa for the way she was.

The way she treated people did eventually catch up to her. Marissa is the only friend in Jennifer's friend group who has never been married or had any children. She's in her early forties now and still has to be the center of attention. She's been in and out of romantic relationships for the last ten years. She cannot keep a relationship because of the way she behaves. Jennifer and the others almost feel bad for her now. I've heard stories from many clients about that friend who behaves in a similar fashion. I think every group has one of them. It takes a lot to deal with these types of people. The need for attention and approval takes all the energy out of a room. I am fascinated by why people put up with these types of people. My close group of friends used to include someone like this; however, he burned so many bridges over time that we didn't want to be around him any longer. Making everything about yourself pushes people away. Relationships are a give-and-take. You have to be willing to invest in others if you want them to do the same with you.

It takes strong relational intelligence to deal with high-maintenance friends. To a high-maintenance personality, everything is urgent—the problem with their kids, the annoying coworker at work, and the troubles with their family. You get sucked into the drama of their world. Relationally intelligent people know how to assess situations and handle these types of people appropriately. They've taken the time to understand how a high-maintenance friend is wired and how to respond to their needs. They are skilled at setting boundaries and making sure their friend doesn't step on their toes. The sense of entitlement many high-maintenance friends tend to have can also be challenging to navigate. Relationally intelligent people can separate themselves from the emotions of the moment and behave in a helpful fashion. This sometimes means giving a little more to their high-maintenance friend in the situations and circumstances that demand it.

Because high-maintenance people are seldom satisfied, intimacy with them forces relationally intelligent people to come up with ways to deal with constant arguing and complaining. Even if high-maintenance friends are given extra care and attention, they will invariably find something wrong with the solution or service they receive. They always seem to feel the need to ask for additional adjustments to gratify their need to feel validated and served. If you have a friend like this in your group, I believe it is important to set guardrails around the relationship. Most high-maintenance people live in a perpetual state of drama that they create in their minds. If you are around one of these types of people for an extended period, you will observe frequent periods of meltdown during the course of a day. Even small inconveniences or mistakes become crises. I've found that you have to treat these behaviors as what they are. It usually takes an empathetic and caring person to just listen and hear out a high-maintenance friend. If they are given the attention that they are demanding, it usually calms the situation down.

I would caution you to be careful about what you share with high-maintenance friends, however. They are obsessed with details—theirs and yours. They are highly focused on the too-much-information and the none-of-your-business particulars of others. They will usually ask more questions than they should and are quick to spread gossip around. They can hurt people with their words and create unnecessary drama that doesn't need to take place. It is extremely difficult for these types of individuals to see outside of the moment and into the bigger picture. Instead, they hold fast to their personal opinions and the credit they should receive for keeping everyone informed. So keep your guard up. Give them enough information to quench their incessant need for details, but don't let them in too closely. Such boundaries will save you the heartache of dealing with problems later on. Using your relational intelligence to deal with these types of people will help you navigate the relationship. It will also protect you from the potential damage they can cause.

Relational intelligence is an important skill to practice in all our closest friendships. People who are relationally intelligent build more lasting bonds with others. They are skilled at establishing rapport and forming early positive connections with people. They take time to learn about their friends and sow into the relationships. They embrace individual differences and are eager to learn about different people's backgrounds and experiences. This enables them to have a wide variety of friends in their social circles. They develop trust by being compassionate and by making sure to honor their commitments with others. They cultivate influence and have a positive impact on others because they want to see their friends develop and grow. Make sure you invest time in developing your most personal relationships. You'll be amazed at the lifelong friendships you create with others.

---

1   C. R. Knee, "Implicit Theories of Relationships: Assessment and Prediction of Romantic Relationship Initiation, Coping, and Longevity," *Journal of Personality and Social Psychology* 74 (1998): 360–370.

2   P. M. Van Lange and C. E. Rusbult, "Interdependence Theory," in *Handbook of Theories on Social Psychology*, eds. P. M. Van Lange, A. W. Kruglanski, and E. T. Higgins (Thousand Oaks, California: SAGE Publishing, 2012), 251–272.

3   R. Larson, R. Mannell, and J. Zuzanek, "Daily Well-Being of Older Adults with Friends and Family," *Psychology and Aging* 1 (1986): 117–126.

4   D. I. Walker, R. Curren, and C. Jones, "Good Friendships among Children: A Theoretical and Empirical Investigation," *Journal for the Theory of Social Behavior* 46 (2016): 286–309.

5   E. E. Graham, "Turning Points and Commitment in Post-Divorce Relationships," *Communication Monographs* 64 (1997): 351–368.

6   T. Docan-Morgan and V. Manusov, "Relational Turning Points Events and Their Outcomes in College Teacher-Student Relationships from Students' Perspectives," *Communication Education* 58 (2009): 155–188.

7   T. W. Farmer, D. B. Estell, J. L. Bishop, K. O'Neal, and B. Cairns, "Rejected Bullies or Popular Leaders? The Social Relations of Aggressive Subtypes in Rural African American Early Adolescents," *Developmental Psychology* 39 (2003): 992–1,004.

8   M. Popper and O. Mayseless, "Internal World of Transformation Leaders," in *Monographs in Leadership and Management: Volume 2, Transformational and Charismatic Leadership—The Road Ahead*, eds. B. J. Avolio and F. J. Yammarino (New York, New York: Elsevier Publishing, 2002), 203–229.

9   R. D. Arvey, M. Rotundo, W. Johnson, Z. Zhang, and M. McGue, "The Determinants of Leadership Role Occupancy: Genetic and Personality Factors," *The Leadership Quarterly* 17 (2006): 1–20.

10 W. M. Bukowski and B. Hoza, "Popularity and Friendship: Issues in Theory, Measurement, and Outcome," in *Peer Relationships in Child Development*, eds. T. J. Berndt and G. W. Ladd (New York, New York: Wiley Publishing, 1989), 15–45.

11 M. Azmitia and R. Montgomery, "Friendship, Transactive Dialogues, and the Development of Scientific Reasoning," *Social Development* 2, no. 3 (1993): 202–221.

PROFESSIONAL
RELATIONSHIPS

You can build more relationships at work in two months
by becoming interested in other people than you can in
two years trying to get other people interested in you.
—Dale Carnegie

We spend most of our lives at work. The relationships we build with colleagues and coworkers are critical to our development as professionals. These types of relationships develop over time. They can start by being on the same team with others. Working closely with someone day in and day out allows you to learn about how people are wired and what makes them tick. You learn about how they think about their work. You pick up on habits and behaviors that can help you be more effective in the work that you do. You get exposure to different ways of thinking. You learn how to collaborate and accomplish collective goals. You develop ways to influence the activities of others. You find ways to fit in and establish credibility in the eyes of the people who matter most. Our professional relationships can be some of the most important ones in our lives. Good professional mentors or role models help us develop the skills we will need to succeed both inside and outside our career.

I've found that you can learn just as much from strong role models as you can from bad ones. In my days at Sears, I learned more about how not to treat people based on the things I saw from some of my coworkers. They were competitive with others and were regularly engaged in counterproductive work behaviors. Some of these behaviors included lying, manipulation, and pitting people against one another to get an advantage over people. These toxic relationships can cause a lot of problems for team members. They can lower people's motivation and cause some to ask for a transfer to a different business unit or even quit a job. When the relationships are strong, though, people tend to flourish. This is the most important factor for relationships between managers and their direct reports. These partnerships are critical to how both parties develop relationships with other colleagues across organizations. When there is a healthy partnership between leaders and the people they oversee, growth and development are accelerated. I've seen this time and time again in the companies with whom I work. I regularly encourage my clients to sow into relationships with their people, as it is the best way to drive performance and productivity.

Some of the most impactful relationships we develop on a professional level happen organically. I've had this happen several times in my career. One of my strongest professional relationships is with Janet, a seasoned consulting psychologist and leadership advisor. I met Janet about two years after I completed my doctoral degree. At the time, I was starting to build connections both inside the firm for which I was working and outside with colleagues in our industry. I met Janet at an annual conference for business psychologists. I was an eager young consultant who was actively networking and looking to build relationships with more senior people in our field. Most of the folks that I met didn't really take time to get to know me. They introduced themselves, made small talk for a little bit, and moved on to others. Janet didn't do that, though. She came right up to me and introduced herself during the cocktail hour reception the first night of the conference. We talked for most of the evening. We discussed my background, the firm where I was employed, and the research I was interested in doing. She shared some of her experiences about the conference, told me about her practice, and invited me to a breakout session she was leading the following day on women in leadership and diversity and inclusion.

The next day, I went to her session, and she introduced me to the rest of the consultants on the panel. Their presentation was compelling. Janet and one of her colleagues had a roundtable discussion with three women who were senior executives in the sales and marketing fields. They talked about the challenges facing women in corporate America. They discussed the importance of building teams made of diverse leaders. They highlighted research on the treatment women received compared to men in senior leadership roles. After the discussion, Janet invited me out to lunch to explain more about the conference and how to network effectively and meet new people. She told me about some of the key stakeholders at the conference every year. Later that day, she introduced me to others and helped me get to know a number of different people. We exchanged numbers at the end of the conference and began communicating frequently over the next year. We would get together every few months for coffee or a meal to discuss our professional endeavors and the work we were doing with our clients.

The following year, Janet was voted on to the board of directors for our professional business psychologists society. She quickly asked if I wanted to help chair the annual conference that year. She connected me with the right people and helped me secure a position on the conference planning team. Over the next eight to twelve months, she began mentoring me across a number of different areas. I always found her to be extremely helpful and supportive of the work I was doing. It didn't matter what questions I had for her or the projects with which I was involved; she always made time for me. A year later, she encouraged me to apply for a role on the board as the treasurer for the professional society. I won the nomination and became a member of the board. It was a three-year term. We got to work very closely together over that period. I found Janet to be insightful about people and relationships. She had strong relational intelligence and modeled the right behaviors when she was interacting with others.

Our relationship grew over the next five years as both of our careers began to prosper and grow. We developed a great deal of trust during that period. I could go to her for counsel or advice about clients. She began leveraging my research and the work I was doing on leadership and influence. We got to work on several consulting engagements together. Janet had a passionate and fiery work ethic. She was candid and direct, and she challenged people to expand their thinking. I saw her do this with colleagues and clients. People resonated with her approach to leadership development. As our relationship continues to develop over the years, we have become strong friends. When I struggled with addiction and lost both my job and my marriage, she was one of the only people to whom I went for support. I trusted that she had my best interests at heart. She never criticized or judged me. She lovingly helped and supported me through that challenging and extremely difficult period.

When I started my own firm, she helped me get things off the ground and provided guidance in building my business. Today, Janet and I work together regularly. I attribute the evolution of our professional relationship to the type of leader and consultant she is. She's been an inspirational role model to me during different seasons of my career. I also try to be a good colleague and friend to her as she continues to develop and grow. We have both added value to each other's lives. We have been a stable point in each other's career trajectories over the years. We all need colleagues and coworkers in our lives who provide this guidance and support. I've now looked for ways to pay this forward with younger consultants I have mentored over the last several years. The relationship Janet has built with me is a reference point for the connections I look to develop with others. I've learned how to give others guidance and support. I've gone out of my way to help others get exposure to the work we do. I attribute my ability and interest in doing so to the investment Janet made in me early in my career. It has served as a foundation for the way I support others in my professional life.

DEVELOPING WORLD-CLASS NETWORKS

Networking is a powerful thing for building relationships and learning about others. I regularly recommend that my clients do it consistently with those with whom they work. I've seen many leaders dramatically improve their relationship-building skills by connecting with people from different parts of their organizations and industries. A few years back, I started working with Jonathan, a senior executive in the telecommunications industry. Jonathan was an outgoing, playful, and gregarious leader. He easily established rapport with leaders at all levels of his organization. He learned this skill early in his career. He knew that if he wanted to grow professionally and align himself with the right people, he had to make connections with stakeholders from different functions and business units.

When Jonathan was promoted into a vice president role, he started going out of his way to meet new leaders as they integrated into the organization. He connected with cross-functional business partners. He requested time with people above him to introduce himself and learn about the work they did. At first, this was to help him cultivate an understanding of how he could better support the initiatives of his leaders. People gravitated to Jonathan because he took time to build relationships. Over a three-year period, he built a strong network across the organization, and leaders began coming to him to share ideas and solve problems together. Jonathan became known as a master networker. He did such a good job of connecting with people that his boss's manager started inviting him to senior-level meetings and leveraging him to drive business-related projects. Because Jonathan was an extremely hard worker and knew the ins and outs of the business, he got involved in many different projects and initiatives. The leader of his division started handing him more and more responsibilities. They became close friends and partners. This helped advance Jonathan's career for a number of years.

Six months before I began coaching him, there was major restructuring and organizational change across the enterprise. The division president that Jonathan knew so well, and had worked closely with for years, was exited from the organization. Because Jonathan had invested so much time in getting to know this leader and his team, his major alliances were with just one group of people. All these relationships had now changed. Leaders from other parts of the business began assuming responsibility for the key leadership roles in Jonathan's business unit. Jonathan began to try and build relationships with these leaders, but he started to get a reputation for talking too much and sharing information with the wrong people. What had worked so well for him earlier in his career seemed to have backfired. People didn't trust him to keep information they shared close to the vest. He never did anything to break trust or damage relationships, but a few leaders felt he had developed a reputation for being a busybody. His new manager and HRBP chalked this up to Jonathan having poor EQ skills and a lack of political savvy.

When the next round of promotions came, Jonathan was overlooked for a key senior vice president role and was told he had to work on his executive presence and relationship-building skills. This was highly frustrating and disappointing given that he had spent so much time networking with people for years. Yet all the leaders with whom he had connected had left the organization or moved outside his area of responsibility. When we met for one of our first coaching sessions, Jonathan explained what had happened and his frustrations with the organization. He believed he was overlooked because of the alliances he had built over the years and that other leaders became jealous of the senior-level relationships he had developed. Although this may or may not have been the case, perceptions are always reality for people. I empathized with his perspective but recommended that we conduct a 360-degree assessment to determine if his EQ and political savvy skills were the main problem. Jonathan agreed that this would be the right approach to take, so we pulled together a list of twelve to fifteen people with whom I could speak. The findings were compelling. Most of the people that he worked with were highly complementary about his leadership style and the brand he had created over many years. However, there was a small pocket of people—and they happened to be the key decision-makers—who felt that he had not taken the news about not getting the promotion well. They spoke about how he communicated his frustrations with the wrong people and did not like his etiquette in some key leadership meetings following the promotion decisions.

When I shared the feedback with him, Jonathan was blown away. Although he was upset about the decisions that were made, he felt that he wasn't engaging in any inappropriate behaviors or complaining about being overlooked. I told him that even though this might have been the case, we had to work on how he read a room and the impressions he left on others. I admired Jonathan for taking the feedback to heart and for committing to start practicing behaviors that would leave a positive impression on his colleagues. We put together three goals in his personal development plan: develop his EQ, cultivate a deeper understanding of how to strengthen his political savvy, and work on developing his impression management skills. Over the course of the next several months, Jonathan made a concerted effort to drive the appropriate behavioral changes. He listened more and leaned into conversations with people. He asked questions and didn't step into meetings to take up all the airtime. He solicited feedback from his manager and other key stakeholders about the behavioral changes he had implemented. He also began networking with the people who had moved over to his business unit from other parts of the organization. Because of his frustrations with the promotion decisions, he had stopped trying to connect with others for a while. Though networking was one of his strongest suits, he had neglected to invest the necessary time to consistently do it.

By the end of our coaching engagement, Jonathan had dramatically improved his leadership skills. He had developed a better understanding of how to read a room and engage with people in the appropriate manner. Afterward, he took time to establish rapport by asking questions rather than broadcasting the things he knew. He embraced individual differences with others and didn't have to be the smartest person in the room. He developed trust by honoring his commitments and delivering results. When the next round of promotions was made, Jonathan was given a senior vice president role overseeing a larger team. Many of the leaders with whom he had networked and built relationships became his direct reports. They trusted him and bought into his vision. I saw him make dramatic improvements to how he led people.

I learned three valuable lessons from working with Jonathan. First, networking is not a one-time event. You have to consistently invest in building new relationships throughout your career. What you did yesterday to establish connections with others may not always work today. You have to adapt and adjust your approach to meet the needs of different stakeholders. Two, you always have to manage the impressions that you leave on others. Just having relational capital with certain people does not mean that you stop investing in new partnerships and alliances. Networking and building relationships must be a continual priority if you're going to learn how to have a positive impact on others. Lastly and most importantly, it takes strong relational intelligence to understand how to influence people. You have to treat every relationship differently. Certain things that help build a relationship with one leader won't necessarily work with others. You have to learn how to read people and situations, then flex your style to connect with different stakeholders.

Networking is often defined as behaviors that are aimed at building, maintaining, and using informal relationships that possess the potential benefit of facilitating work-related activities or outcomes for people.[1] People who build dynamic networks are skilled at developing a wide variety of relationships with different types of people. They use their relational intelligence to get to know others and invest the appropriate amount of time to build long-term relationships. They are curious about people and find value not only in how they can benefit from having a network but also in the deep connections they build with others. Much of the work industrial-organizational psychologists have conducted on networking behaviors has made it clear that the quality and scope of an employee's network has a substantial impact on their ability to solve problems, learn new things, and build sustainable relationships over time. Many books and articles that have been published suggest that networking behaviors, such as going out for drinks to discuss business matters informally or staying in contact with former colleagues, are essential to career success.[2]

Some of the best networkers with whom I've worked place a strong emphasis on how they build relationships with people. They have a large repertoire of skills they use to establish rapport with colleagues. They're playful and humorous. They have high energy and are passionate about their work. They ask incisive questions and are great active listeners. They are empathetic and seek to understand the emotions of others. They value diversity and appreciate individual differences. They go out of their way to make others feel comfortable. They develop trust by investing in relationships. They look to give more than they want to receive. They're the type of people who are easy to get along with. They use their influence for the greater good. These qualities enable them to build lasting relationships across organizational boundaries.

I've found that many high-potential employees are usually skilled at using their relational intelligence to build strong networks. These types of employees value the connections they build with others. They do more than just perform well on the job. They seek to establish relationships that will enhance their visibility and connectivity to key stakeholders across their organizations. Research by organizational psychologists supports these observations. Researchers have found three important features of high performers' networks. The first is structural. High performers have a greater tendency to position themselves at key points in a network, and they leverage the network around them better when implementing plans. The second is relational. High performers tend to invest in relationships that extend expertise and help them avoid learning biases and career traps. The third is behavioral. High performers value networks and engage in behaviors that lead to high-quality relationships, not just big networks. Employees who do well in these three dimensions are more likely to be successful than those who pay little to no attention to their networks.[3]

Most people engage in networking behaviors to help build developmental relationships. However, the degree to which people network depends on a number of different factors. Researchers have found five types of networking behavior: maintaining contacts, socializing, engaging in professional activities, participating in the community, and increasing internal visibility.[4] Gender, socioeconomic background, extraversion, self-esteem, and attitudes toward workplace politics have also been found to be related to networking behaviors of leaders and professionals. Networking has been found to have a direct relationship to valuable career outcomes, such as enhanced promotions and compensation, given that engaging in networking behavior is one means a person can use to develop their social capital. Social capital often refers to the structure of people's contact networks—the pattern of interconnection among the various people to whom an individual is tied.[5] Social capital constitutes a valuable resource. The relationships a person has with others can provide access to new information, resources, and opportunities. A more diverse network of relationships can extend one's reach into different social circles and consequently enhance the quality of their connections with others.

Although developing strong networks is beneficial to everyone, there are differences in their benefits to men and women. Research has found that networking behaviors typically favor men over women. Historically, one explanation for this may be that work assignments, task forces, or committees in which women are involved are less prestigious than men's. Research has found that women traditionally have less access to influential people and powerful coalitions in organizations.[6] The concept of the "good old boys' club" comes to mind around the discrepancies that have existed for many years. However, in the last fifteen to twenty years, these dynamics have changed dramatically. With the proliferation of management development programs geared toward cultivating leadership skills in women, the benefits of networking have been more balanced. I've found that women tend to be exceptional network developers. Women are more empathetic and relationship-oriented than many of their male counterparts, and this contributes to their ability to build diverse networks both inside and outside their organizations.

People build networks for many different reasons (e.g., work performance, career advancement, or job searching). Research assuming the networking for work performance perspective conceptualizes networking as a practice that enables managers or leaders to access interpersonal resources that are necessary and useful for facilitating work-related activities.[7] Specifically, managers network to develop informal relationships with professional colleagues to access interpersonal resources that facilitate task performance or leader behaviors. Within career management literature, networking is often regarded as an essential behavior for maintaining and advancing one's career because it enables people to acquire resources (e.g., information, influence, or friendship) from network contacts, which can be leveraged for career success. The perceived breadth and depth of one's external network has been shown to promote perceived control over a person's career, security in one's employment situation, and the perception that someone is valued by current or alternative employers.[8] Networking in the job search context explicitly entails developing and using network contacts who are capable of providing information concerning alternative employment opportunities for people. Studies within this perspective suggest that the more intensely one networks, the more likely one is to acquire quality job information from their contacts.[9] Also, when conceptualized as a network of contacts that a person can approach for job leads, networking is positively related to one's ability to acquire and act on high-quality job offers.

We all need to build networks as we continue to develop and grow. People with strong relational intelligence have better opportunities to do so. Relational intelligence enables people to build relationships that can benefit both themselves and others. Although someone can use networks to get to desired professional outcomes, networks can also be used to add value to others. Employees who become great networkers do it over time. They learn from past experiences and find new and different ways to connect with others. They are not afraid to make themselves vulnerable and walk into situations with a learning orientation. Becoming a world-class networker should be a goal for every relationally intelligent person. You get to sharpen and refine your interpersonal skills through the exposure you get to different types of people.

FORCES OF NATURE: EVERY TEAM HAS ONE

We have all worked with that one person who is extremely difficult to get along with. They are usually stubborn and always have to get their way. They love the spotlight and rarely share credit with others. They engage in counterproductive work behaviors, like lying, manipulation, and intimidation. They create problems between people. They like to pit teammates against one another. They spread rumors and talk behind people's backs. Several years ago, I worked with a CFO succession candidate in the real estate industry. Chris was the type of leader others wanted to be around. He built relationships easily with people. He was caring and compassionate toward colleagues. He partnered effectively with leaders across the enterprise. He invested time in developing and growing the capabilities of his people.

We started working together when he was given additional responsibilities over investor relations and corporate strategy for his organization. One of the mandates from the board and the CEO was for Chris to bring together a team of cross-functional colleagues to map out a three- to five-year strategy for the business. He needed to assemble a group of leaders from all parts of the organization. When we started our coaching work together, we discussed the types of people he needed on the team. He needed folks who were innovative and who thought about the future direction of the business. He needed practical people who would challenge ideas. He needed folks who understood the culture and had years of institutional knowledge about the company's history. He had to find good partners who would work together collaboratively. His CEO allowed him to pick most of his team members, but he wanted Chris to add Jennifer to the team. Jennifer had a history of being a challenge to work with. She always had to be the smartest person in the room. She was combative and often caused problems for others. Chris's CEO liked her though, and she frequently went to him when issues started to surface. He would often side with her on major decision-making, which frustrated others. In the first meeting I observed, I could see why she was so hard to work with. It was Chris's meeting, but she had to be in the spotlight. She challenged others' ideas with little to no awareness of the impact she was having on the room. Chris tried to move the meeting along, but she was constantly interrupting and slowing things down. He split the team into small committees that would be responsible for focusing on different parts of the strategy. Jennifer insisted on being involved in the highest visibility part of the plan. She bullied her committee members and pushed for her ideas to be implemented.

Over the next six months, she wreaked havoc on the team. People didn't trust her, and they didn't want to work with her. Over this period, I learned that Chris had great relational intelligence. He invested time to strengthen his relationships with all the members of his team. He took time to listen and to make sure all points of view were heard. Given that Jennifer was such a problem, he went out of his way on multiple occasions to appease her. He would regularly go to her for input but did most of this behind the scenes. This ensured that her ideas were heard and that he never put her down in front of others. It was extremely challenging to get her to work with others, but he found ways to keep Jennifer from derailing the team. He even found ways to build trust with her despite her actions and behaviors. In the end, the team developed a strong strategy that they shared with the C-suite and the board. Employees were aligned with the approach the team wanted to take for the future. Chris had made it work because he built individual relationships with all his colleagues, including Jennifer even though she was difficult to work with.

I learned three valuable lessons about relational intelligence from my coaching work with Chris. First, patience plays a big role in dealing with difficult people. Relationally intelligent leaders don't have to get their ways all the time. They can adapt, adjust, and go with the flow. Second, they know how to influence without authority. Even though Chris was the leader of the strategy team, he never used or abused this power. He made everyone feel that their opinions mattered. When Jennifer pushed hard to get her way, he would redirect the energy to positive outcomes rather than negative ones. Lastly, relationally intelligent leaders embrace individual differences with challenging people by making them feel valued and appreciated. Even though they have to work with difficult personalities, they know how to peel the onion back a few layers and get at the main concerns or issues of these types of people.

Counterproductive work behaviors (CWB) consist of behaviors that harm or intend to harm organizations or people in organizations. They remain a costly issue for organizations and their employees. For example, it has been reported that up to 75 percent of employees, on at least one occasion, have engaged in negative and destructive behaviors (e.g., verbal aggression, combativeness, or interpersonal conflict) in their organizations.[10] Given the cost and frequency of CWB, organizational psychologists have examined its environmental and individual predictors. Some researchers have linked occupational stressors with CWB. Others have looked for the link between people's personalities and their engagement in negative work behaviors. These factors contribute to acts of physical or verbal aggression, sabotage, work avoidance, or purposefully flawed work. Over time, interpersonal conflict has garnered an increased amount of attention by organizational psychologists, and many studies have documented its potentially detrimental relationship with outcomes such as depression, job satisfaction, and intention to quit. Concerning its relationship with CWB, studies have found that interpersonal conflict is associated with sabotage, interpersonal aggression, and hostility.[11]

Conflict between employees has consistently been found to have the strongest relationship with CWB. This usually has to do with a number of situational variables and organizational constraints. Organizational constraints are situations that prevent employees from using their abilities to achieve heightened job performance. Many of my clients deal with challenges related to lack of resources for projects or limited buy-in from senior management in the attainment of goals and objectives. Situations as these are often the breeding ground for CWBs. In particular, conflict between employees tends to happen when there are alignment issues between different functions or business units. Employees who do not have support from their leaders to drive key initiatives often seek out other means to move their agendas forward. Such means can often result in bullying or causing interpersonal conflict with colleagues. This was the case with Jennifer and many of her coworkers. Even though Chris had backing from senior management to develop the organization's strategy, the details of the plan were undetermined. Jennifer pushed her agenda forward often at the expense of others.

Narcissism is often found to be an important personality predictor of CWB. The trait reflects self-aggrandizement with those high on narcissism having fantasies about control, admiration, and success. As I've discussed in the chapter on cultivating influence, narcissists come across as arrogant, aggressive, and self-promotional. In the workplace, a narcissist's sense of entitlement and felt exemption from all the standards that apply to others leads to poor-quality social exchanges and negative perceptions of them by others. Studies have found that narcissistic employees tend to provide less individual consideration for their colleagues or coworkers.[12] I've seen this time and time again in the organizations I work with. The narcissists tend to be the employees who cause the most problems for others. They cause interpersonal conflict by having to get their way and becoming combative and aggressive when others disagree with their goals or objectives.

There are several ways to deal with difficult employees. You can either give in to them or challenge their behaviors. Relationally intelligent people know how to balance the give-and-take required to effectively partner with these types of individuals. First, they invest time to understand the underlying motivations of challenging coworkers. This entails getting to know people on a personal and professional level. Several years ago, I worked with a senior executive who had to deal with a lot of conflict from one of their cross-functional colleagues. The difficult employee regularly lashed out at people and was verbally abusive. Rather than fight back, I advised my client to go out of their way to build a relationship with the person. She did simple things to establish rapport (e.g., asking about the colleague's personal life and finding ways to connect with them about things outside of work). She solicited feedback from the aggressive colleague to ensure the person felt their concerns were being taken into account. She found ways to include the person in key decisions that were being made. This mitigated the person's CWBs and created more opportunities for collaboration.

Second, relationally intelligent leaders are great at building trust with difficult employees. They honor their commitments to such individuals and go out of their way to offer a lending hand or to be a supportive resource in times of change or uncertainty. These tendencies build strong alliances that usually help prevent conflict. It doesn't work all the time, but I have seen clients who build trust consistently reduce the tension and friction that exist when difficult employees try to get their way. Lastly, relationally intelligent people cultivate influence on difficult coworkers by seeking to find mutually agreed upon goals that will make the other person feel valued and appreciated. In many cases, people who are forces of nature struggle with some form of poor self-esteem or insecurity. The relationally intelligent person can identify these issues and are empathetic toward them. This creates a personal connection that garners alignment and commitment from a person who presents problems. So next time you see a person engaging in CWBs and causing interpersonal conflict, stop to look at the situation more deeply. The most difficult and challenging colleagues usually have more issues under the surface that others aren't taking the time to understand. If you invest in building the relationship, you can make your workplace a better environment for your people and teams.

SERVICE WITH A SMILE: BUILDING EXCELLENT CUSTOMER RELATIONSHIPS

Early in my career, I had the privilege of working with many great management consultants. Greg was one of my first professional mentors. He quickly took me under his wing when I joined his consulting firm. Greg was a thirty-year veteran of the leadership and management consulting field. He had served in many different roles during his tenure at the firm. One thing I respected about him right away was the way he served our clients. He was great at getting to know people and building relationships. It didn't matter what level a person was in their organization. Greg always found ways to connect and deliver excellent customer service. He was an active listener and sought to understand the perspectives of others. He always exceeded our clients' expectations by going out of his way to ensure our work was of the highest quality. He honored his commitments and was consistent in both his words and actions. He was never overly aggressive or assertive when it came to selling our services. Clients knew Greg had their best interests at heart, so they easily followed his advice and counsel. Many of the leaders with whom he worked saw Greg as a trusted advisor rather than a vendor or consultant. This was the result of the time and energy he poured into relationships.

I can vividly remember the first consultant engagement I got to work on with Greg. We were doing a CEO succession project for a midsize consumer products company. It was early in my career, so there was a lot I needed to learn. The night before our first meeting with the CHRO, Greg sat me down at dinner and took me through objectives for the next day. He mapped out how we would approach initial conversations with the CEO and CHRO. He walked me through the interview protocol for the conversations we would have with each of the board members. He outlined the engagement from start to finish in a clear and concise manner. He also told me about the importance of delivering excellent service to our clients. Such service was more than just doing a good job on the engagement. It was about investing in getting to know these leaders and establishing rapport. It was about really taking the time to understand their needs and embracing who they were as leaders.

Greg had an incredible knack for playing at the right level with clients. He could spend the morning with the CEO and fully engage the client in a discussion. That afternoon, he could be on the factory floor and make connections with assembly-line workers. He had a way of connecting with people and making others feel valued and appreciated. Greg was skilled at quickly getting to the underlying psychology and makeup of his clients, then leveraging the information to drive impact. I saw him do this time and time again with different stakeholders. He developed trust by making sure we always delivered exceptional work. He also taught me the art of delivery. Many times, it wasn't "what" we were saying to our clients but "how" we said it that made the difference. He knew how to deliver tough feedback and have a difficult conversation. At the same time, he created an environment of psychological safety, where people could let their guards down and be authentic with our team. This came from the time he spent cultivating relationships.

As I got to know Greg on a deeper level, I was amazed at his relational intelligence. He was a resource to our clients as they navigated obstacles, challenges, and adversity. He knew how to develop effective strategies and coping mechanisms for managing people's stress and anxiety. He always made himself available to the key stakeholders in an engagement. It didn't matter the time of day or how busy he was with other duties or responsibilities; he was there for our clients. He made sure they could always come to him when they needed to. This also had a positive impact on our consulting team. Greg treated his people the same way he treated his clients, which created trust with the team. He created a culture of autonomy and empowerment. This also encouraged us to deliver excellent services to the clients we worked with during an engagement. It pushed us to bring our best to any piece of work we touched.

Greg was also skilled at balancing his work and personal life. He had challenges like any of us did, but they never affected the way he showed up for clients. He brought the highest levels of professionalism to our work. His methods galvanized our team and made each of us bring our A game when we interacted with our clients. I learned three valuable lessons from Greg. First, as management consultants, we must always look the part. Appearance, verbal and nonverbal behaviors, and our knowledge and expertise were critical. Greg taught me how to show up in a room with different clients, how to balance influence with partnership, and how to drive impact that led to repeat business and referrals. Second, he showed me that working with clients was a long-term game. You must always be mindful of where the next piece of work could come. Greg truly understood clients' needs and anticipated how those needs would evolve over time. Third, he taught me how to have swagger as a consultant. Clients hired us for our expertise, but there was a fine balance between confidence and arrogance. Greg taught me how to walk that line. He helped me hone the skills needed to be the expert in the room but showed me how to influence people without authority or positional power. This was one of the major keys to having long-term relationships with our clients. They wanted to feel that we were in it with them, and that we were always there to support their initiatives. Delivering great service to our clients or customers did not happen overnight. It required hard work, discipline, and a commitment to excellence. All these start and end with relationship building. You cannot influence people if you do not first win their hearts and minds.

Customer service is an organizational behavior cocreated by three organizational constituents: management or ownership, coworkers, and customers. Researchers have described how influences from these three constituents can affect service provider behavior during service encounters.[13] There are several customer variables, such as demographics, behavior, mood, and affect, that impact the nature of the relationships. Contextual variables, such as organizational environment, structure, leadership, and coworkers, also play a role. Service orientation plays an additional critical role in the relationships between employees and customers. Service orientation is a set of attitudes and behaviors that affect the staff of any organization and its customers.[14]

Several models have been developed highlighting the extent to which employees' customer orientation is related to consumers' perceptions of a service organization's performance, showing that elements of employee performance, physical goods quality, and service quality influence consumers' perceptions of overall customer service quality. One model, in particular, presents customer orientation as a service practice that assesses the degree to which an organization emphasizes, in multiple ways, meeting customer needs and expectations for service quality.[15] Employees delivering service on the front lines have an influence on how customers view their experiences with services. Relationally intelligent employees are more likely to build the types of relationships that lead to repeat business and sustainable partnerships over time. Factors like establishing rapport and understanding customer needs before offering services play a critical role in the quality of the relationship. Developing trust is also important for the relationship to grow and customers to come back for repeat business.

Standards and practices of organizations represent an important part of a company's mission, as they provide guidelines for how products and services are produced, delivered, and evaluated. Managerial philosophies and values influence an organization's internal business practices, which, in turn, influence employee and customer interactions and behaviors. If standards for service delivery set the stage for desired performance, then employees involved in the service process should use the existing standards as a guide to offer support to others to ensure that appropriate service-related behaviors are ultimately delivered to the customers. To deliver exceptional customer service, coworker support also plays a critical role. Coworker support is the degree to which employees believe that their coworkers are willing to provide them with work-related assistance to aid in the execution of their service-based duties and responsibilities. In most instances, coworkers' perceived support is vital to the accomplishment of work-related tasks but influences more than just tangible issues, such as areas like morale. Coworker support, whether formal or informal, is usually void of hierarchical differences, likely supplements formal support offered by managers, and should be based on the espoused organizational standards for service delivery.

Customer orientation is the important service providers place on their customers' needs related to service offerings and the extent to which service providers are willing to put forth time and effort to satisfy their customers.[16] Customer orientation is a product of the customer service process and is influenced by exposure to and relationships with the customers, coworkers, and leaders involved in the service process. It represents a service provider's level of commitment to their customers. Service providers who routinely modify their service delivery to anticipate and meet the needs of their customers are customer-oriented. For example, customer-oriented behavior may involve offering a customer more choices and suggestions to enhance their service experience. When service providers receive support from their coworkers and managers while performing their duties, it will likely lead to a stronger commitment to the service process, particularly when the supportive actions of others are based on the organization's standards for service delivery.

How customers react to service experiences is the main concern for people in the business of providing service. Role theory is useful in describing connections between employees' and customers' perceptions. Role theory suggests that when both parties conceptually understand and accept their roles in the customer service experience, their expectations are more likely to be met or exceeded.[17] If either customer or service provider senses a process violation, their satisfaction with the experience is likely to be negatively influenced, as people involved in the service episode will attempt to reconcile their perceived differences. Research conducted by organizational psychologists has indicated that service providers' positive perceptions of service processes are linked with customers' positive perceptions. When service providers have a high level of commitment to their role in the service process, realized as customer orientation, they are more likely to be motivated to consistently offer their customers a level of service that is satisfying.[18]

Customer satisfaction, service quality perceptions, and decisions to remain loyal or to switch service providers are significantly influenced by the attitudes and behaviors of employees. Poor core service can be compensated for by having peripheral strengths. In this sense, friendly types of behaviors of the service staff have proved to improve service outcomes. The range of friendly types of behaviors includes friendliness, familiarity, caring, politeness, responsiveness, trustworthiness, helpfulness, and understanding. The development of all these skills is critical to relationally intelligent employees. When we work on client engagements, there is a high standard of service and quality etiquette we expect from our consultants. When these behaviors are consistently displayed, they lead to excellent customer service. How we deliver our services is just as important as what we are providing.

At our firm, we select employees who embody our core values and practices. Some of the must-have values for our people include reliability, ability to get in the trenches with our clients, high-decency quotient, curiosity, passion for our work, political savvy, proactive initiative, and strong relational intelligence. I've found that over time, relational intelligence is the greatest factor in how we grow our business. When our team members take time to cultivate dynamic relationships with clients, it leads to exceptional quality of service and repeat business over time. Relational intelligence also plays a role in how we partner on client engagements together. The trust developed between team members challenges everyone to bring their best to the work that we do. Most of our client engagements grow over time as a direct result of our ability to collaborate effectively with key stakeholders.

---

[1]   H. G. Wolff and K. Moser, "Effects of Networking on Career Success: A Longitudinal Study," *Journal of Applied Psychology* 94, no. 1 (2009): 196–206.

[2] A. R. Nierenber, *Nonstop Networking* (Herndon, Virginia: Capital Books, 2002).

[3] R. Cross and R. J. Thomas, "How Top Talent Uses Networks and Where Rising Stars Get Trapped," *Organizational Dynamics* 37, no. 2 (2008):165–180.

[4] M. L. Forret and T. W. Dougherty, "Correlates of Networking Behavior for Managerial and Professional Employees," *Group and Organization Management* 26 (2001): 283–311.

[5] H. J. Raider and R. S. Burt, "Boundaryless Careers and Social Capital," in *The Boundaryless Career*, eds. M. B. Arthur and D. M. Rousseau (New York: Oxford University Press, 1996), 187–200.

[6] D. J. Brass, "Men's and Women's Networks: A Study of Interaction Patterns and Influence in an Organization," *Administrative Science Quarterly* 29 (1985): 518–539.

[7] F. Luthans, S. A. Rosenkrantz, and H. Hennessey, "What Do Successful Managers Really Do? An Observational Study of Managerial Activities," *Journal of Applied Behavioral Science* 21 (1985): 255–270.

[8] S. N. Colakoglu, "The Impact of Career Boundarylessness on Subjective Career Success: The Role of Career Competencies, Career Autonomy, and Career Insecurity," *Journal of Vocational Behavior* 79 (2011): 47–59.

[9] T. A. Lambert, L. T. Eby, and M. P. Reeves, "Predictors of Networking Intensity and Network Quality among With-Collar Job Seekers," *Journal of Career Development* 32 (2006): 351–365.

[10] P. E. Spector and S. Fox, eds., "The Stressor-Emotion Model of Counterproductive Work Behavior," in *Counteproductive Work Behavior: Investigations of Actors and Targets* (Washington, DC: American Psychological Association, 2005), 151–174.

[11] P. Y. Chen and P. E. Spector, "Relationships of Work Stressors with Aggression, Withdrawal, Theft and Substance Abuse: An Exploratory Study," *Journal of Occupational and Organizational Psychology* 65 (1992): 177–184.

[12] C. J. Resick, D. S. Whitman, S. M. Weingarden, and N. J. Hiller, "The Bright-Side and the Dark-Side of CEO Personality: Examining Core Self-Evaluations, Narcissism, Transformational Leadership, and Strategic Influence," *Journal of Applied Psychology* 94 (2009): 1,365–1,381.

[13] W. S. Z. Ford and C. N. Etienne, "Can I Help You? A Framework for Interdisciplinary Research on Customer Service Encounters," *Management Communication Quarterly* 7 (1994): 413–441.

[14] J. Hogan, R. Hogan, and C. M. Busch, "How to Measure Service Orientation," *Journal of Applied Psychology* 69 (1984): 167–173.

[15] B. Schneider, S. S. White, and M. C. Paul, "Linking Service Climate and Customer Perceptions of Service Quality: Test of a Causal Model," *Journal of Applied Psychology* 83 (1998): 150–163.

[16] S. W. Kelley, "Developing Customer Orientation among Service Employees," *Journal of the Academy of Marketing Science* 20 (1992): 27–36.

[17] M. J. Bitner, B. H. Booms, and L. A. Mohr, "Critical Service Encounters: The Employee's Viewpoint," *Journal of Marketing* 58 (1994): 95–106.

[18] B. Schneider, J. K. Wheeler, and J. F. Cox, "A Passion for Service: Using Content Analysis to Explicate Service Climate Themes," *Journal of Applied Psychology* 77 (1992): 705–716.

ROMANTIC RELATIONSHIPS AND MARRIAGE

When you realize you want to spend the rest of your life with
somebody, you want the rest of your life to start as soon as possible.
—Billy Crystal

Marriage and romance can be some of the most powerful or destructive relationships in our lives. I'm always amazed when my clients
share stories about how they met their spouses and life partners. I've
heard stories about high school sweethearts and stories of couples
who met in college and grew together over time. There have been
stories about folks who met their spouses at work. Some have met
husbands or wives through online dating; others through friends and
acquaintances. When hearing these stories, I've always been curious
about three things: When did they know they loved their partner,
what has made the relationship stand the test of time, and my favor-
ite question, if their spouse were here with me now, what would they
tell me about them that their colleagues and coworkers don't know?
I usually wait until the end of an assessment interview to ask this
question. It surprises people but gives me a glimpse into one of their
most intimate relationships.

Many years ago, I worked with a senior executive from the food
and beverage industry. Tom was a migrating executive looking to take
on a new challenge with a larger organization. During our assessment
interview, we discussed some of the people in his early childhood
who left a positive impression on how he built relationships. He
talked about the values and beliefs his parents instilled in him, things
like hard work, treating people with respect, and having empathy

for others. When I asked him about people outside his immediate family, he talked about the relationship between his aunt and uncle, Mary and Bob. Bob grew up in the 1940s, during World War II. As a young child, he developed a strong attachment to his mother. They were extremely close given that Bob's father was away at war. Bob referred to himself as a mama's boy. He constantly looked for recognition from his mother. Although they had a very strong relationship, there was an unhealthy Oedipus-like complex that started to form. Bob's mother had unrealistic expectations about the relationship. She expected Bob to do everything she wanted. Bob wanted to please her emotionally, so he did what he could to keep her happy. This changed dramatically when Bob was in his early twenties.

One night, Bob was out with friends at a nightclub, and he met a beautiful woman. There was instant chemistry between the two of them. It was a love at first sight type of story. Bob and Mary danced all night and opened up to each other. Bob was lovestruck and a week later asked Tom's aunt to marry him. Mary was shocked at Bob's boldness. She was Jewish, in the process of getting a divorce, and had an infant. Bob was Catholic and still finishing college. When Bob's mother found out about the news, she exploded in anger and rage. "How could you do this to me!" she accused. She was furious that another woman was taking away her son. His mother kicked Bob out of her house and told him she never wanted to see him again. "You're not my son! I want you out of my life!" she retaliated. These words were devastating to Bob. The person to whom he was closest growing up had disowned him.

Over the next six months, Bob formed an incredibly tight bond with Mary. They were inseparable. They had an intense and passionate relationship. Theirs was the type of love that was once in a lifetime. Shortly after they got married, they started having children. Bob and Mary poured all their love in their family. Everything was about their children. At the same time, Bob started working for an insurance company and became a very motivated and driven individual. At his core, Bob was an introvert. He had been shy and reclusive most of his life. However, selling insurance did something to him internally. It lit in him a fire and passion to succeed. His incessant need for recognition propelled him to the top of the sales force. Bob won every sales competition and became the top sales leader in the entire company. People around the country emulated his methods. With the success came fame and fortune. Bob was making hundreds of thousands of dollars a year. During this period, he developed a drinking habit. At first, drinking was great. Having a few drinks made him fun to be around. Mary loved all the attention and energy he poured into the relationship. Life couldn't have been any better.

Over time, though, his drinking habit became worse. Bob also started using drugs. Slowly, this damaged his marriage. He hid things from Mary. He stopped taking work seriously. He began to miss work, and his drinking and drug use became worse. Mary knew Bob loved her deeply, but she couldn't understand why he wouldn't stop using. They started fighting all the time. He was verbally abusive as the substance addiction became worse. Bob hit rock bottom when he lost his job. The thing that had defined him and had become part of his identity was destroyed. This sent Bob into a deep depression. He wanted to take his own life. Although Mary was devastated, she stuck by Bob's side throughout all of it. She checked him into a rehab facility and did all she could to help him turn things around. She should have left Bob many times. He had several relapses that had a tremendously negative effect on their marriage and the relationships he had with their children. She didn't leave him though. Mary was committed to their marriage and wasn't going to give up on him.

Years later, when Tom was an adult, he asked his aunt about her marriage and why they had never gotten divorced. Mary told him that despite all the negative things that had taken place in their lives, she always knew Bob loved her deeply. Although she didn't understand alcoholism early on, Mary did all she could to learn about the disease. She also had great empathy and compassion for Tom's uncle. The damage Bob's mother had caused when they got married left a scar on his life for many years. Mary believed this was the underlying cause of many of the problems he had as an adult. Bob never reconciled with his mother, and he spent years in therapy, working through the issues that she had caused. Mary stood by his side through all of it. Their marriage was a testament to the power of love and commitment in their relationship.

Tom learned several valuable lessons from his aunt and uncle's relationship. First, communication and understanding are critical to making a marriage work. Before the addiction and substance abuse, Mary and Bob were open and honest about everything. They didn't keep secrets and were genuine and authentic. They cared deeply about each other and encouraged each other to grow. This intimacy was one of the reasons his uncle excelled at his career. Mary had been by his side, pushing and championing him to succeed. Second, although forgiveness is very hard, it is one of the greatest displays of love one can extend to another person. When trust is damaged so severely, it takes courage and vulnerability to believe in a person again. Tom's aunt never gave up on her husband. She believed in the power of love, and this enabled her to forgive and move forward.

Lastly and most importantly, Tom learned that marriage is hard work. You have to be willing to change, evolve, and grow together. Sometimes, one partner will carry the other. Sometimes, one partner will have to shoulder more of the burdens. Mary realized over time that she was stronger than she would have ever thought. Her unwavering commitment to the relationship stood the test of time. Tom took these lessons into his own marriage. His aunt and uncle were a model of unconditional love. Their unwavering commitment to each other was what made his aunt and uncle's relationship so powerful. It got them through some of the most difficult and challenging seasons. It was a true testament to the power of love.

BUTTERFLIES AND FIRST DATES: THE HONEYMOON PHASE

Life in my mid to late twenties was exhilarating. I had completed graduate school and was making six figures working in NYC. By day, I was learning how to become a leadership advisor and organizational psychologist. At night, I was diving deep into the dating world. This was around the time online dating started to become popular. I was aware of the notoriety of websites like Match.com and eHarmony. Most of the people I knew signed up for memberships but spent little time investing in building their profiles. I didn't do this. I saw such sites as an opportunity to share my story and sell myself. To me, it was nothing different from selling TVs at Sears, making friends in college, or building relationships with colleagues and clients. We are always sharing our brand with the world. Those who take the process seriously usually have more success in all areas of life. The same applies to romantic relationships.

When it came to dating, I was never the type to get drunk with friends and meet women in bars or nightclubs. I found this to be exhausting and draining. I was more interested in getting to know the women I met. Of course, physical attraction and chemistry were important, but I also wanted to understand their stories. I wanted to know what they looked for in a partner. I was curious about them personally and professionally. There was a lot of trial and error in the early days. I quickly realized that talking about myself didn't lead to second dates. Women didn't want to hear a man brag about his accomplishments and successes. They wanted someone who was interested in getting to know them, someone who was curious and asked good questions. They wanted someone who showed a genuine interest in learning about their backgrounds and experiences.

I heard many different things from the women I met. They told me stories about how other men behaved. I heard about men who just wanted sex or one-night stands. Smart women figured these tendencies out quickly. They could easily tell what a man was looking for. It had to do with how men carried themselves and what they typically said. There were stories of men who asked for inappropriate things on the first date. I heard stories about unspoken expectations if a man paid for dinner or took a woman out on a few dates. I heard stories about etiquette and appearance. Women could tell more about a man from how he dressed than from what he said on a first date. I was blown away by how some men treated women. Simple things like holding doors open or pulling out a chair so a woman could sit at a table didn't take place. These gestures were common sense to me, but I found that many men didn't know how important they were.

Many of my close friends were experiencing different things with the women they were dating. They told me horror stories about women they met online. On one occasion, a friend of mine took a woman out for dinner and drinks. Within the first hour of the date, the woman he was with had pounded four drinks. He had barely finished his second drink when she started acting belligerent. Another friend went on a date with a woman who was glued to her cell phone the whole time. She barely made eye contact during their date. I remember one of my friends met a woman for a first date at the beach. I thought it was pretty bold to meet someone for the first time in a bathing suit. The woman showed up with six girlfriends and all their boyfriends. The date didn't last long. It seemed online dating worked for some but was a disaster for others.

Despite people's experiences, online dating has revolutionized the dating process and has produced some of the most profound and widespread changes to traditional courtship that have been seen in decades. A survey conducted by the Pew Research Center, a non-partisan fact tank that informs the public about the issues, attitudes, and trends shaping the world, has found that three in ten US adults say they have used a dating site or app, but this varies significantly by age. While 48 percent of eighteen- to twenty-nine-year-olds say they have used a dating site or app, the share is 38 percent among those thirty to forty-nine and even lower for those fifty or older.[1] Roughly six in ten online daters say they have had an overall positive experience with online dating platforms. While online daters generally say their overall experiences are positive, they also point out some of the downsides of online dating. By a wide margin, Americans who have used a dating site or app in the past several years say their recent experiences has left them feeling more frustrated than hopeful.

Popularity aside, online dating sites provide an important context for understanding how present-day relationships are formed. Online dating relationships do not necessarily follow traditional models of relationship development. Rather than meeting a physical person, online daters are introduced to a virtual profile, and much of their early communication occurs exclusively through mediated channels that filter out the social cues on which people typically rely to form impressions face-to-face. This can have the benefit of leading to feelings of enhanced intimacy, but it may also cause setbacks if partners meet face-to-face and find that their positive impressions are merely idealizations. Such outcomes depend heavily on how two people behave on their first date. When there is consistency between what people post on their profiles and how they appear when meeting in person, the likelihood of a positive experience occurs.

As I continued to learn about online dating and how relationships were initiated, I started to figure out that there were certain things both men and women did that determined if a date was moving in the right direction. Establishing rapport was critical on a first date. Eye contact, hand gestures, and nonverbal cues indicated how interested the two people were in each other. The use of humor, playfulness, and flirting were good signs that the date was progressing. There were also signs that things were not going so well. Short answers, lack of interest, and staring off into space while talking indicated a lack of engagement. Truly taking the time to understand the other person was important. Men and women with strong EQ could pick up on emotional cues from others. Active listeners who asked probing questions demonstrated interest and curiosity. I've found that relationally intelligent men and women know how to leave a positive first impression on others. Their genuine interest in learning about the other person usually leads to more dates.

If a positive first impression is established and intimacy begins to build, the honeymoon phase of a romantic relationship can serve as a foundational building block for later stages of development in the relationship. It's during this period that we get butterfly feelings every time we see our partner. The honeymoon phase is the place where rapport building and understanding others become more involved. Most people see all the good in their partner during this time. They overlook some of the issues that may become problems later on. Impression management is a major factor in the early stages of a relationship. We want to show our partners the best versions of ourselves, and this dictates how we start to build the relationship. It's during this period that we set the tone for how the relationship will develop over time. Candid and honest connection during this phase despite wanting to set the best impression sets the stage for embracing individual differences and developing trust. If you're evasive, it opens the door for trust issues and doubts later on in the relationship.

Relationally intelligent people make the most of the honeymoon phase. They are able to figure out ways to connect with their partners on a variety of levels. This stage is not just about chemistry and physical intimacy. It is a chance to invest time in getting to know what's most important to a partner and to share dreams, goals, and ambitions. Relationally intelligent people have intellectually stimulating conversations with new partners. They encourage their partners to develop and grow. They are genuine and authentic in how they approach the new relationship. When a solid foundation has been established, romantic relationships can mature over time. If the relationship is not grounded in honesty and integrity, it will crash and burn quickly as the two people start to really get to know each other.

WHEN REALITY KICKS IN: WHAT DID I GET MYSELF INTO?

I had a close group of friends from college that I spent most of my time with in my late twenties. We were an inseparable band of brothers. Each guy in the group played a stereotypical role for men in their early careers. I had one friend who was a homebody. We always went to his place on Sunday afternoons for football in the fall and basketball in the spring. One friend was a maestro of planning nights out in the city. He always had some restaurant, bar, or lounge we all had to try. I had a cheap friend who never wanted to pay for anything. He always bought the first round of drinks so we would all know he had spent money and then asked all of us for drinks for the rest of the night. We had a hot-tempered friend who was always looking for trouble. After a few drinks, he was the one who usually started fights.

Then there was Frank. Frank was the self-proclaimed player in the group. Women fawned over him, and he was in and out of relationships all the time. I was the resident psychologist on staff. My friends came to me to discuss their love lives and careers. Frank and I regularly talked about his relationships, as he wanted to brag about conquests or get my advice on how to deal with challenging women. I heard all types of crazy stories about his love life. Most of the time, he was the winner in those situations, but that was only until he met Kristin. She was a fiery and passionate Irish woman who was five or six years older than Frank. He was mesmerized by her beauty. I always had to listen to stories about how gorgeous she was. "This is the one, Adam! I'm telling you, brother. My player days are coming to an end," he would say. They weren't though, and I had a front-row seat to their chaotic and destructive relationship.

When Frank met Kristin, he was dating three other women. Kristin knew he was up to no good from the start, but their chemistry and physical intimacy drew them to each other. He called me right after their second date. "I cannot tell you how amazing she is in bed, man," he said. "I've never felt like this before." I asked him if he thought it was too quick to be sleeping with her. He knew nothing about her. She didn't know much about him. This didn't bother Frank. "I know what I'm doing, man. Don't be a bitch." I smiled and listened. "Okay, Frank. I'm sure you have it all under control," I had responded. Three weeks later, he called me in a panic at 2:00 a.m. He had lied to Kristin and had told her that he was out with the guys while he was on a date with a different woman. She sat in the parking lot of his apartment complex the entire night to wait and see when he was coming home. When she did see him with another woman, she lost her shit. This was the first of many incidents when he lied and then tried to cover his tracks.

As I got to learn about Kristin, I found that she also seemed to be shady. It was almost like tit for tat between the two of them. One would lie and do something to hurt the other person, and back and forth they would go. This went on for months. Every time there was a big falling out, I would get a call the following day. "She's fucking crazy, bro! How am I letting this woman get to me?" Frank would say. I told Frank he was crazy for staying in the relationship, but that didn't stop him from continuing to pursue her. Several months later, Frank told Kristin he wanted to commit to her in an exclusive relationship. He was lying but felt he had to do so to prevent her from seeing other men. I told him he was taking a major risk and playing games where someone could get hurt. "I got this, bro. Let me do me," Frank only said.

One night, the two of them were on a date in the city. At this point, reality had set in. Kristin didn't trust Frank, and he felt the same. I'm not sure what kept them together; there was zero trust in the relationship. At one point in the night, Kristin caught Frank eyeing another woman at the bar. She started arguing and fighting with him immediately. They were both drunk, which didn't make things better. Kristin got violent and started making a scene. The bouncers had to come over and escort the two of them out of the bar. On the ride home, Kristin started getting physical with Frank as he drove through the Lincoln Tunnel. She hit him repeatedly. They swerved in and out of traffic. When they finally got back to his place, she attacked him in his apartment. He tried to lock himself in the spare bedroom, but she punched a hole through the door. Frank called the cops immediately, and Kristin started a fight with them when they arrived on the scene. They took her away in handcuffs, and I got a call early that morning. I've never heard Frank in so much of a panic as I did that night. He was stunned by how quickly things had unraveled. He almost got killed in a car accident. He never spoke to Kristin again after that. Frank was the type of person who had to learn things the hard way. It was a lesson he never forgot, that although things might seem great in the early phases of a relationship, lying and deception could lead us down a dark path.

Most romantic relationships don't have these types of extremes. However, we learn a lot about our partners when the reality phase kicks in. We learn about the underlying personality quirks and blemishes of another person. We learn about their dark side. Everyone has one. The reality phase is where most romantic relationships can be derailed quickly. We don't really start to get to know someone until we reach this phase of the relationship. I've found that two people can work through this stage if they have established a solid foundation in the honeymoon phase. Frank and Kristin did not have such a foundation. The games they both played left the other person in a constant state of suspense and anxiety. Relationships built on suspicion and doubt can blow up in our faces. I've seen it happen again and again with friends and family when they get into destructive relationships. I'm always amazed by how they cannot see this when it starts to occur. People tend to be blinded to some of the most obvious issues.

Romantic relationships are an important source of many adults' subjective well-being. Unfortunately, some people find themselves in unsatisfactory relationships that they are not able or willing to leave. According to attachment theory, individual differences in mental representations of adult romantic relationships explain romantic relationship dynamics.[2] These differences are assessed along two dimensions: attachment anxiety and avoidance. Adults high in attachment anxiety are uncertain about their partner's love and intentions to remain in the relationship and often have unhappy relationships. By contrast, adults high in attachment avoidance tend to eschew closeness and intimacy in romantic relationships. Their relationships are characterized by psychological distance. Because anxiously attached people are theoretically the most likely to remain committed to unsatisfying relationships, their level of relationship satisfaction is often low.[3] These relationships will seem likely to break up quickly, but many do not. We see this time and time again with partners who constantly fight but do not take action to end the relationship.

During the reality phase of a relationship, people evaluate the quality of their relationship in a variety of ways. One of the most common ways is that people assess the extent to which their relationships meet personal standards or ideals.[4] Some people evaluate their relationships in comparison to other people's relationships. In addition to personal standards and social comparison, there are several other important means of relationship evaluation. People may evaluate their relationships by examining behavioral information (e.g., how frequently they experience conflict), listening to feedback from others, or comparing their current relationships to past relationships.[5] Relationship evaluation processes (REPs) give us a glimpse into how people navigate the reality phase of a relationship. In most instances, REPs determine if a person will remain in a relationship or end it.

Prominent theories that focus on personal standards or ideals suggest that people evaluate their relationships based on intrapersonal factors. Interdependence theory suggests that people compare their relationship outcomes (based on costs and rewards) to an internal standard known as a comparison level. This theory predicts that people are more satisfied when their relationship outcomes meet or exceed their comparison level than when outcomes fall short.[6] Social psychologists have found that people often compare their current partner and relationship to ideal standards based on dimensions of warmth, attractiveness, and status. Research surrounding this framework has shown that greater consistency between people's perceptions of their relationship and their ideals predicts greater relationship satisfaction. Reductions in ideal-perception consistency over time predict decreases in satisfaction and often lead to breakups.[7]

Researchers have also investigated people's use of social comparison to evaluate their romantic relationships. Experiments that have manipulated relationships' social comparison emphasize the effect of social comparison direction (i.e., upward versus downward comparison). For example, people often evaluate their relationship less favorably after hearing about another person whose relationship has been going very well (i.e., upward comparison) rather than on one whose relationship has been going poorly (i.e., downward comparison). In most instances, social comparison direction on relationship quality depends on how people interpret the comparison. Engaging in social comparison, regardless of the direction, is often associated with worse relationship quality. I've seen this with friends or acquaintances who run into challenges during the reality phase. They compare the problems and difficulties they experience in their relationship to the issues they observe in other relationships around them. This often leads to larger discrepancies between their relationship and what they believe a good relationship should look like.

Although research is mixed on the evaluations people make about the quality of their relationships, I've learned three valuable lessons from serving as Frank's therapist during his tumultuous relationship with Kristin. First, although people say that love is blind, that can't be further from the truth. There are always signs early on in a relationship. People need to be aware and attuned to these issues. Don't get lovestruck or infatuated just because the sex or physical intimacy is so great. I've heard stories from friends about their great sex lives while the rest of the relationship is chaotic and dangerous. Second, once trust is broken, that's the end of things, especially in the dating world. It's more challenging with marriage, as I'll discuss later in this chapter. However, when it comes to dating, you usually cannot damage trust and expect the relationship to work. Men and women will continually second-guess someone they catch in a lie. If you really care for someone you're dating, don't do it. You may not be able to recover from the damage you do.

Lastly and most importantly, the reality phase hits every relationship. Most people aren't aware that this is part of the natural evolution of any relationship. We don't live in a Disney fairy tale world. The quicker people can move past the honeymoon phase and see their partner for who they really are, the more likely the relationship will work in the long term. Either it will work, or you will find out it's not the right relationship for you. Relationally intelligent people don't run from this process. They start to embrace the individual differences that surface during this stage. They accept people for who they are and don't try to drive change that may not be welcome or appreciated. It takes courage to see someone's flaws and weaknesses and still commit to the relationship. This can only happen if a solid foundation has been built from the start. The ebbs and flows of any relationship will include seasons of joy and frustration. When we are aware of this and have started to build trust with our partners, we can weather the storms together.

Fully Committing to the Relationship: The Adjustment Phase

Over time, I've developed close friendships with many of my clients. When you work with someone for years, you get to know about many aspects of their lives. I've learned how people have overcome trials and tribulations that have made them who they are. I've heard personal success stories about overcoming obstacles and adversity. I've heard about the joys of having children and the legacy people want to leave to others. I've heard about relationships built during difficult periods in their lives. I've also heard about challenges in close personal relationships and the impact such challenges have on the way people view others.

I started working with Tony over ten years ago. When we met, he was a single man in his early thirties and was considered a high-potential employee for his organization. Tony had a knack for connecting with people and inspiring others. He built strong relationships by finding commonalities with others and aligning on key values and beliefs. In the early years, our coaching work focused on expanding his influence with and impact on leaders at his level and those who were more senior in his organization. Tony was skilled at building trust and honoring his commitments to people. Colleagues found him to be consistent and disciplined in achieving his goals and objectives. Our relationship flourished because we were always candid and honest with each other. I was direct with Tony when he needed to hear tough feedback. I didn't pull any punches, and I often challenged him to grow.

As our relationship evolved over time, Tony and I became good friends outside of work. We both had a passion for golf and regularly played together on weekends. I went on several golf trips with Tony and his close friends from college. It was fascinating to see a different side of him outside of work. Then Tony met his wife, Ashley, through colleagues at work. They had an instant connection and fell in love quickly. After about a year of dating, they got engaged and moved in together. Given that our relationship had grown so close during those years, he often came to me for guidance and input on his relationship with Ashley. In the beginning, most of the feedback he requested was about positive things in their lives. He wanted to get my thoughts on ideas for their wedding, and he was curious about the ways he could strengthen and grow their relationship. But he also came to me for advice and input on challenges they had during the engagement.

Tony and Ashley came from different worlds. Although they both had tough upbringings, Ashley had a more difficult and turbulent childhood. Her father was murdered when she was six, and her mother was in and out of rehab facilities during her years in grade school. Ashley moved around a lot and had difficulty making friends.

Given the challenges she faced at home, she would often get in fights with other girls at school. She developed a mean streak and formed a tough outer shell that made her hard to get along with. In Ashley's household, conflict was avoided at all costs. When she got into a fight with other family members, she turned inward and sought out isolation to process her feelings. Ashley was an introvert, so the time alone helped her think about things in a deep way. She often processed her thoughts and emotions through writing and poetry.

Tony also grew up in a single-family household. His father raised him for most of his life because his mother had abandoned the family when he was nine years old. His father was a disciplinarian and displayed tough love for his children. He taught Tony the value of hard work and dedication. He also taught Tony about honesty and integrity. Although these were good values to instill in a child, his father was not loving and supportive. Tony didn't learn how to be empathetic toward others and didn't understand how to manage his emotions. In his household, if an argument or conflict started, you had to hash it out and come to a resolution. Tony was an extrovert and often shared his perspectives before thinking through what he wanted to say. You had to fight for airtime in his family, as his two older brothers dominated most of the conversations.

You can imagine how their upbringings and past experiences had a negative effect on their relationship. For the most part, Tony and Ashley got along great. He rarely talked about disagreements or arguments they had. Tony was very loving toward Ashley and put her before everything else in his life. I admired how committed he was to their relationship. There were only two or three fights I remember him telling me about that turned out really bad. These were all early in their relationship. All the fights started over stupid and insignificant things. On one occasion, Tony and Ashley started fighting over who was using the printer. Ashley was printing out color photos, and Tony got annoyed that she was using up all the ink. He snapped at her, and she fought back. Name-calling went back and forth, and before long, Tony was screaming. Ashley tried to retreat into the bedroom to calm down. Tony followed her because he wanted to finish what he had to say. The fight got worse until it ended with Ashley grabbing her keys and leaving his place.

On another occasion, they were getting ready to go to a relative's house for the Christmas holidays. They had been arguing the night before, so tensions were high. Tony made a comment that rubbed Ashley the wrong way, and she started cursing at him. He told her that if she wanted to scream and yell, she could stay home by herself. He left her that day and went to the family party on his own. This enraged Ashley, and she left him a goodbye note saying she wasn't coming back. He couldn't find her for two days, and this damaged the trust in their relationship. When Ashley did return, they worked things out and didn't have another fight for well over a year. During this time, I remember Tony talking about how good things were going. They were planning their wedding. It was an exciting time in their relationship.

Several months before their wedding, however, things took an unexpected turn. It was the week before Easter, and Ashley and Tony were fighting on and off about how they were going to spend the holiday. Resentments were building on both sides over things about which they should have talked but didn't bring up to avoid a fight. Early one Saturday morning, they started arguing over text while Ashley was at work. The texting got vicious, and Tony told Ashley not to come home that evening if she was going to keep fighting with him. She took this personally, packed three bags, and told him she was leaving. Then he tried to calm her down and to talk things over peacefully, but Ashley didn't want to hear anything he had to say. She left that afternoon and took a flight to visit family out of the country. This enraged Tony, and their fighting continued for two weeks. Things got so bad they almost called off the wedding and broke up.

When they finally started speaking again, so much trust had been damaged and destroyed. They decided to go to couples counseling to try to save their relationship, but it did not go well for several weeks. When I met with Tony that month for our coaching session, he was distraught with sadness and frustration. I told him therapy would help but that he had to look at things differently. They both had played a role in how things unraveled, so they each had to look at what caused the fight to get so out of hand so quickly. Over time, they began to understand that it wasn't that they were trying to hurt each other intentionally. There were different ways they had learned how to handle conflict from years of picking up bad habits from their families. They needed to understand how trauma from their past was having a negative impact on their relationship. There were things that had happened in both of their lives that contributed to how they viewed the world. When they understood how to embrace their individual differences and process things differently, their communication started to improve. Tony and Ashley grew closer as a result of their couples counseling and found new ways to handle conflicts together. They both learned how to manage their emotions better, which helped them navigate future challenges as a couple.

The adjustment phase of any relationship is a time when two people need to embrace their individual differences the most. Embracing individual differences requires moving past understanding on a surface level. It is a time when people have to put aside their pride and truly seek to grow the relationship. Many people make mistakes during this phase when they try to change certain things about their partners. In most instances, they need to self-reflect and change things about themselves. True intimacy is developed when each partner makes an effort to grow together. It requires sacrifice and being vulnerable with each other. It requires humility and a commitment to learning about underlying issues that cause people to view the world in different ways.

Social psychologists who study romantic relationships have found many factors that contribute to the growth that takes place during the adjustment phase. Self-disclosure is defined as the process by which people reveal personal information about themselves to others. In romantic relationships, self-disclosure is especially important in the development of intimacy and is related to greater levels of personal and relationship satisfaction. In fact, self-disclosure is greater in romantic couples who stay together and in couples who are more satisfied with their relationship primarily because self-disclosure facilitates intimacy and increases the quality of one's relationships.[8] Certain personality and relationship differences predict self-disclosure. With regard to personality variables, high self-esteem has consistently been linked to greater amounts of self-disclosure. People with high self-esteem report more openness with their romantic partners and friends.[9] Additionally, trust that has been developed and the level of responsiveness between two partners contributes to the amount of self-disclosure that takes place. If the adjustment phase involves developing deeper trust with a partner, people are more willing to self-disclose and share intimate aspects about themselves.

Self-concept clarity is another important factor that impacts the connection between two people during the adjustment phase. Self-concept clarity is defined as the degree to which a person's self-concept is clearly and confidently defined, temporally stable, and internally consistent.[10] When people have taken the time to cultivate a deep understanding of their self-concept, they are more likely to embrace the unique personality characteristics of their partners. In the case of Tony and Ashley, the work they did in couples counseling helped them further explore how their personal experiences shaped how they viewed the world. Once they got clear about their individual self-concepts, therapy enabled them to work together to create a shared concept of the relationship and how to support each other. Tony told me this step was the turning point in the work they did with their therapist. Once he had a better understanding of how his childhood experiences had affected the way he dealt with conflict, he could adjust his approach in the moment to meet Ashley's needs. Ashley also learned about how her upbringing contributed to the way she behaved when they had fights. This knowledge helped them resolve conflicts in a more healthy and productive fashion.

Intimacy, the sense of closeness between two people, is a fundamental component of healthy romantic relationships. It promotes mental, physical, and emotional well-being. For a relationship to endure the test of time, greater levels of intimacy must be developed during the adjustment phase. Relationally intelligent people know how to build intimacy by understanding individual differences and using information about their partners to develop greater levels of trust and commitment. Social psychologists have found two primary process models of intimacy. The most widely known conceptual framework, the interpersonal process model of intimacy (IPM), suggests that intimacy increases when a person discloses their personal thoughts or emotions to their partner, the partner responds supportively, and the partner's response is perceived as validating and caring.[11] People who self-disclose to a romantic partner and perceive their partner's response as supportive tend to experience increased intimacy with their partner.

The second model of intimacy is a behavioral interpretation of personal interactions when a person expresses vulnerability. This is absolutely critical for a relationship to thrive during the adjustment phase. Emotional disclosures that reveal the innermost self and involve experiences of vulnerability typically elicit high responsiveness from our partners. Because vulnerable disclosures are at risk of interpersonal punishment and involve insecurity and feelings like pain, sadness, or shame, they can be some of the most powerful moments in the development of a romantic relationship. When handled with care, the vulnerable disclosures we make to our partners strengthen the bonds we have with them. Sharing personal information is a way of communicating trust and a desire to offer one's true self. As a romantic relationship evolves, vulnerabilities regarding childhood events and past memories of hurt or personal secrets become less common. New vulnerabilities start to unfold, including vulnerabilities that occur in the context of the relationship. How two people handle and react to these vulnerabilities determines the extent to which the relationship will grow.

Social and emotional support is an important part of a happy and healthy romantic relationship. Because relationally intelligent people take time to invest in their partner's life, the support they provide strengthens the relationship. Social and emotional support during the adjustment phase is about adapting and adjusting to the needs of your partner. Personal sacrifices become critical during this stage of a relationship. Sacrifices are diagnostic situations in intimate relationships, as they can signal that a person is invested in the relationship and attentive to their partner's needs. Not surprisingly, when people receive a sacrifice, they are more likely to feel cared and loved by their partners. Sacrifices need to be made by both partners for the relationship to move beyond the adjustment phase. The give-and-take that takes place in a relationship must support the ongoing growth and development of each partner. Relationally intelligent people are skilled at navigating through life's challenges together. Their commitment to the relationship and the trust they develop over time enable them to put their own feelings and needs aside when they have to. Relational intelligence in long-term relationships also opens the door for cultivating influence, having a positive impact on a partner's life, and helping them reach their full potential.

MARRIAGE IS HARD WORK: DEVELOPING LASTING INTIMACY

Clients often ask me if executive coaches ever work with their own coach. I laugh when I am asked this question and tell them the best coaches always do. If we want to get better at our craft, we have to strive for continuous improvement. Coaching is a process where there is always more to learn and grow. However, you'll be surprised who coaches actually turn to for guidance and support. I've had colleagues tell me they've worked with their mentors for years. Often, an experienced and seasoned leadership advisor will take someone under their wing. They develop a relationship that lasts decades as both consultants advance in their careers. I've had other colleagues talk about people who have spoken life into them from outside our profession. Personal trainers, life coaches, and therapists are people they turn to for insight and wisdom.

In my life, I've had many mentors and trusted advisors. At different points in my career, I've sought out different types of people who have helped me achieve my goals. I've worked with my therapist for years. He's always been a great sounding board for relationships professionally and in my personal life. I've sought out spiritual advisors and pastors with whom I've developed relationships over the years. These are men who have challenged me to grow in my faith and believe in the impossible. I've worked with my personal trainer for a long time. He's been the one to push me to my physical limits and pat me on the back when I finish those few extra burpees. Despite all these people, my most intimate romantic relationships have been with the ones who have inspired and challenged me to grow the most. They have encouraged, loved, and supported me along my journey. They have gotten me to better understand, accept, and appreciate who I am at my core. It takes people who genuinely and authentically love us despite our flaws and weaknesses to help us reach our full potential.

I've seen the powerful effect of healthy marriages on many of my long-term clients as well. The people that I have worked with for years often credit much of their growth and development to their husbands or wives. It's our partners who see every side of us. They understand our hopes and dreams. They know our worries and fears. They've seen us at our best, and they've helped us through some of the most challenging and difficult periods. True intimacy is about having a positive influence on our partners. It's about helping our spouses understand how they can develop and grow over time. It's also about doing work on ourselves. We have to grow if we want our partners to come along on the journey. Relational intelligence needs to be a commitment both partners make. Marriage is about constantly pouring into the relationship. It's doing the little things when we don't want to. It's consistently putting someone else's needs before our own. It's about intentional generosity and sowing positivity.

It is commonly believed that marriage is a lot of work, but what kind of work sustains the most intimate of relationships? In response to this question, intimate relationship scholars have explored the concept of "emotion work," which refers to supportive behaviors that foster a partner's positive emotions (e.g., listening attentively to a partner's thoughts and acknowledging their emotions).[12] Related to this is the study of relational developmental systems (RDS), which frames human development as a relational process involving continual, bidirectional transactions between an individual and their intrapersonal (e.g., cognitions), interpersonal (e.g., spouse), and sociocultural (e.g., gender norms) contexts over the course of a life span. Grounded in the worldview of relationism (a paradigm that focuses on processes within, change throughout, and relations among developmental systems) and the principle of holism (the need to consider context to derive meaning), an RDS perspective suggests that person and context mutually constitute each other and evolve together over time. As such, a person's cognitive and behavioral trajectories will inevitably shape and be shaped by their relational environments. Marriage is one of the primary vehicles for this process to occur. Our worldview and that of our spouse are shaped by how we grow in the relationship together.

Studies conducted by social psychologists who focused on marriage and intimate relationships found many benefits to relationship well-being from doing emotion work. In one study, researchers analyzed cross-sectional data from 205 married women and found that spouses' emotion work (e.g., sharing thoughts and feelings or expressing concern for a partner's well-being) was positively associated with women's martial stability and satisfaction.[13] In a separate line of research, psychologists found that men and women were most satisfied with their marriage when they provided similar levels of emotion work (e.g., attempting to relieve a partner of their negative mood). Providing emotion work also predicted higher daily relationship satisfaction, love, commitment, and closeness for both men and women.[14] It is no wonder that marriages thrive in the long term when both partners commit to the emotion work that is required to sustain the relationship. Relationally intelligent people have the EQ and empathy required to meet their partner's needs. They also listen attentively, ask probing questions, and do the work necessary to continue to invest in the relationship.

Successful marriages create a safe environment where each partner can develop their sense of purpose. This is critically important, as finding purpose leads to better-quality relationships across all areas of our lives. When studying sense of purpose, researchers have found three essential components: thoughts, feelings, and behaviors. Regarding thoughts or cognitions, sense of purpose is positively related to hope, which involves both the perception that people can find opportunities and pathways around obstacles and the motivation to take action to achieve their goals.[15] As such, purposeful people have the ability to get around relationship obstacles and continually seek to grow both inside and outside the relationship. When considering feelings or emotions, studies have found that purposeful people report greater positive emotions daily and that these contribute to romantic relationship quality. This makes sense, as it is easier to be in a relationship with a purposeful partner who is generally happy and handles stressors within and outside of the context of romantic relationships. Lastly, regarding behaviors, purposeful people tend to be better at organizing their short-term and long-term activities. They tend to engage in more relationship-promoting behaviors, like remembering important dates and keeping promises. Such engagement strengthens the bond with a partner and leads to more fulfillment in the relationship. When both partners have a sense of purpose, it leads to high levels of relationship quality. It also strengthens the bonds of trust, as each partner looks for ways to encourage, support, and champion their spouse.

The concept of I-sharing, a sense that one's subjective experience overlaps with that of at least one other person, is critical to the success of marriage and long-term romantic relationships.[16] I-sharing is different from simply sharing an experience in that it hinges on a shared reaction. People can share an objective experience (e.g., hearing a joke) but fail to I-share if they have different subjective experiences of that event (e.g., laughing versus cringing). Most people are drawn toward I-sharers because they give us a sense of existential connection and a feeling of kindred spirits. I-sharing is particularly important in romantic relationships based on the suffocation model of marriage. This framework suggests that expectations surrounding marriage have shifted over time to become increasingly orientated toward self-expression needs.[17] Historically, marriages were viewed as an outlet for meeting physiological (e.g., food and safety) or basic companionship needs, but they are now viewed as an outlet for meeting higher-order psychological needs, such as esteem and self-actualization. With these evolving requirements for a relationship partner, the importance of finding "the one" increases. We want partners who will be our best friends, who will help us discover ourselves, and with whom we share a passionate sexual relationship. Relationally intelligent people take the time to do their due diligence in finding ideal partners to meet those needs.

Other related constructs that have been linked to long-term relationship satisfaction are empathic accuracy and emotional similarity. Empathic accuracy occurs when one partner accurately understands another's feelings. Understanding a relationship partner's feelings indicates, at the very least, an understanding of the partner's subjective experiences even if those experiences are not shared. Work on emotional similarity more directly suggests that the sharing of subjective experiences is critically important to marriage functioning. I-sharing encompasses more than just empathy and shared emotional responses. It often involves perceptions of shared thoughts and motivations as well as feelings. I-sharing also hinges on the recognition of shared subjective experiences, unlike emotional similarity. When I-sharing takes place, both partners develop greater levels of trust and commitment to the marriage. I-sharing enables them to navigate turbulent times in the relationship as well as handle some of the storms of life.

Marriage requires consistent work to make it successful. Lasting intimacy is a verb. It is active and alive. The most successful marriages progress over time, as each partner is committed to ongoing personal growth and development. If one partner starts to regress, it can have detrimental effects on relationship satisfaction and quality. Relationally intelligent people understand the importance of the ever-evolving nature of their marriage or romantic relationships. As people who will continue to change and grow, partners with high relational intelligence embrace those changes and actively seek to incorporate them into the relationship. Some of the most enduring aspects of successful marriages are when each partner cultivates influence that has a positive effect on their spouse's mental, physical, and emotional development. Relationally intelligent people build dynamic, life-changing relationships that help their spouses reach their full potential.

---

[1] E. A. Vogels, *Ten Facts about Americans and Online Dating* (Washington, DC: Pew Research Center, 2020).

[2] M. Mikulincer and P. R. Shaver, "The Attachment Behavioral System in Adulthood: Activation, Psychodynamics, and Interpersonal Processes," *Advances in Experimental Social Psychology* 35 (2003): 56–152.

3   J. J. Feeney, "Adult Romantic Attachment: Developments in the Study of Couple Relationships," in *Handbook of Attachment: Theory, Research, and Clinical Applications*, 3rd ed., eds. J. Cassidy and P. R. Shaver (Guildford Press, 2016).

4   G. J. O. Fletcher and J. A. Simpson, "Ideal Standards in Close Relationships: Their Structure and Functions," *Current Directions in Psychological Science* 9: 102–105.

5   H. A. Wayment and S. Campbell, "How Are We Doing? The Impact of Motives and Information Use on the Evaluation of Romantic Relationships," *Journal of Social and Personal Relationships* 17 (2000): 31–52.

6   J. W. Thibaut and H. H. Kelley, *The Social Psychology of Groups* (New York, New York: Wiley Publishing, 1959).

7   G. J. O. Fletcher, J. A. Simpson, G. Thomas, and L. Giles, "Ideals in Intimate Relationships," *Journal of Personality and Social Psychology* 76 (1999): 72–89.

8   J. H. Berg and R. D. McQuinn, "Attraction and Exchange in Continuing and Noncontinuing Dating Relationships," *Journal of Personality and Social Psychology* 50 (1986): 942–952.

9   D. Gaucher, J. V. Wood, D. A. Stinson, A. L. Forest, J. G. Holmes, and C. Logel, "Perceived Regard Explains Self-Esteem Differences in Expressivity," *Journal of Personality and Social Psychology* 38 (2012): 1,144–1,156.

10 J. D. Campbell, "Self-Esteem and Clarity of the Self-Concept," *Journal of Personality and Social Psychology* 59 (1990): 538–549.

11 H. T. Reis and P. R. Shaver, "Intimacy as an Interpersonal Process," in *Handbook of Personal Relationships: Theory, Research, and Interventions*, eds. S. Duck, D. F. Hay, F. Dale, S. E. Hobfoll, W. Ickes, and B. M. Montgomery (Oxford, United Kingdom: John Wiley & Sons, 1988), 367–389.

12 R. J. Erickson, "Why Emotion Work Matters: Sex, Gender, and the Division of Household Labor," *Journal of Marriage and the Family* 67 (2005): 337–351.

13 R. J. Erickson, "Reconceptualizing Family Work: The Effect of Emotion Work on Perceptions of Marital Quality," *Journal of Marriage and the Family* 55 (1993): 888–900.

14 K. E. Holm, R. J. Werner-Wilson, A. S. Cook, and P. S. Berger, "The Association between Emotion Work Balance and Relationship Satisfaction of Couples Seeking Therapy," *The American Journal of Family Therapy* 29 (2001): 193–205.

15 C. R. Snyder, K. L. Rand, and D. R. Sigmon, "Hope Theory: A Member of the Positive Psychology Family," in *Handbook of Positive Psychology*, eds. C. R. Snyder and S. J. Lopez (Oxford University Press, 2005), 257–276.

16 E. C. Pinel, A. E. Long, M. J. Landau, K. Alexander, and T. Pyszczynski, "Seeing I to I: A Pathway to Interpersonal Connectedness," *Journal of Personality and Social Psychology* 90 (2006): 243–257.

17 E. J. Finkel, C. M. Hui, K. L. Carswell, and G. M. Larson, "The Suffocation of Marriage: Climbing Mount Maslow without Enough Oxygen," *Psychological Inquiry* 25 (2014): 1–41.

THE CALL TO ACTION

An idea not coupled with action will never get
any bigger than the brain cell it occupied.
—Arnold Glasow

On March 16, 2020, the world changed forever. A month before that, in mid-February, my partner and I had been doing our weekly grocery shopping. Things were starting to unravel in China. I had watched CNN earlier that evening and had heard of the potential spread of coronavirus around the globe. As we walked down the toilet paper and paper towel aisle at ShopRite, I had an eerie feeling. "We better stock up on paper products, hon. A storm is coming." She laughed and said I was being dramatic. I went outside and got a second shopping cart. She consented and loaded up on paper towels, toilet paper, and nine cases of water. She took a picture of her crazy boyfriend in the parking lot carrying all the water to the car. We all know what started happening six or seven weeks later.

For over two years, most of us were isolated in our homes. We had little contact with the outside world. Many of us couldn't spend time with older parents and grandparents. Our children weren't allowed to go to school. We started working from home. Zoom video meetings became the norm. As the pandemic raged on, many of my firm's clients began shifting their work-from-home strategies. Several of my clients made the decision to extend work from home well into 2022. Some companies decided that employees never had to come into an office again. The CEO and CFO of one of our largest financial services clients made public pronouncements of their decision to work from home permanently. This was good news to some employees' ears but very frustrating for others.

After about six months of working from home, I started to see certain behaviors emerge from some of the teams I was coaching. Zoom fatigue began to creep in at the end of people's days. Employees were multitasking on calls. People were distracted by work-life responsibilities. Patience and respect for colleagues started to diminish. Capacity for work drained as people became increasingly exhausted working twelve- and sometimes fourteen-hour days. Some of my clients talked about the fear of burnout. Work relationships began to suffer. People lost human connection. The power of sitting face-to-face with someone in the same room was removed. People forgot how to build relationships.

New hires suffered the most. Because everyone was stuck working from home, they didn't have the right opportunities to establish rapport. They didn't have ways to learn about cultural norms within a team, business unit, or organization. It was hard to support leaders on their executive integration. Networking came to a standstill, which had a negative effect on building partnership and alliances with others. Opportunities to spend physical time together, getting to learn about and understand others, had been removed. Of course, we tried to artificially recreate this via videoconferencing, but it was not the same. Companies did start focusing more on diversity and inclusion given the events leading up to the Black Lives Matter movement, but the sense of community and camaraderie that came with building inclusive cultures was missing. Developing trust with people was difficult. Trust requires face-to-face interaction and being in the same room with people to flourish. Cultivating influence was even harder. If relationships are not given the space to develop and grow, getting people to follow one's lead is challenging. Many employees acted out of compliance rather than because they were truly being inspired by their leaders.

I also saw social and relational challenges develop with many of my clients' children. One of my clients whom I have been coaching for several years talked at length about the developmental issues that his eight-year-old son had been struggling with. At the peak of the pandemic, Mark and his wife had to balance caring for their son while each of them did their full-time job. They rotated shifts to homeschool their son while the other had meetings. Their son was an only child, which exacerbated his issues, as he spent hours by himself on his iPad or in front of the TV, playing video games. When the vaccine started to become available and people were allowed to meet together in large groups again, Mark took his son to a family party at his relatives. His son was socially awkward and was afraid to interact with others. He chose to sit outside in the yard by himself on his mother's iPhone rather than play in the house with his cousins and the other kids. Mark was sad and concerned about how to deal with the situation. He tried to encourage his son to come into the house and socialize, but he wanted to be left alone. I've heard similar stories from other clients.

As a result of the pandemic, relationship building is more important than ever before. We need it as colleagues and coworkers. The human connection that makes relationships thrive has to be restored. Our children need it to learn how to interact face-to-face with others. Many of them have lost a year or two of connection at a critical stage in their lives for social, emotional, and relational growth. Personally, I've made it a point for all our consultants to have face-to-face meetings with our clients when circumstances permit. As organizational psychologists and leadership advisors, we influence our clients best when we get in the trenches with them. You have to work face-to-face to have meaningful and sustainable impact. Practicing the five skills of relational intelligence is critical as we reengage and restore relationships across all areas of our lives. When I sat down to begin writing this book, I didn't realize how important it would be given what we have been through. The call to action demands that we spend more time reconnecting intentionally with others. Without in-person interaction, we miss out on some of the most powerful experiences in life. Having dynamic, deep connections with others strengthens our mental, emotional, and social well-being.

RELATIONSHIPS NEED TO BE RESTORED

Today, we have more ways to communicate, but we're connecting less than ever. Our lack of connection is affecting our children.

It's affecting how we work. It's affecting how we live our lives. We are desperate for connection. Through the innovations of technology, we call ourselves connected, but nothing could be further from the truth. We live in a social media, instant gratification culture. We've lost the art of process when it comes to building and sustaining relationships. The time has come to rectify some of these issues. Relational intelligence is the path to restoring the connections with others that we have lost. Developing the five skills outlined in this book will help you cultivate deep, meaningful, long-term relationships with others. I've found that relationally intelligent people have better-quality relationships across all areas of their lives. They know how to have a positive and lasting impact on others. This enables them to have more satisfaction and fulfillment in all that they do.

Establishing rapport is the first critical step to building a strong, dynamic relationship. This skill focuses on the initial stages of communication between two people. It is the starting point for understanding others, embracing individual differences, and developing trust. Rapport creates a safe environment for people to establish a positive connection. When two people establish rapport, a state of affinity starts to take shape. There are many factors that come into play when establishing rapport. Similarities and differences between two people can impact the interaction. Your interest in getting to know another person plays a vital role. The views you hold about yourself can impact how you come across to others. The perspectives you have about culture, upbringing, and past experiences affect the way you engage with people. The words that are used early on play an important role. How you communicate is just as important as what you are trying to say. Verbal and nonverbal cues show interest in the person and what they are saying. The use of humor lightens the mood and puts people at ease. You cannot progress to further stages of developing a lasting relationship unless time has been put in to establishing rapport.

Understanding others is about taking the time to get to know people on a deep level. It is about learning how others are wired and what makes them tick. Understanding others is about using EQ to understand both our own feelings and the emotions of others.

Relationally intelligent people are able to control their emotions, so they make a strong, positive impression. They have good active listening skills. Active listening enables them to attentively and truly take in what another person is communicating to them. Relationally intelligent people are curious and inquisitive. They ask probing questions to learn about the background, history, and experiences of people they meet. They are empathetic. They can put themselves in other people's shoes. Understanding others does not happen overnight. It is an ever-evolving process that must take place over time. Relationally intelligent people seek to understand in a genuine and sincere manner. The investment they make during this early stage of relationships sets the foundation for growth.

Embracing individual differences is about acknowledging that we all come from different backgrounds and experiences and accepting people for who they are. It's having a favorable reception toward people who think, act, and behave differently than we do. It's about appreciating racial and ethnic diversity. It's acknowledging the differences in how gender makes an impact on the way people think and the value they bring to the table. It's choosing to embrace people's sexual orientations. It's understanding that cross-cultural differences impact how we interact with the world. Embracing individual differences is about showing people common decency and treating others the way we want to be treated. When we are accepting of people who are different from us, we are able to more effectively communicate with them. This helps strengthen the quality of relationships we have with others. We may not agree with the practices or beliefs of others, but we can still connect with them. Relationally intelligent people know how to leverage their differences with others to get superior outcomes. At work, this is about being inclusive, which translates to greater levels of creativity, problem-solving, and innovation. With family, friends, and loved ones, it's about being exposed to diversity of thought, which helps us develop and grow. We cannot build strong relationships with people if we are not exposed to new and different ways of thinking. You may have an affinity toward certain types of people with similar values and beliefs, but operating with a closed mindset limits our ability to have a positive impact on the lives of others.

Developing trust is about being vulnerable and risking exposure to others' actions and behaviors. In order to trust others, we must first know, understand, and trust ourselves. We have to know how we're wired and how this translates into our relationships. When trust develops, people are able to let their guards down and open up more. There is a feeling of psychological safety that starts to take place. To develop and maintain trust, people must continually sow into the relationship. Deposits into the bank account of trust must be made on a regular basis. Withdrawals of trust can have a negative effect on our relationships, though small withdrawals are more tolerable than major ones. Trust is also about commitment and consistency. It's showing up the same way each day for the people who are most important to us. When trust is developed in our professional lives, it translates to higher levels of cooperation, team effectiveness, and job performance. It enables leaders to galvanize and motivate their people. In our personal lives, it helps us grow closer to family and friends. It strengthens the bond between romantic partners. Developing trust is the most important skill of relational intelligence. Trust takes surface-level relationships and turns them into dynamic partnerships with others.

Cultivating influence is the most powerful skill of relational intelligence. Influence is the capacity to have a positive impact on the lives of others. It's about helping people become better versions of themselves. It relates to character development, growth, and encouraging people to realize their fullest potential. When I talk about influence, I'm not referring to social media influencers and people who affect the purchasing decisions of others. I'm not talking about celebrities like Beyoncé, Kim Kardashian, or Taylor Swift. I'm talking about building deep, long-term relationships with others and how this opens the door to helping people improve the quality of their lives. Influence is not about manipulation or getting people to do what we want them to do. Dynamic, life-changing relationships help us mature and grow. When we cultivate influence, we have a desire to support others. In the business world, cultivating influence is about leadership. It's about the use of noncoercive tactics to direct and coordinate the activities of others. It is used to accomplish goals and guide people to collective desired outcomes. The most successful leaders use their influence for the greater good.

In our personal relationships, cultivating influence is about wanting the best for others and helping them get there. Parents influence and shape the way children mature and grow. Great friendships challenge people to see the world differently. Our closest friends are there to give us insights, support, and wisdom. In most intimate romantic relationships, the influence partners have on each other shapes an ever-evolving understanding of the world. Our spouses know the most about us. They know all the good, bad, and ugly. They use this information to inspire us to be better versions of ourselves. Cultivating influence happens over time. We have to earn the respect of others before we can effectively influence them. At its best, influence works both ways between two people in a relationship. It can only happen if trust has been firmly established. We have to believe that others have our best interests at heart if they are going to make an impact in our lives.

Using the five skills of relational intelligence is critical for building sustainable, long-term relationships. I've also found that relationships thrive when we have the right focus. I believe the only thing you're ever entirely in control of is your focus. So many factors in life are beyond our control, but one thing you can always control if you learn how to do it and are committed to it is your focus. I think that many relationships fail not because of a lack of connection but because of loss of focus. Sometimes, what we call failure in relationships is just broken focus. It's the reason why the excitement that exists when relationships start tends to falter over time if we aren't committed to putting in the work required to maintain the relationship. We haven't damaged the relationship per se, but we've lost the focus on making the relationship grow.

Having the right focus in our relationships is an ever-evolving process. Focus comes through our commitment to making our relationships grow. The focus may shift depending on the type of relationship we are considering, but the same skills need to be practiced across all areas of our lives. In our work and professional relationships, focus often comes down to alignment on goals and strategic objectives. It's about partnering with others to get to collective outcomes that drive positive results for our organizations. It's how leaders direct their efforts to help their people maximize performance. It's how team members interact with one another to get to superior outcomes for the business. It's how leaders mentor and coach their people. When leaders have the right focus on developing talent, they find ways to connect on deeper levels and build positive relationships with their people.

In our most intimate relationships, it can be difficult to keep that right focus. Is your focus on changing your partner or on continually growing so you are the best version of yourself for them? True happiness is not finding the right people; it's about being the right person for others. If you find the right person and you're not committed to personal development, what do you think you're going to do to that person? The only way you will have the right people in your life is if you're consistently growing into the right person you want to be. You cannot always control the types of people who come into your life, but you can control the type of person you become. The object of relationship, the object of love and compassion, is not that someone else will complete you. But we often treat relationships like two halves are going to become whole. I've found that if you bring two different halves into a relationship, you're going to have hell, not whole. This applies to relationships across all areas of our lives. Building relationships is hard work. It takes time, diligence, and commitment.

TENDING TO THE GARDEN

Although the five skills of relational intelligence build upon one another, the process of maintaining and sustaining our relationships is constantly changing. There may be times when trust withdrawals are made. This can have a negative effect on the degree to which we are willing to be influenced by another person. There will be times when our understanding of people and our ability to embrace individual differences will change. This should happen in a progressive fashion as we are exposed to new and different people. One of my clients recently said it best when he was discussing the relationships he had with each of his direct reports: "I continually take time to work on the relationships with my people," he said. "As their needs and interests change, I want to make sure I am aligned with their goals. The only way I can do that is to consistently sow into the relationships."

I like to use the analogy that relationships are like a garden. No visit to a garden is useless. You must continually tend to the soil. The best relationships are about maintenance, love, and growth. You want people to feel valued and appreciated. We must continually nurture the relationships that are most important to us in a variety of ways. Nurturing relationships is about tending to the needs of your colleague, spouse, partner, or friend and the relationship. Leaders tend to the needs of their people so they can develop and grow. Parents tend to the needs of their children as they mature and become adults. Tending to the garden happens in the big things and in the day-to-day small events of life. Intimacy is active and alive. Relationships are constant work. I've found that most people don't know how to do this work instinctively. It has to be practiced and refined over time. You have to be willing to be there for people as a source of support.

Several years ago, I worked with an executive vice president in the media and entertainment industry. Colin was a confident, direct, and assertive leader. He spent most of his career with one organization where the culture was competitive, cutthroat, and aggressive. After a headhunter enticed him to take on a new challenge with a smaller organization, he joined a company that had more of a collaborative and engaging culture. When he first joined the organization, Colin did all the important things a new hire should do. He made his rounds to all the key leaders and important stakeholders throughout the company. He asked questions about their areas of the business. He solicited input and asked folks about what they felt his team needed to accomplish. He shared knowledge, insights, and wisdom he had picked up over his career. He did the maintenance, surface-level relationship building work most newly onboarded executives should do.

Once he felt he had made the initial connections that were needed, he quickly jumped into action and execution mode. He outlined his strategy and plans for the enterprise. He started articulating a vision to leaders without gathering the necessary buy-in and alignment from others. He quickly developed a reputation for having sharp elbows and operating like the proverbial bull in a china shop. He would push back and challenge the ideas of others. If people didn't align with his strategy, his frustrations quickly showed. This caused problems with leaders across the enterprise. People found him to be combative and difficult to work with. Yet he didn't understand why his messages weren't landing with the business. He had been asked to drive change for the business and was bringing in great ideas. He couldn't understand why his vision wasn't landing.

Seven months into his tenure, I was asked to come in and serve as his executive coach, supporting him on successfully integrating into the culture. From the start of our partnership, I found Colin to be a passionate and intense leader. He put you on edge and on the defensive as soon as you started speaking with him. I noticed this in one of our first coaching sessions. He came across as aggressive and domineering. We talked through our process and discussed conducting a stakeholder 360 interview. He thought this was a great idea, and I began conducting interviewers with his colleagues and coworkers. The conversations were compelling. Numerous stakeholders commented on Colin's interpersonal style. He was pushy. He came across as the smartest guy in the room, and everyone had to know it. When he came to a conclusion, people had to quickly align with his approach. He didn't give people the opportunity to shape strategy collectively. It was his way or the highway. You can imagine how this behavior was received by a collaborative and highly congenial culture. People worked together collectively, and he was not fitting the mold. His tendencies made cross-functional colleagues not want to work with him. He stopped putting in the maintenance work and tending to the garden of relationships. This prevented his team from accomplishing their goals.

When I shared the feedback with him, Colin was shocked that people viewed him in this way. He felt he had put in the necessary work to get to know what his colleagues needed. He had done a thorough assessment of the organization and knew what changes needed to be made. He was brought to the company to shake things up and drive change. Although these things were true, it was the "how" that he was missing. It didn't matter how brilliant his plans or strategies were. If he couldn't sell his vision and bring others along for the journey, he wasn't going to win people over. Once he understood this, we were able to outline goals for his executive development plan.

We had three goals for our coaching work. First and most importantly, Colin had to continuously tend to the garden. The company's culture was built on a solid foundation of relationships. Connections with colleagues had to be a consistent investment. There was not a one-size-fits-all approach to leadership. Colin had to go out and build individual relationships with each of his key stakeholders, which required work. Here, the goal wasn't about winning like he did for his former employer. Competition was not one of this new company's cultural pillars. A mindset shift needed to take place. Second, Colin had to talk less and listen more. Everyone knew he was bright and smart. People didn't want to hear about it all the time. They wanted him to be curious, to ask more about the culture and how things got done across the business. Yes, Colin had knowledge and subject matter expertise from his former employer, but those things were not the only factors that mattered. His ability to serve as a trusted thought partner would work in their culture. Lastly, he had to slow down and bring others along for the journey. People wanted him to scale back the intensity. The world did not revolve around him and his timelines. People placed a high emphasis on respect and treating colleagues with common decency. He had to align himself with these principles.

Once we ratified our development plan with his manager and HRBP, we quickly began to take action to make the necessary behavioral changes. Colin was stubborn at times, and I had to give him some tough, direct feedback when it was needed. He would often complain that the problems with the company were mostly cultural and that he had been told to change this. I agreed with him. But to change the culture, he had to adjust his style. People would only follow his lead if they believed he had the best interests of the enterprise at heart. Over time, we began to see progress. Colin made it a priority to continually invest in relationship development. He slowed down to take in insights and input from others. He strategized with people more rather than tell them what the strategy needed to be.

By the end of our coaching engagement, Colin had made a complete turnaround. He still had his edgy and passionate fire, but he knew how to channel it. His focus became more about alignment and collaboration rather than championing his own ideas and opinions. People began to enjoy working with him. They trusted his vision for the future. They bought into his strategy for the enterprise. Working with Colin taught me a valuable lesson: we get the most accomplished alongside others when we make relationships the priority. Colin did have ideas that would change the company's future trajectory. That was why they brought him into the mix. However, it was the investments he made in developing key stakeholder relationships that garnered him the buy-in and support from others. You cannot win people's minds if you do not first tend to the garden and win over their hearts.

In our personal lives, tending to the garden is about the continuous work we must put into our relationships to learn, understand, and support the growth of those closest to us. It's about how we make an impact on our loved ones. It's about caring for others' needs. It's about promoting mental and emotional health and wellness. As someone who has lived with bipolar disorder for a long time, I've started to see a shift to destigmatize mental health disorders over the last several years. People with mental health challenges have begun to be viewed with more care and empathy. I recently began watching a docuseries Oprah Winfrey started with Prince Harry called *The Me You Can't See*. It focuses on the immediate need to replace some of the shame surrounding mental health with wisdom, compassion, and honesty. The series features stories that help lift the veil on the current state of mental health. Hopes are that this will spark a global conversation. I'm in full agreement with the hosts that the time has come to view people for who they are and not what categories they represent. We need to humanize the idea of mental health. As human beings, we are wired for connection and community. Developing and using relational intelligence is a path to making this happen. Understanding others and embracing individual differences give us a snapshot into other people's worlds. These skills allow us to understand people's narratives and the life events that shaped who they are today.

The fruits of the garden can be some of the most rewarding aspects of our lives. When we consistently tend to our relationships, we see people develop and grow. We see people reach their full potential. We see leaders empower and unleash the capabilities of their people. We see parents raise children who can change the world. We see friendships that stand the test of time. We see marriages blossom and flourish. I find it so beautiful that we all have opportunities to make an impact on the people around us if we are intentional in our actions. Tending to the garden is not just about others, though. It's also about our own personal journeys. That's the great thing about life-changing relationships. All parties benefit from the process. Influence is a two-way street. When people have each other's backs and they can count on one another, the possibilities are endless. It just takes focus, commitment, and the desire to continuously grow.

EMBRACE THE PROCESS: EVERY DAY IS AN ALTAR CALL

In the Christian world, the altar call is a summons to the altar at a worship service to those wishing to show their commitment to Christ. When it comes to the people closest to us, we must make daily altar calls to show our investment in relationships. We can consistently give and extend grace that helps relationships prosper and grow. In my life, I've found grace in adaptation. The way you build relationships is constantly changing. You have to be a student of people and a lifelong learner. There will be a lot of trial and error. You will make some mistakes. You'll hurt people in the process, and others will let you down. Embrace these things. Don't get bitter. Don't get resentful. Don't be driven by your feelings and emotions. Make commitments to people. Honor those commitments. Be a person of your word. Show up consistently for others in the good and in the bad times.

We have to strive for daily altar call connections with our family, friends, and coworkers. Life and relationships are all about the process. Relationships are never a means to an end. In today's world, we are obsessed with data, analytics, and outcomes. Most people want things yesterday. We live in an impatient and instant-gratification-driven culture. This is sad. It needs to change. Relationships should never be transactional. Of course, some relationships will have transactional components, but you can ask yourself, are you more concerned about immediate needs or possibilities for the future? I have built a leadership advisory firm where we pride ourselves on the authentic relationships we build with our clients. Relationships are our primary driver. They are why we exist. Relationships are what get me out of bed, ready to tackle each day. Yes, my firm does leadership advisory work. We have the best management consultants in the world working on executive assessments, senior team effectiveness, executive coaching, and transformational change. But we do not simply provide services to our clients. We provide our clients with an "experience" they have never had before. It's something they will not get with any other leadership advisory or management consulting firm. Our clients begin a relational experience the first time they meet one of our team members, and they experience it because we are solely focused on the relationships we build with their people and teams. Relational intelligence is an essential skill set required in any attempt to connect, build, and maintain successful relationships. Without it, it is inconceivable to construct meaningful, long-lasting, impactful partnerships with others.

In relationships, process is the point of it all. It's the journey that makes relationships memorable and impactful. Nothing else matters quite as much as relationships. Great relationships help us change, evolve, and grow. Though there is energy extended and lost, we can anticipate the entropy. Engaging honestly with entropy gets us to true and lasting empathy and intimacy. It challenges us to tackle our blind spots and weaknesses, face them with courage and conviction, and drive true, lasting change. I can only tell you this because I've seen it happen in my life. I've seen how relational intelligence has enabled me to touch the lives of so many people in a meaningful and impactful way. It's my superhero power. My purpose, calling, and mission in life is to help people identify, unlock, and unleash their true relational and leadership potential. I've been blessed with the God-given ability to influence people, which has become a responsibility I take seriously. This responsibility is demonstrated in my commitments to people and relationships. It shows up in the work I do as a leadership advisor and organizational psychologist. It's in the promise I give to my clients. They know I am in the trenches with them as their trusted advisor and friend along the journey. Influence and the relational intelligence skills that lead to it appear in how I show up for my family and friends. It's in being a loving and supportive son to both of my parents. It's in being a role model and resource to my siblings. It's in being a thought partner and trusted ally to my closest friends.

Relational intelligence will change your life. Learn and practice these skills if you want to see dramatic improvements in the quality of all your relationships. You will become a better person. I promise you this. I say this from personal experience. I see it happen with all my clients. I've seen relational intelligence transform the people closest to me. At the end of the day, life is about relationships. When your relationships are strong, they serve as gateways to your growth. Our lives are changed by the people around us. It saddens me that for many people, this happens by chance. We let our surroundings dictate who we become. With relational intelligence, you can be intentional about how you build relationships with others. I'm a firm believer that if we want anything positive in our lives, we have to be intentional and proactive about it. If you are intentional about how you build relationships with others your life will be transformed.

ABOUT THE AUTHOR

Dr. Adam C. Bandelli is the Founder and Managing Director of Bandelli & Associates. The firm believes that the growth and development of people is the highest calling of leadership. His team embraces the power of relational intelligence. This is demonstrated in the authentic and genuine relationships the firm's consultants build with their clients. They challenge leaders to embrace diversity of thought. They empower senior executives to capitalize on their greatest talents, skills, and core capabilities. They inspire clients to be bold, take calculated risks, and drive sustainable change. Adam has twenty years of management and consulting experience in the firm's service offerings, including board consultation, senior executive selection, leadership development, pre-investment due diligence, organizational culture, and transformational change.

Adam is also the author of *What Every Leader Needs: The Ten Universal and Indisputable Competencies of Leadership Effectiveness,* which has received strong reviews from prominent business leaders. As an expert on executive leadership and relational intelligence, Adam works with CEOs and senior executives to strengthen their abilities to inspire and influence their people, teams, and organizations. Adam has worked with leaders around the world in organizations ranging from small start-up firms through global Fortune 100 companies. He has consulted to a diverse set of industry sectors, including private equity, financial services, consumer products, manufacturing, medical devices, retail, energy, pharmaceuticals, sports and entertainment, nonprofit, and telecommunications.

Prior to founding Bandelli & Associates, Adam was a Partner at Korn Ferry, where he led the private equity assessment practice for North America. Earlier in his career, he was a Partner at RHR International, where he served as one of the firm's leaders on CEO succession and leadership development. Adam received his doctoral and master's degree in industrial-organizational psychology from the University of South Florida and his bachelor's degree concentrating in psychology and business management from Fairleigh Dickinson University. Acknowledged as a world-renowned thought leader on relational intelligence, transformational leadership, and organizational effectiveness, he is a frequent speaker at Fortune 500 companies, leadership retreats, and business and professional meetings.

As a former athlete, Adam spends his recreational time long-distance running and CrossFit training. He has competed in several marathons, including the TCS New York City Marathon. He is an avid golfer and usually spends his weekends on the golf course with clients, colleagues, and friends. His family is active in their church and volunteer in their local community. For more information on Adam, his firm, and their leadership advisory consulting service offerings, visit www.bandelliandassociates.com. **Leadership Matters. Without It, People Fail.**

CPSIA information can be obtained
at www.ICGtesting.com
Printed in the USA
BVHW041741300622
640990BV00003B/4/J

9 781638 856740